Public Policies in East Asian Development

Facing New Challenges

Edited by F. GERARD ADAMS
and WILLIAM E. JAMES

 PRAEGER

Westport, Connecticut
London

Library of Congress Cataloging-in-Publication Data

Public policies in East Asian development : facing new challenges /
    edited by F. Gerard Adams and William E. James.
        p. cm.
    Includes bibliographical references and index.
    ISBN 0–275–96444–2 (alk. paper)
    1. East Asia—Economic policy. 2. East Asia—Economic policy—
Case studies. 3. Economic forecasting—East Asia. I. Adams, F.
Gerard (Francis Gerard), 1929–   . II. James, William E.
HC460.5.P83   1999
338.95—dc21   98–56628

British Library Cataloguing in Publication Data is available.

Library of Congress Catalog Card Number: 98–56628
ISBN: 0–275–96444–2

First published in 1999

Praeger Publishers, 88 Post Road West, Westport, CT 06881
An imprint of Greenwood Publishing Group, Inc.
www.praeger.com

Printed in the United States of America

The paper used in this book complies with the
Permanent Paper Standard issued by the National
Information Standards Organization (Z39.48–1984).

10 9 8 7 6 5 4 3 2 1

Contents

Preface

This volume is one of a series of books based on research conducted at the International Centre for the Study of East Asian Development (ICSEAD), Kitakyushu, Japan, during the past eight years. It brings together chapters from the most recent of a series of economic study workshops concerned with macroeconomics and policy for East Asian development held at ICSEAD in Kitakyushu in November 1996.

ICSEAD was started by the City of Kitakyushu to serve as a vehicle for the internationalization of the city and to bring the city closer, in an intellectual way, to its neighbors in East Asia. In 1987, the city authorities approached the University of Pennsylvania to collaborate on the establishment of the ICSEAD, helping to organize the research program, running conferences, designing and editing publications, and carrying on active research. This represents a unique collaboration between a unit of the city government in Kitakyushu and a leading American university. This collaboration has been responsible over the years for numerous research studies at ICSEAD, at Penn, and at other cooperating institutions. The research was coordinated by F. Gerard Adams at the University of Pennsylvania and by Takeshi Katsuhara and, since 1995, by Shinichi Ichimura at ICSEAD. It has brought together leading experts from Japan, the United States and Canada and from many developing East Asian countries. Economists from many international organizations—the World Bank, the International Monetary Fund (IMF), Organization for Economic Cooperation and Development (OECD), Asian Development Bank—have also participated.

The research covered in this volume emphasizes the broad dimensions of economic policy, domestic and international, in East Asia.

The role of policy is a central question with regard to East Asian development. Some economists have argued that *active* development policy lies behind the success of East Asian development. It has been suggested that industry-specific industrial policy strategies, and the promotion of basic and/or high-technology industries have advanced development in several countries—Japan, Korea, Taiwan, and so on. On the other hand, other scholars have seen a more limited policy role for government that focuses on the basic macroeconomic stability, balance of payments equilibrium, infrastructure, education, and so on. There is far from consensus on this important issue being studied by ICSEAD.

The 1997 crisis in East Asia casts a new perspective on questions of policy. On one hand, one may ask whether policies or the lack of appropriate policies is responsible for the crisis. On the other, one may pose questions about the nature of policies needed, in the short run and in the long term, to extricate the East Asian countries from the crisis and to renew the rapid growth process.

Increasing recognition of the high costs of pollution are turning thinking in many rapidly industrializing countries in East Asia toward pollution control. In this regard, Japan has set important precedents.

Finally, the international dimensions constitute an important policy sphere. International linkages, increasingly advanced by regional economic integration under Asian Free Trade Area (AFTA), Asia Pacific Economic Cooperation (APEC), and other multinational global trading partnerships, will have an important impact, as documented in Project LINK's scenario studies.

While the East Asian countries appear to be linked together by a common growth process, the diversity of experience and of policy among them is striking. The policy spectrum has ranged widely from a high level of government intervention in Singapore and Korea to relatively freer markets in Thailand, for example. For this reason, it is important to look at many of countries individually, as we do in this volume.

We are grateful to the many participants in our research efforts—economists from Japan, the United States, Canada, and the many countries of East Asia who have worked with us over a long time.

I

Public Policies for Economic Development

The principal reason for raising the question, How did East Asia achieve its miracle? is, of course, that many countries would like to duplicate that experience. They want to create their own "Miracle." As the literature documents, there remains much disagreement about the ingredients essential to achieving rapid economic progress, although policy is widely seen as one of the important pieces. In various respects, the countries of East Asia have followed a common policy pattern, though in many particulars their individual policies have been quite different. This part of the volume is concerned with an overview of the policy issues.

The first chapter, by F. Gerard Adams and William E. James, "Policy Perspectives in a Post-Asian Crisis World: Toward a Taxonomy," categorizes policies, particularly between broad-based macrostabilization and macrodevelopment approaches, on one hand, and more narrowly interventionist, sector-specific policies, on the other.

The second chapter, by F. Gerard Adams, "Policy Challenges to Revive the East Asian Miracle," is concerned with recent developments, the swing from "miracle" to "meltdown" in East Asia. It asks what can be done to regain the rapid rate of development that has characterized East Asia for the past two decades.

The third chapter, by William E. James, "Trade Trends and Policy Issues in East Asian Developing Economics," is concerned with trade policy in East Asia and its interaction with development.

The fourth chapter, by F. Gerard Adams and Heidi Vernon, "Sector-Specific Industrial Policies and Southeast Asian Economic Development," deals with thinking and experience with industrial policy. Some economists have argued that industry-specific policy initiatives have played an essential role, while others have argued that free market forces can accomplish the task with little industry-specific intervention. The chapter concludes that sectoral industrial policies may have their time and place but are not a generic prescription for rapid economic development.

The fifth chapter, by Hidefumi Imura and Takeshi Katsuhara, "Industrialization and Environmental Policy in East Asia: A Comparative Study of Japan, Korea, and China," is concerned with the important environmental problems that are developing in the region and that will be aggravated if continued growth is not matched by improved energy utilization and pollution control. The study projects pollution loads associated with rapid East Asian development, considers how environmental policy in Japan helped to alleviate the problem, and discusses how similar policies have the potential to alleviate it in other parts of Asia.

1

Policy Perspectives in a Post-Asian Crisis World: Toward a Taxonomy

F. Gerard Adams and William E. James

In 1997, the upward path of East Asian development, what had been termed The East Asian Miracle (World Bank, 1993), was rudely interrupted. The crisis, which combined elements of the business cycle, financial failure, and exchange rate contagion, has proved to be a challenge to policymakers. Prior to the 1997 crisis, while the boom was still in full swing, economists argued at length about the basis for East Asian growth and the role of policy in facilitating it.[1] Since then, discussions have focused on the policy failures that brought about the crisis and the policy steps, both within the countries and at the international organizations, needed to reestablish stability and growth.

This chapter on policies for growth and stability introduces this volume by viewing economic policy from a taxonomic perspective. In the first two sections, we consider the policy objectives of East Asian economic development. Then we begin our study of policy approaches. Policy must promote long-term development. It must provide internal and external stability. In the process, policymakers must be concerned with issues of trade and foreign investment. A critical consideration is to distinguish between policies that operate within the "market" framework, without deliberate intervention, and those that may be called "interventionist." We raise a series of basic questions to distinguish between policies. Finally, we apply these perspectives to recent East Asian policy experience and attempt a reconciliation between different views about policy approaches to the current East Asian crisis.

As is typical in the economics profession, there has been much disagreement about policy prescriptions. These discussions reflect disagreements about theory and, sometimes, about underlying facts or statistics. Inevitably, they also reflect sociopolitical biases: preferences for free markets versus proactive policy intervention, or belief in the effectiveness of authoritarian versus democratic government.

On the other hand, at least among economists trained in the Western tradition, there is also a great deal of agreement about the kinds of policies that promote growth and stability. We consider various dimensions of public policy and its impact on economic development, recognizing the areas of consensus and those of disagreement.

POLICY OBJECTIVES IN ECONOMIC DEVELOPMENT

Policymakers in a less developed country (LDC) are likely to place greater emphasis on economic transformation and development than in the industrial world. Survey evidence suggests that businesspeople and advanced students in Thailand view economic growth as the primary objective. Except in times of crisis, stabilization objectives like price stability, balance of payments equilibrium, and full employment are considered less important. A fair income distribution and environmental considerations take an even lower place among policy priorities, though they may get high marks in some political circles.

From this perspective, the East Asian economies achieved signal success in the past 30 years. Not only was the rate of growth very high but expansion was relatively stable with few serious cyclical interruptions. Price and balance of payments performance varied among the East Asian countries but was generally within tolerable limits. In this respect, the achievements of East Asia have been commendable. With respect to macroeconomic stability, the East Asian economies compare markedly with Latin America, whose instability, high levels of inflation, and debt problems during the 1970s and 1980s proved a barrier to sustained growth (Adams and Davis, 1993).

Unfortunately, internal and external excesses have now caught up with many of the East Asian countries. The 1997 crisis can be characterized not just as a traditional business cycle or balance of payments/exchange rate crisis. It is the result of important policy failures. In some respects, these are apparent in statistics, for example, in the overvaluation of exchange rates and in the excessive current account deficits (and associated capital inflows) and in government budget deficits. But there were also other aspects of policy failure that cannot be easily supported by data, for example, inadequate supervision of banks and finance companies in Thailand or excessive indebtedness by corporate conglomerates in Indonesia and Korea.

THE EAST ASIAN GROWTH PROCESS

The fact that East Asian economic development is a linked process in which many countries participate suggests that growth in the area has not simply been a result of independent but parallel policy choices by the developing countries in the region. The process suggests a linked *development ladder*, which has been considered at length in Adams and Ichimura (1998). The idea is an extension of the traditional *flying geese* analogy, where some countries lead others in advancing their industries toward higher levels of sophistication, to an international *product cycle* view. The East Asian countries participating in the development process are naturally shifting their relative competitiveness. As countries move up the *ladder*, their stock of capital rises, and their technological capacity reaches a higher level, but at the same time their labor costs increase, and their exchange rate becomes less favorable. This gives them advantages in the production of more sophisticated products but reduces their competitiveness in more simple goods. In turn, this process opens a slot, the industries in which the more advanced country is no longer competing, that can be filled by other countries in the region. These, situated on lower rungs of the ladder, gain competitive advantage as a result of the fact that they are not so far advanced: they have lower labor costs, for example. Shifts in revealed comparative advantage from primary products to more advanced products reflect this development process. On one hand, there are new opportunities. On the other, there are countries waiting in the wings, ready to compete.[2]

Economic development policies must recognize and respond to the development process. On one hand, it is important to maintain competitiveness. The exchange rate counts! On the other hand, it is necessary to look ahead and to facilitate the process of industrial adaptation. In this regard, an open, competitive market structure as well as investments in infrastructure and in human resources are of particular importance.

POLICY AND THE 1997 CRISIS

As we have noted, until the mid-1990s, the record of growth and stabilization policies in East Asia has been quite good. While cyclical fluctuations have not been avoided, the exchange rates of the Southeast Asian countries have maintained a considerable degree of stability with respect to the U.S. dollar, and business cycle fluctuations have been modest. The continued growth of export markets and the requirements for massive domestic investment have contributed to stable growth. At the same time, the central banks have played a major role in maintaining internal and external stability.

Moreover, substantial progress was being made in liberalizing the economies and opening them to international trade and capital movements. The scope of government regulation was being reduced. Under the ASEAN Free Trade Area agreements (AFTA) tariffs among the East Asian countries were being cut. International capital flows were widely deregulated.[3]

However, in many countries of East Asia, the makings of cyclical and foreign exchange crisis were already apparent in 1996. Excess speculative investment and borrowing—in Thailand for real estate investment, in Indonesia and Korea for industrial projects, in Malaysia for infrastructure—were already recognized. The deterioration of the trade balance as exports slowed and imports continued to grow rapidly in 1996 undermined the capital inflows that had made it possible to maintain foreign exchange rate stability.[4] In the case of Thailand, loss of confidence in the Bank of Thailand related to problems in the balance sheets of financial institutions and failure of the government to implement appropriate policy to control the budget deficit contributed to a sudden depreciation of the baht. The contagion was not long to spill to neighboring countries.

At this point serious questions remain about the appropriate policies to lead the East Asian countries out of the crisis and to produce a resumption of the East Asian growth process. These policy issues include:

—How to restore confidence in the financial system and in the currency

—How to meet external and internal debt obligations

—How to make the East Asian countries competitive again in international markets

—How to rebuild industrial and financial system institutions

—How to develop sufficient internal demand

—How to deal with the immediate social fallout of the crisis

We note that there is substantial disagreement among economists with respect to the policies required to achieve these objectives. We discuss policies to deal with the crisis and steps toward resumption of growth in Chapter 2.

TOWARD A POLICY TAXONOMY

Policies can be classified from the perspective of a number of criteria. We discuss the considerations in detail here, recognizing that some of them may not be mutually exclusive.

Growth versus Stabilization

In the developing world, growth is a primary objective, as we have noted. Development involves transformation: from rural to urban, from production of primary products to more sophisticated goods and services, from labor-intensive production methods to capital-intensive high technology. Growth policies focus on long-run development in contrast to the shorter time horizon of stabilization policy. Moreover, growth policy considers growth of saving and investment, the building of infrastructure, the acquisition of modern technology, and the development of human capital. In contrast, stabilization is concerned with the internal and external macroeconomic balances of the economy, the avoidance of inflationary pressures and of balance of current account disequilibrium. Because these policy directions interact—indeed, conflict in some cases—there is often disagreement among government officials and/or among political interests. For example, concern with long-run growth by increasing the inflow of foreign capital may not be consistent with stability in the international accounts or with soundness of the banking system.

Market-based versus Interventionist Policies

Despite the fact that the East Asian economies have based their development on the operation of private enterprise and the free market (with the exception of the socialist economies, which are, themselves, turning to a market economy), there has always been and continues to be substantial government intervention. Some of this intervention is directed toward protecting domestic interests—for example, protective tariffs and import quotas as well as barriers to foreign enterprise—and other interventions reflect a lack of confidence in the operation of the market or dissatisfaction with its results, sometimes specifically with respect to development objectives. Some interventions are, of course, appropriate even in a market economy. These include the traditional tasks of government to provide for infrastructure, defense, and military and concerns with public health, consumer protection, antitrust, and the law. One public function, recognized as increasingly important in view of recent failures, is fiduciary supervision of banks and financial companies.

With respect to development policy, the distinction between intervention and the market involves the classic debate among development economists of whether it is sufficient "just to get prices right" (Hughes, 1995) or whether incentives should be distorted, perhaps in line with long-run judgments about market outcomes (Wade, 1990). The distinction here is about whether relying on market prices without significant government intervention will yield an optimal development path. The counterargument is that biasing incentives, in favor of exports or investment, for example, will improve development performance. Wade argues that such interventions will be helpful so long as they are consistent with long-run prospects for comparative advantage. The nature of these interventions is discussed under the next heading.

Focused or General Interventions

The difference between policies that are intended to influence markets in general terms, and those intended to influence markets in industry-specific or even project-specific terms is an important distinction. It is elaborated in our discussion of industrial policies in Chapter 4. Aggregate or general interventions are broad policies, available to all sectors without explicit preference—though they benefit some sectors more than others. They include favorable interest rates or investment incentives as well as generally applicable tariff rates. Focused interventions select out for preference specific sectors or industries, often so-called sunrise industries. The difference is essentially one of whether investment decisions are made by profit-seeking enterprise managers or whether they are influenced by public officials. The clearest distinction is that between privately owned firms and state enterprises that are directly controlled and funded by governments. But there are many other instances, as well, when industrial policy calls for decisions by public officials about industry- or product-specific incentives or even about particular projects. In the East Asian countries, there has been considerable collaboration between business decision makers and government officials. While at times that may have been advantageous to the pace of development, we can point to numerous instances when it has not.

Domestic versus Externally Oriented Industrial Development Policies

Policy must, of course, be directed toward the achievement of domestic development objectives. However, a critical distinction in the field of trade and industrial development is between policies that are domestically versus externally oriented. Can development aims be achieved by protecting domestic industries or by opening the economy to participation in world markets? This is the classical distinction between "import substitution" and "export promotion." Most developing countries, in East Asia as elsewhere, began their development efforts with a strategy of import substitution, hoping by promoting domestic production in place of imports to save scarce foreign exchange and to industrialize. While in many instances, import substitution policies still apply, the swing toward export promotion has been seen as a major factor in East Asian development. By orienting development toward industries participating in world markets, the East Asian countries have learned to produce products competitive with respect to quality, design, and price with production in the industrial world. They have also been able to attract foreign investment, intended for export production and often for meeting the needs of their domestic markets.

Export promotion has not always corresponded to other aspects of market opening. Thus, many countries have continued import barriers and tariffs, though these have been reduced in recent years, and have limited the participation of foreigners in many aspects of their domestic economies. Trade policies are discussed in detail in Chapter 3.

INSTITUTIONAL CONSIDERATIONS

The structure of the economy and of its institutions has clearly played an important role in the development of the East Asian economies. By and large, the successful East Asian countries have been market economies, but the role of government institutions should not be underestimated. Some of these countries, like Korea and Taiwan, had a high level of institutional development early on. Effective government agencies cooperating with private business may have facilitated development (Wade, 1990). Others have built institutions that have served as a means to provide a setting for economic development by private firms and sometimes by public enterprises. Central banks, planning agencies, stock exchanges, and financial institutions are good examples. Institution building is very much part of the East Asian development process.

Recent experience suggests that much institution building is still required. The crisis reflects institutional failures in various dimensions, for example, with respect to financial market supervision. There is clearly a need for building up regulatory institutions without imposing unnecessary rules.

A most fundamental example of the importance of market- based institutions lies in the turn from planned/command economy in China and Vietnam toward what has been termed "socialist market economies." Since 1979 China has seen rapid expansion of locally owned and controlled "town and village industries" (TVEs) and of private and joint venture enterprises that face a hard budget constraint and that are guided by market incentives. These have been quite successful. On the other hand, the traditional, state-owned enterprises (SOEs), many in heavy industry, have not done well, with a large proportion having large losses. Reorganization of the SOEs is in the works, with the idea of creating a small number of large conglomerates similar to the chaebols in South Korea. So far the overall growth record of the China has been been exemplary.[5]

ECONOMIC VERSUS SOCIOPOLITICAL CONSIDERATIONS

Public policy cannot be guided by economic aims alone. Social and environmental conditions are important. For many years, a primary concern has been the deleterious impact of industrialization and primary resource development on the environment. More recently, the social cost of stabilization policies—high interest rates, budget balancing, and their implications for growth, economic activity, and employment—has been the heart of controversies about IMF policies in East Asia (Sachs, 1997). Such matters often dominate the debate and influence political decision making. A view of recent developments in Indonesia and Malaysia illustrates how political considerations, in their own right, also influence policy, sometimes at the cost of policies that produce undesirable economic outcomes.

Sociopolitical aims have high priorities in national policymaking, sometimes at the expense of important economic objectives. In some cases, this is a matter of broad national imperatives, like the *bumiputra* policy in Malaysia or establishing national unity in Indonesia or upgrading the "northeast" in Thailand. In other cases, political considerations reflect the fragmentation of political power or the need to cater to specific political constituencies. The issue does not appear to be so much whether the government is autocratic or democratic. Whether governments can take policy actions that may be unpopular or painful is usually a matter of political strength. Insecure governments have often been reluctant or unable to institute appropriate economic policies, regardless of whether they were democratic or authoritarian. For this reason, pressures from the IMF to change policies have sometimes been useful when governments have been unable to implement these policies on their own. As recent history demonstrates, the IMF often gets the blame for policies that should have been and, probably, would have been implemented in any case.

POLICY FOR ECONOMIC DEVELOPMENT IN EAST ASIA

Does the experience of East Asian development point to a policy stance that will consistently advance rapid development? The 1997 crisis suggests that this is not quite as simple a question to answer as we might have thought. There is, nevertheless, substantial consensus on longer-term development policies, even as there is disagreement about the short term. We consider the longer-term aspects here and then briefly discuss the short-term issues (these will be considered in greater detail in the next chapter).

Policies for growth in East Asia have characteristically combined building the internal economy with emphasis on competitiveness in export markets and reliance on foreign investment and technology. While these economies are known for their outward trade orientation, there has also been much emphasis on building the stock of capital—human as well as physical—and technical change needed for economic advancement. However, detailed policy strategies have varied between countries, as the "country papers" in this volume demonstrate.

Inward versus Outward Orientation

We have already noted the importance of outward trade orientation as an engine of growth in East Asia. Consensus on the importance of exports as an earner of foreign exchange has caused many countries, in Latin America and elsewhere in Asia as well as in East Asia, to seek export markets. Promotion of inflows of direct foreign investment, closely related to export policies, has also been a mainstay of development policy. Whether these policies will work as well in the future, when there will be more and bigger competitors, for example, China, and advanced country markets are more saturated is an open question.

The extension of openness to import markets for goods, services, and, particularly, to financial flows is an important question. Trade policy, export promotion, and foreign investment are discussed in greater detail in this chapter and in Chapter 3.

Infrastructure and Industrial Policy

There is little disagreement among policymakers and economists that inward-oriented policies are also important. High rates of saving and investment have been important contributors to growth. While most countries promote saving and encourage both domestic and foreign investment—the Board of Investment (BoI) of Thailand, for example—high savings rates and private investment are not simply attributable to public policy. Natural forces like growth, culture, and demographics account, in large part, for high rates of saving and investment. The East Asian countries do take responsibility for investment in infrastructure—roads, ports, mass transportation, communications, sanitation, and so on. Where this was clearly a public sector task only one or two decades ago, it has increasingly been shifted toward the private sector either directly or indirectly.

Governments are also concerned with investments in human capital, for example, education, public health, and science and technology, all very important in economies that are rapidly shifting up a development ladder. In this respect, the record of performance is much stronger in some countries, like Taiwan and Korea, than in others, like Thailand, Indonesia, and the Philippines.

As we have noted, a related issue is whether these policy interventions should favor specific sectors or involve the establishment of "national" enterprises. Some East Asian countries—Korea and Taiwan, for example—have followed policies similar to those of the Ministry of International Trade and Industry (MITI) in Japan during the 1950s and 1960s: to advance specific industries that were seen as central to industrialization such as steel, cement, or chemicals. Wade (1990) argues that such policies have been consistent with the long-run perspectives of the market. Other countries, like Hong Kong before its merger with China, have had little, if any, industry-specific policies or, like Thailand, have carried them out in a substantially *ad hoc* manner. Still other countries have tried to advance particular mass production industries—the Proton Saga automobile in Malaysia—or have tried to achieve technological leapfrogging, as in the Indonesian aircraft industry. Have interventions with the operation of the market been useful? This issue is discussed in more detail in a survey of Southeast Asian industrial policy in Chapter 4.

Trade and Exchange Rate Policy

Trade policies in the East Asian developing economies have been gradually liberalized, with an emphasis on export promotion gaining precedence over import substitution in most cases. The completion of the Uruguay Round in 1994 and the creation of the World Trade Organization (WTO) in 1995 have intensified the liberalization process in the region. Though some important East Asian economies (China, Vietnam, and Taiwan) are not presently members of WTO, all aspire to membership in the near future. Taiwan has already adopted trade practices that conform to WTO standards, and China is moving in the same direction with a program of unilateral tariff reductions and improvement in the protection of intellectual property and other commercial practices.

The tendency of East Asian economies has been to undertake liberalization measures unilaterally as a means of spurring greater efficiency and competitiveness. This can be seen in Indonesia, where MFN tariffs have been steadily reduced from over 20% in 1990 to about 11% in 1997. Regional initiatives, including the ASEAN Free Trade Agreement (AFTA) and the APEC Bogor Initiative of 1993, are moving ahead as well. The AFTA scheme for intra-ASEAN tariffs of 0–5% will be fully implemented by the year 2003, unless policy responses to the 1997 crisis get in the way. While the target dates for the Bogor Initiative are 2010 in the case of developed members and 2020 in the case of developing members, individual action plans for trade and investment liberalization are already being implemented by all members.

Vietnam is now a member of ASEAN and will bring its trade policies into conformance with the other members of the AFTA within a few years.

The steady reduction of protection in the region has greatly facilitated trade within the region and with other parts of the world. The rising share of East Asian developing countries in global trade (export basis) rose from about 10% in 1986 to almost 15% in 1996, according to the WTO.[6] The East Asian countries have had a sharp slowdown in trade expansion in 1996, and this may be expected to continue in 1997 and 1998 with the severe financial and currency turmoil in the region. As traditional tariff and nontariff barriers come down in the region, there is likely to be mounting pressure to adopt new, contingent forms of protection. The rise of antidumping petitions in the region in recent years is indicative of this dangerous trend.

Exchange rate policies have varied substantially between East Asian countries. The details of individual countries' policies cannot be adequately covered here (see the country chapters later). However, East Asia has had success in the past in avoiding serious problems associated with excessive real appreciation by periodically adjusting the nominal exchange rate and keeping inflation well under control.[7] In recent years there has been a tendency for the Southeast Asian countries to adopt a dollar peg with varying degrees of flexibility. This policy was carried to the extreme in Thailand with disastrous results. The fixed peg of the Thai baht to the U.S. dollar coupled with a large interest rate differential spurred the excessive expansion of domestic investment fueled by inflows of short-term private capital.[8] The financial crisis is discussed in greater detail in Chapter 2.

Hong Kong has maintained a currency board approach to manage its exchange rate and has maintained a fixed nominal exchange rate vis-à-vis the U.S. dollar since the mid-1980s. This approach requires a strong and well-regulated banking system and sufficient foreign reserves to provide backing to the local currency. China, by way of contrast, had discreetly devalued in 1990 and again in 1994. The rapid expansion of Chinese exports following the devaluations put tremendous competitive pressure on the Southeast Asian countries.

The currency crisis that began in Thailand and spread across Southeast Asia and to Korea has forced all these countries to adopt a freely floating exchange rate policy. The extent to which the currencies in Thailand, Korea, Indonesia, Malaysia, and the Philippines depreciated was far in excess of what any standard economic model would have predicted. Hence, expectational contagion or, in some cases, political factors that are not easy to introduce into an economic model lie at the core of the problem. With the massive depreciation, import compression has begun. A surge in exports can be expected with some time lag. The threat of competitive devaluation in East Asia is present, though, so far, China has avoided this course of action. The severe weakening of the Japanese yen against the dollar would place enormous pressure on Korea and, eventually, on the other East Asian countries. The consequences for the U.S. current account may be severe, with the potential for a protectionist backlash. We discuss trade and foreign exchange policy in more detail later and in Chapter 3.

Crisis Policy

The 1997 crisis has drastically changed policy priorities. Emphasis has shifted from growth to stabilization. The stabilization policies that are required focus on altogether different considerations than growth and development policies. They call for a rethinking of exchange rate and international financial market policies. Is exchange rate stability consistent with liberalization of international capital flows, for example? They require more conservative monetary and budgetary policies. They require more careful fiduciary supervision of banks and other financial institutions and more careful monitoring of the business cycle situation. But governments have been reluctant to take stabilization measures that impose social burdens or that may impede long-run growth—though stabilization and restoration of confidence are clearly essential if development is to continue.

The International Monetary Fund (IMF) has assumed a leading role in guiding the restructuring of the East Asian economies in the face of the recent crisis. The IMF has made its financial aid packages conditional on the implementation of conservative policies seeking, on the macrolevel, to minimize internal and external deficits to reduce inflationary pressures and, on the microlevel, to shut down failing banks and businesses and to liberalize trade and foster competition. Such a policy mix imposes social costs such as unemployment and business failures in the short run in the hope of restoring confidence and achieving greater dynamism in the long run. It has been the source of many disputes (Radelet and Sachs, 1998).

Some economists have supported more moderate policies (Sachs, 1997). Others have pushed for even greater emphasis on free market (Feldstein, 1998) and still others have advanced specific remedies like the currency board (Hanke and Schuler, 1994) that risk even more drastic readjustments. Past experiences with IMF restructuring lends much support to the idea that crises, like that of East Asia, can be remedied and that growth can be resumed by following IMF prescriptions, even though the medicine may be bitter for a period (Corbo et al., 1987).

We consider the 1997 crisis and the policy responses to it in greater detail in Chapter 2. It is clear that "one size fits all" policies, common to all of the countries involved, are not likely to apply. The historical record of the various East Asian countries shows a diversity of strategies, reflecting the initial situation, the nature of political and social organization, and the resources specific to each country. It is important, consequently, to see policies at the country level. The later chapters of this volume demonstrate many aspects of uniqueness of the policies of each country, as well as the common threads of policy that have been apparent throughout the East Asian region.

NOTES

1. For recent discussions see Adams and Ichimura (1998). Opinions have ranged widely from "free market" views (Hughes, 1995) to "governed market" perspectives (Wade, 1990).

2. As a result, in the mid-1990s, competitive pressure of China and Vietnam made it increasingly difficult for Thailand and Indonesia to compete in labor-intensive product markets at the then-prevailing exchange rate.

3. Indeed, capital flow liberalization has been seen as a source of the 1997 crisis. Excessive capital inflows, many of them short-term, were a central factor in the difficulties of Thailand, Indonesia, and Korea. Countries, like China, that did not free their international capital markets avoided some of the difficulties.

4. There has been much discussion on whether the crisis originated from fundamental factors like excess investment within each economy, from fundamental shocks like trade failures originating outside, or from panic in the international financial system (Radelet and Sachs, 1998).

5. The Chinese transition experience has been astonishing not only in comparison with other Asian countries but, particularly, with respect to the transition economies in Eastern Europe. However, the Chinese situation has always been very different fro that in the European economies.

6. *World Trade Organization Annual Report 1997*, Vol. 2 (Geneva: WTO Secretariat). These figures are derived from figures and tables on pp. 59–63 of the report.

7. For discussion see Bijan Aghelvi and Peter Montiel, "Exchange Rate Policies in Developing Countries." In Emil-Maria Claassen, ed., *Exchange Rate Policies in Developing and Post-Socialist Countries* (San Francisco: International Center for Economic Growth, 1991).

8. See Manuel Montes, *The Currency Crisis in Southeast Asia* (Singapore: Institute of Southeast Asian Studies, 1998).

REFERENCES

Adams, F. G., and I-M Davis. (1993). "The Role of Policy in Economic Development: Comparisons of the East and Southeast Asian and Latin American Experience." *Asian-Pacific Economic Literature* 8(1), pp. 8–24.

Adams, F. G., and S. Ichimura, eds. (1998). *East Asian Development: Will the East Asian Growth Miracle Survive?* Westport, CT: Praeger.

Corbo, V. M. Goldstein, and M. Kahn. (1987). *Growth-Oriented Adjustment Programs.* Washington, DC: IMF, World Bank.

Feldstein, Martin. (1998). "Refocusing the IMF." *Foreign Affairs* (March/April).

Hanke, S. H., and K. Schuler. (1994). *Currency Boards for Developing Countries: A Handbook.* San Francisco: ICS Press.

Hughes, H. (1995). "Why Have East Asian Countries Led Economic Development?" *The Economic Record* 71(212), pp. 88–104

Radelet, Steven, and Jeffrey D. Sachs. (1998). "The East Asian Financial Crisis: Diagnosis, Remedies, Prospects. *Brookings Papers on Economic Activity.* Vol. 1, pp. 1–90.

Sachs, Jeffrey D. (1997). "IMF Is a Power unto Itself." *Financial Times* December 11.

Wade, R. (1990). *Governing the Market: Economic Theory and the Role of Government in East Asian Industrialization.* Princeton, NJ: Princeton University Press.

World Bank. (1993). The East Asian Miracle: Economic Growth and Public Policy. New York: Oxford University Press.

2

Policy Challenges to Revive the East Asian Miracle

F. Gerard Adams

A time when the headlong rush to development of East Asia has hit a roadblock is an appropriate point to consider what happened in East Asia and what kind of policies can revive the East Asian miracle. While the IMF claims some success for its structural adjustment approach, some economists (Sachs, 1997; Feldstein, 1998) argue that the IMF's approach is wrongheaded and that the type of stabilization policy promoted by the IMF imposes too heavy a burden.[1] Are policies needed beyond the traditional stabilization measures to give the East Asian economies a jump start and to set the East Asian growth process back into rapid motion? What kinds of policies will serve that purpose?

In this chapter, first I ask what went wrong in East Asia and how that is likely to affect future economic and social prospects. Short-term prospects are quite dire, particularly for Indonesia, but there is basis to remain moderately optimistic about the long-run viability of the region. Then, I turn to policy. What are the challenges for policy? What are the basic stabilization policies, the elements of the IMF conditionality package? What, if anything, can be done about the social and employment problems resulting? Finally, I turn to policies for the longer run. What policy approaches will help to put East Asian development back on track? Our discussion deals in detail with Thailand, though we note its applicability to other East Asian countries.

WHAT WENT WRONG?

The crisis began "officially," so to speak, with the devaluation of the Thai baht on July 2, 1997. This event came as a big surprise to financial markets. Not until August did the crisis hit Indonesia and still later in the year engulf Malaysia and

Korea. Contagion effects were to spread to the currencies of many other countries, including those of Latin America and Russia. As a result, much of the discussion has been in terms of a financial/exchange rate panic (Radelet and Sachs, 1998b). But the roots of the crisis undoubtedly lie deeper, and its beginnings should have been apparent in various dimensions of the affected economies at least a year or two earlier (Corsetti et al., 1998a, 1998b).

The 1997 economic crisis in Southeast Asia has its roots in the disequilibria resulting from the exceedingly rapid growth of the previous decade and in important policy failures. The question is not so much why there was a crisis but, rather, why the expansion lasted so long without interruptions. The example of Thailand illustrates the situation clearly (Mingsarn Kaosa-ard, Chapter 11 in this volume). Similar problems were apparent in other East Asian countries as well, though some like Taiwan and, perhaps, China have avoided much of the problem.

With hindsight it is now clear that the Southeast Asian countries—Thailand in particular—were greatly overextended. Investment, foreign borrowing, and speculation were based on unrealistic expectations. The excessively large current account deficit was offset by foreign borrowing, much of it at short term.

The proximate cause of the crisis was the slowdown in exports, already apparent in Thailand in 1996, when exports showed zero increase compared to double-digit growth in previous years. Much of this slowdown was thought to be attributable to the appreciation of the dollar, to which the baht was pegged, and to the weak economies of countries that served as important markets for Thai products, particularly Japan and Western Europe. But there is also evidence that Thai products were no longer competitive with other supplier countries. Production of athletic shoes and garments was being shifted from Thailand to China and Vietnam. In part, this is simply the operation of the economic growth ladder process, discussed in the previous chapter.

The growth process in East Asia involved evolution of the economies from suppliers of primary and labor-intensive products to more automated processes and more technologically advanced goods and to services. As countries achieved higher per capita income, exchange rate appreciation and increasing wages reduced their competitiveness for labor-intensive products relative to other countries in the region. Each country, in turn, gradually shifted its production to more sophisticated goods as competitive pressures from its neighbors mounted in the more traditional products. This produces a linked development ladder tying the development of the more backward countries to that of their more advanced neighbors. It also means that the various East Asian countries compete with one another as suppliers and that some of them lose competitiveness as others gain. Costs in Thailand increased quickly with shortages of skilled labor and infrastructure bottlenecks. In that respect, the competition of China appears to be an important factor in the East Asian situation. This competition was exacerbated when the Chinese renminbi was adjusted in 1994 and as Chinese production capabilities improved in the 1980s and early 1990s. In other words, the export problem that precipitated the financial crisis reflects the operation of the development cycle process in East Asia exacerbated by currency overvaluation. At the same time as exports lagged, the booming economy stimulated imports, so that in 1996 Thailand was running a trade deficit of 8% of gross domestic product (GDP).

It is important to emphasize that the problem also has aspects of a business cycle. In Thailand in the 1994–1996 period, massive investment in hotels, offices, and condominium buildings in addition to public infrastructure projects caused excessively rapid growth. The expansion was financed, directly and indirectly, by a huge capital inflow, much of it in the form of short-term money. Demand pressures affected labor costs, as we have noted, and the costs of construction materials and land. At the same time, there were signs that investors may have been overly optimistic. Excess capacity in the Thai real estate sector was already apparent in 1995 and 1996, and it was clear that the high levels of construction investment were unsustainable. In other East Asian countries, there was also a cyclical swing, though somewhat different in nature, with massive industrial investment in Korea and large infrastructure projects in Malaysia, for example.

The situation was abetted by serious policy failures. The Bank of Thailand (BoT), itself embroiled in the Bangkok Bank of Commerce scandal, did not deal with overexpansion and excessive foreign capital inflow. Indeed, in an attempt to widen the financial role of Thailand in the East Asian region, the BoT had set up the Bangkok International Banking Facility (BIBF), permitting "offshore" banking. The intent was to obtain money abroad and to rechannel it toward Cambodia, Laos, and other neighboring countries. In practice, the BIBF opened a channel for foreign money to flow into Thailand. Such flows became very large. The problem was not so much liberalization of capital flows as it was incomplete liberalization. Since domestic rates remained high, largely controlled by local banks, an interest rate differential between domestic rates and world rates of some 7% attracted a vast flow of foreign capital. At about the same time, the government budget was allowed to slip into deficit.

In late 1996 and the first half of 1997, as financial markets lost confidence, a flight of capital ensued that brought down the baht and had similar effects on other Southeast Asian currencies, except that of China. As the inflow of capital was suddenly reversed, the BoT used much of Thailand's foreign exchange reserve in a vain effort to maintain the baht-dollar exchange rate. Note that devaluation would have, and did, cost borrowers in U.S. dollars dearly. As the condition of finance companies and some banks began to deteriorate, the BoT failed in its fiduciary duties of bank and finance company supervision. Finally, responding to an IMF request, in mid-1977, two-thirds of the finance companies were "suspended," though not until they had borrowed the equivalent of $20 billion from a government fund.[2] Most commercial banks were in dire straits and needed recapitalization or closure. The resulting liquidity crunch severely affected investment, construction, auto sales, and many other aspects of the economy. Even exports were hindered by the lack of credit financing.

The consequences of these developments unfolded only gradually as bankruptcies, industrial shutdowns and unemployment increased (see Figures 2.1–2.4.).

Figure 2.1
Thai Exchange Rate, 1997–1999

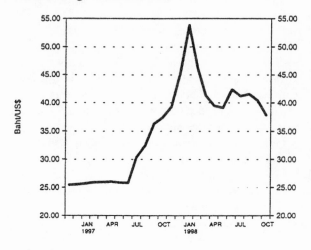

Figure 2.2
Thai Merchandise Trade Balance, 1997–1998

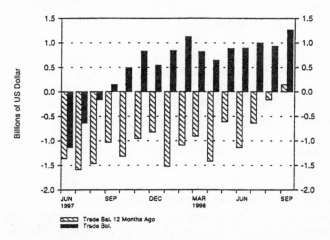

While the magnitude of the crisis had not been anticipated, it soon became clear that the short-run prospect was serious, as economists were sequentially lowering their forecasts for 1998 and beyond. The slowdown in 1997 was followed by full-fledged recession in 1998, with a decline in GDP estimated between 6% and 8%. How long this situation would last depended on the speed and forcefulness with which the government put credible policies into place. Initially, that was uncertain because of the political instability in Thailand at the time of the crisis. But since the accession of the Chuan government in late 1997 and its collaboration

Figure 2.3
Thai Manufacturing Output, 1997–1998

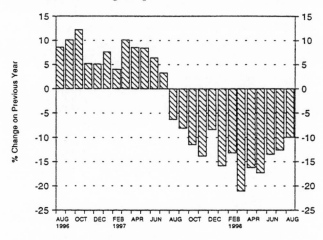

Figure 2.4
Thai Rate of Inflation, 1997–1998

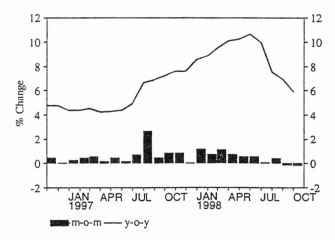

with the IMF, a political basis for stabilization has been established, even if the process of change was taking longer than had been hoped.

In 1998, what started out as a recession turned into a depression. Regardless of whether one agrees with our view of the business cycle basis for the crisis, the slowdown clearly reflects sharp declines in domestic demand. Statistics showed drops of auto sales of 80% and declines of investment of 16%. A survey of business sentiment (Adams and Vernon, 1998) showed that there were widespread cutbacks in production and plant closings and efforts, by almost all respondents, to cut back inventories and investment. The primary motive was lack of demand, though lack of liquidity also played an important role. Only exports were expanding, though they were held in check by a shortage of outbound shipping containers and, as we have noted, by lack of export financing. The business cycle aspects of the decline of domestic demand have some positive elements for the future in that once excess inventories have been used up and excess investments absorbed, there will be a bottoming out of the demand decline and a basis for some expansion. In the second half of 1998, steps were finally being taken to resolve the banking crisis. Some banks sought foreign capital; some were taken over. Only very few of the finance companies were able to present a feasible reorganization plan. Assets held by finance companies were to be divided between those that were good and those that were not good and were to be sold at auction. A bankruptcy law was passed, but it does not appear that many ventures would go through the formal bankruptcy process. There was hope that the recession would bottom out in the latter half of 1998 or early 1999, so that modest growth could resume (Table 2.1).

The timing and severity of the crisis were different in other East Asian countries. The impact on real GDP has been considerably more severe in Indonesia than in Thailand, Malaysia, and South Korea (Table 2.1). Some countries, like Taiwan, China, and Vietnam show only a mild slowdown, but none has escaped unscathed. Exchange rate depreciation in Indonesia, Malaysia, and South Korea followed the decline of the baht by some months, prompting the notion that the crisis was caused by contagion of expectations from Thailand to other East Asian (and, more recently, South American) countries (Table 2.2). The political problems of Indonesia accounted for much greater currency instability and inflation there than elsewhere in the region (Table 2.3). An abrupt turnaround in the current account, from deficit to surplus, is apparent in all the developing East Asian countries, except Singapore and Taiwan, as trade patterns changed and as foreign lenders and investors sought to withdraw capital (Table 2.4).

For the longer term, there is reason for guarded optimism. Thailand is well placed as one of the countries in the East Asian growth process. It was the first one to be hit by crisis, and it may well be the first to recover. The depreciation of the baht restored the competitiveness of Thai export products. Thailand participated effectively in the East Asian development process in the past and, given appropriate policies, may well be able to do so again in the future. In late 1998, other East Asian countries were also showing signs of stabilizing, and there was hope that the area could resume its growth. Much, however, depends on policies, to which we now turn.

THE ROLE OF THE IMF

The IMF has played a pivotal role in dealing with the East Asian crisis.[3] It has offered its financial support. In accord with IMF practice, its loans have been conditional on restrictive economic policies. As Feldstein (1998) emphasizes, the IMF stretched its mandate from traditional emphasis on macroeconomic policies like the government deficit and monetary policy to a more interventionist posture.

Table 2.1
Real Gross Domestic Product in East Asia

	1996	1997	1998	1999	2000	2001	2002
Japan	4.1	0.8	-2.1	0.4	1.9	3.2	3.0
Hong Kong	5.0	5.3	-4.0	-1.5	1.0	3.0	3.8
Singapore	6.9	7.8	0.3	2.1	4.5	5.4	5.8
South Korea	7.1	5.5	-6.0	0.6	4.8	5.6	5.6
Taiwan	5.7	6.8	5.2	5.4	5.6	5.7	6.0
Indonesia	8.0	4.6	-13.5	-3.9	3.2	4.3	6.0
Malaysia	8.6	7.8	-4.1	0.9	3.3	5.6	6.4
Philippines	5.8	5.2	0.7	3.7	5.5	5.9	6.0
Thailand	5.5	-0.5	-6.8	0.9	2.6	4.1	5.5
China	9.7	8.8	7.0	8.0	8.2	8.5	8.7
Vietnam	9.4	8.8	4.9	7.4	8.6	8.6	9.0

Note: Annual percentage changes. Actual: 1996, 1997; estimated: 1998; forecast: 1999–2002.

Source: The WEFA Group, *Asia Economic Outlook*, Fourth Quarter 1998.

Table 2.2
Exchange Rate Indexes

	1996	1997	1998	1999	2000	2001	2002
Japan	15.6	11.2	14.4	0.9	-14.6	-6.2	-1.9
Hong Kong	-0.0	0.1	-0.0	-0.1	-0.0	-0.0	-0.0
Singapore	-0.5	5.3	13.0	1.1	-2.6	-2.2	-3.1
South Korea	4.3	18.3	43.0	-12.1	-3.5	-2.3	-1.0
Taiwan	2.7	5.3	19.1	8.5	-10.6	-15.8	-3.7
Indonesia	4.2	24.2	273.4	-7.6	-5.9	3.5	3.2
Malaysia	0.5	11.8	39.6	-3.2	1.9	1.3	1.0
Philippines	2.0	12.4	34.2	-0.6	4.1	4.1	4.0
Thailand	1.7	23.8	40.8	3.9	1.1	1.1	1.5
China	-0.4	-03	0.2	7.0	1.8	1.8	1.7
Vietnam	-0.8	11.7	6.8	4.9	3.6	3.1	3.0

Note: Annual percentage changes, local currency in billions of U.S. dollars. Actual: 1996, 1997; estimated: 1998; forecast: 1999–2002.

Source: The WEFA Group, *Asia Economic Outlook,* Fourth Quarter 1998.

Table 2.3
CPI Inflation

	1996	1997	1998	1999	2000	2001	2002
Japan	0.1	1.7	0.6	0.6	1.0	1.2	1.7
Hong Kong	6.0	5.7	3.6	3.7	3.8	3.9	4.0
Singapore	1.4	1.9	0.9	2.2	2.0	2.3	2.1
South Korea	5.0	4.4	7.2	10.5	8.4	4.9	4.8
Taiwan	2.3	0.9	1.8	2.7	3.5	3.4	3.4
Indonesia	8.0	6.6	74.6	36.2	17.5	9.8	6.7
Malaysia	3.5	2.7	6.0	7.3	5.7	3.8	3.7
Philippines	8.4	5.1	9.7	10.7	9.6	6.0	5.8
Thailand	5.8	5.6	10.4	9.3	7.8	5.6	4.5
China	8.3	2.8	0.2	3.3	4.4,	4.8	5.1
Vietnam	4.5	3.5	8.1	7.5	7.8	8.1	8.4

Note: Annual percentage changes. Actual: 1996, 1997; estimated: 1998; forecast: 1999–2002.

Source: The WEFA Group, *Asia Economic Outlook*, Fourth Quarter 1998.

Table 2.4
Current Account Balance

	1996	1997	1998	1999	2000	2001	2002
Japan	66.81	94.06	107.23	156.07	218.98	237.48	234.98
Hong Kong	-2.03	-6.00	1.74	0.42	0.56	0.81	1.20
Singapore	14.72	14.80	15.82	11.88	11.46	11.34	11.43
South Korea	-23.01	-8.85	41.03	39.26	22.86	13.21	4.81
Taiwan	11.03	7.78	3.56	6.14	5.08	4.94	4.62
Indonesia	-7.66	-4.62	8.68	7.39	3.03	-0.98	-2.35
Malaysia	-2.97	3.81	10.18	8.05	4.89	1.75	-1.92
Philippines	-3.95	-4.30	3.03	1.36	0.82	1.02	1.29
Thailand	-14.69	-2.92	10.12	8.06	3.72	0.25	-3.24
China	7.24	28.77	28.10	24.32	19.60	13.21	12.47
Vietnam	-3.42	-1.74	-0.99	-0.18	0.26	-0.76	-0.87

Note: Annual percentage changes, local currency in billions of U.S. dollars. Actual: 1996, 1997; estimated: 1998; forecast: 1999–2002.

Source: The WEFA Group, *Asia Economic Outlook,* Fourth Quarter 1998.

It urged the elimination of trade barriers, cronyism, corruption, even price controls on fuels and rice. Arguably, some of these features of East Asian economies were at the source of their troubles, for example, in Indonesia. Some economists would take the position that clearing the decks of market interventions might advance progress and, with it, confidence in the East Asian economies. But so long as the East Asian economies showed considerable success despite market imperfections, one could argue that the IMF was intervening in aspects of economic management that did not relate closely to balance of payments problems. Coming from a different perspective, Sachs (1997) took a position that the restrictive policies being imposed on these countries were too stringent. He felt that recovery and stability would not be possible in an atmosphere of social disarray and recession resulting, precisely, from IMF policy prescriptions. High interest rates would drive into bankruptcy even the soundest firms, the ones that might lead the recovery. Such views were based on the notion that the fundamentals of most of the East Asian economies were all right and that the problem was one of temporary illiquidity and financial panic rather than of solvency. By seeking closure of insolvent financial institutions, the IMF may have caused panic and brought down finance companies that might otherwise have survived. Radelet and Sachs (1998b) write that "while Asia economies had flaws that needed mending, those weaknesses didn't come close to accounting for the depth of the crisis. . . . The IMF's policies . . . merely fanned the flames of panic." A still different perspective was that of Hanke and Schuler (1994), whose proposal to establish a currency board arbitrarily linking the Indonesian money supply to foreign exchange reserves at a fixed ratio and fixing the exchange rate had a brief moment of glory.

Initially, the IMF's policies may well have been too rigorous. This reflected a view of the crisis as a single-country problem, failing to recognize that it would quickly spread. It also reflected expectations, in common with many economists, that the crisis would be much less serious than it turned out to be. Finally, the IMF began its agreements with Thailand and other countries on the supposition that all outstanding debts would be repaid, making no effort to seek accommodation by the creditors. Not until December 1997 did it become apparent with regard to Korea that foreign lenders needed to be persuaded to ease credit terms and extend further loans. It is apparent that even greater accommodations will have to be made for Russia, where *de facto* default occurred.

The IMF has shown flexibility in recognizing that there is reason for concern with regard to the social and economic implications of stabilization policies. In the case of Thailand, the bargaining for the "fifth letter of intent," August 1998, allowed the government of Thailand to ease its fiscal stance, from an initial surplus of 1% GDP to a more realistic deficit of 3% and eventually to 5%, which would permit some modest "pump priming." The agreement also foresaw a gradual decline of interest rates.

Altogether, we must judge the IMF's approach a qualified success. To gain some perspective, it is important to remember that the IMF's purpose is to stabilize the international financial system. It is not to save the creditor banks or even to smooth life in the countries in crisis. A year into the crisis, we must admit that the IMF has succeeded only in part. The international financial system is operational, but the crisis has spread from the countries directly affected—Thailand, Indonesia, Korea, the Philippines, and Malaysia—to Russia, Brazil, and elsewhere.

LIBERALIZATION VERSUS CONTROLS

Gradual liberalization of domestic markets, international trade, and financial flows has been a hallmark of East Asian development. Like most developing countries, the East Asian countries began with extensive systems of controls and other forms of government intervention into their economics. As the economies developed, many of these regulations have been abolished or have become ineffective. As we note in Chapter 4, sector-specific industrial policies have faded even in countries, like Korea and Taiwan, that once put substantial priority on such interventions. Trade policy has become more liberal, with elimination of quotas and reduction of tariffs. As we note in Chapter 3, further progress in this direction is being made in the framework of AFTA and APEC. International capital flow controls have also been reduced or eliminated, as we have noted in the discussion of Thailand's BIBF. A priority on economic liberalization has consistently been a part of the IMF's structural readjustment programs.

Unfortunately, the 1997 crisis may turn out to be a setback to the tendency toward freer markets. Import restrictions are being imposed and tariffs raised as a way to improve the trade balance. A recent example is China, which has reimposed regulations limiting imports and is raising minimum prices of imported goods in order to restrict the import flow. The issue of capital flow liberalization has raised particular controversy. Krugman (1998) has called for capital controls as a way of dealing with the crisis. He argues that controls would avoid the need for raising interest rates to protect the exchange rate. Others have taken the position that liberalization, particularly of capital flows, has come too quickly or that capital flows are inherently speculative and destabilizing. Countries, like China, that have had substantial controls, now strengthened, have had less difficulty than countries like Indonesia or Thailand. Malaysia has reinstituted capital controls. Soros (1998) has proposed imposition of some costs associated with short-term capital movements to "throw some sand in the wheels." Chile, long seen as a pioneer "tiger" in Latin America, has maintained restrictions on short-term capital transactions. Regardless of one's conclusion about the desirability of liberalization of global trade and financial markets, it is probable that the tendency toward liberalization of the past few decades will be interrupted, at least temporarily, as a result of the East Asian crisis.

POLICY CHALLENGES

How can the policy challenges of the crisis be handled? We focus here on policy from the perspective of the East Asian countries. There is, of course, a far broader question with respect to providing a stable framework and a lender-of-last-resort for the world's monetary and trading system. While that is an equally, if not more, important issue, it is outside the scope of control of the developing countries in East Asia.

The principal policy issues for the countries in East Asia can be categorized into three parts:

—Stabilization

—Employment and social welfare

—Growth

There is little question that stabilization is a primary consideration. External stabilization and internal stabilization are closely interrelated, a watchword of the IMF's adjustment programs. To stabilize the currency and to reestablish foreign capital inflows, confidence is essential. This requires not only external adjustment with a positive trade balance but also internal balance as well. For this reason the typical IMF program deals not only with trade, stimulating exports and reducing imports, but also with questions of monetary and fiscal policy. In the case of Thailand, this has meant:

—$17 billion of loan commitments

—increases in taxes (the value-added tax [VAT] was increased from 7% to 10%)

—massive reductions in public spending even for infrastructure capital projects

—tight monetary policy

—closing insolvent finance companies and banks

The primary objective is to restore confidence and to prevent inflation, some of which is inevitable as a result of the currency depreciation. At the same time, the challenge is to put the financial system back on track. This involves taking over insolvent finance companies and banks (Financial Restructuring Authority and Assets Management Committee) and will require special arrangements for debtors (in foreign currencies) who are unable to meet their obligations. In Thailand, as we have noted, the problem was exacerbated initially by political instability; a weak government unable to achieve sufficient consensus was replaced by the Chuan government, which ultimately succeeded in putting in place the requirements of the IMF program.

The category of employment and social welfare policies raises the second dimension of policy measures. Unfortunately, this has been and will be the focus of much controversy. As we have noted, the crisis has inevitable recessionary consequences for demand and output. This is not just the result of IMF-sponsored readjustment measures, as some politicians would argue. Production declined significantly. Employment in industry and in the financial and real estate and construction sectors was falling sharply. A positive consideration is that export industries benefited from the baht devaluation, but the increase was not sufficient to offset the drastic decline in domestic demand. Thailand faced a true recession with unemployment of middle-class people as well as workers. There is little if any public safety net. Macropolicies—increases in government expenditures, tax cuts, and lower interest rates—might represent ways to deal with such a problem from a demand stimulus perspective—hence, the controversy. Should spending and monetary policy be restrained to assure stability and confidence even at high social costs? Or would domestic stimulus to alleviate the social problems once again endanger stability?

The third policy category deals with growth. Of course, the Southeast Asian countries cannot be put back on a true growth path until the excesses of the past have been taken care of, until the banking systems are on solid footing, and until most of the excess supply of housing, and hotel and office space is absorbed. On the other hand, reduced demand pressures may temporarily ease the difficulties of transportation and supply of manpower.

What is needed to resume growth is to enhance competitiveness. This is not only a question of the exchange rate, which has already adjusted to make Southeast Asian goods very competitive. In the longer term, what are needed will be policies that facilitate the transition to the next stage of the development ladder. This means that Thailand will need to develop industries that use more advanced technologies as Taiwan, Singapore, and Korea have in the past decade. Progress is being made. In the Thai case, an example has been the growth of the automobile parts and assembly industry, which represents a more advanced stage of development. In the case of Malaysia, it has been the development of electronics manufacturing. The difficulty is that such development calls for skilled labor and engineering and management expertise, all of which has been in short supply. It also requires more sophisticated infrastructure and supplier industries. There is clearly a role for the public sector in this regard. But investments in physical and human capital take many years to pay off.

Second, there is the question of competition and markets. Internally, the Southeast Asian economies are still subject to many regulations and controls. This is particularly true of the financial, communication, and professional service sectors. Improvements are being forced by increased competition, often on the part of foreign entrants. At the same time the local markets are of limited size. Increased competition and economies of scale would result if there were greater opening between the various economies in the area. From this perspective the progress of the East Asian Free Trade Area (AFTA) is a very welcome step. (AFTA is discussed in greater detail in Chapter 3.)

Finally, there is the challenge of obtaining new technology. It is not so much a question of developing new technology but of acquiring it from the industrial world, where much of it is available, and adapting it to local conditions. Some of the East Asian countries, Taiwan, for example, have made significant strides in raising the level of technology of domestic manufacturing by attracting overseas engineers and professionals. Others, like Malaysia and Indonesia, have gone in for industry-specific industrial and technology policies and have tried to establish national companies to produce automobiles and aircraft to exploit more advanced technologies. Whether technology and industry-specific industrial policies are effective is unclear (see discussions in Chapters 1 and 4). In the East Asian scene much of the improvement of technology has been associated with the operation of private enterprises, particularly those with important international connections. Appropriate technology policy may well be closely related to liberalization and opening of markets to international partnership.

The East Asian crisis in 1997 represents the policy challenge for the East Asian countries and for the IMF for the next few years. While the prospects for renewed growth in the area are positive, it is too early to tell whether the Southeast Asian countries can meet the policy challenges to revive the East Asian growth miracle.

NOTES

1. An interesting summary of contrasting views is, "Would-Be Keyneses Vie over How to Fight Globe's Financial Woes," *Wall Street Journal*, September 25, 1998, A1. Nouriel Roubini's Web site http://www.Stern.NYU.edu/~nroubini/asiaHomepage.html#intro contains references to most of the relevant publications.

2. Earlier in the year, closure of 16 finance companies had caused runs on some banks but had favored those that appeared to have good balance sheets.

3. For a balanced discussion, see Fischer (1998).

REFERENCES

Adams, F. Gerard, and Heidi Vernon. (1998). "The Impact of the East Asian Crisis on Thai Firms: A Micro Survey Study." Unpublished. Boston: Northeastern University.

Corsetti, G., P. Pesenti, and N. Roubini. (1998a). What Caused the Asian Currency and Financial Crisis? Part I: A Macroeconomic Overview." NBER Working Paper W6833. Cambridge, MA: National Bureau of Economic Research.

———. (1998a). What Caused the Asian Currency and Financial Crisis? Part II: The Policy Debate." NBER Working Paper W6834. Cambridge, MA: National Bureau of Economic Research.

Feldstein, Martin. (1998). "Refocusing the IMF." *Foreign Affairs* 77(2), pp. 20–33.

Fischer, Stanley. (1998). "Lessons from a Crisis." *The Economist* October 3, pp. 23–27.

Hanke, S., and K. Schuler. (1994). *Currency Boards for Developing Countries: A Handbook.* San Francisco: ICS Press.

Hughes, Helen. (1995). *Achieving Industrialization in East Asia.* Cambridge: Cambridge University Press.

Krugman, Paul. (1998). "Saving Asia: It's Time to Get Radical." http://www.pathfinder.com/fortune/investor/1998/980907/sol.html.

Radelet, Steven, and Jeffrey D. Sachs. (1998a). "The East Asian Financial Crisis: Diagnosis, Remedies, Prospects." *Brookings Papers on Economic Activity.* Vol. I, pp. 1–90.

———. (1998b). *Financial Times*, Letters to the Editor, April 15.

Sachs, J. (1997). "IMF Is a Power unto Itself." *Financial Times*, December 11.

Soros, George. (1998). *The Crisis of Global Capitalism.* New York: Public Affairs.

Wade, Robert. (1990). *Governing the Market: Economic Theory and the Role of Government in East Asian Industrialization.* Princeton, NJ: Princeton University Press.

World Bank. (1993). *The East Asian Miracle: Economic Growth and Public Policy.* New York: Oxford University Press.

3

Trade Trends and Policy Issues in East Asian Developing Economies

William E. James

TRENDS IN WORLD TRADE AND PRODUCTION: IMPLICATIONS FOR EAST ASIAN DEVELOPING ECONOMIES

World goods and services trade volume has been expanding more rapidly than real world output during the last decade (Table 3.1). This can be seen from estimates of actual growth and forecasts of future growth of world production and trade volume. The high elasticity of world trade with respect to world output may be explained by:

1. Improvements in transport and communications technologies that have lowered the cost of conducting international transactions;
2. Liberalization of international trade through elimination of traditional nontariff barriers coupled with tariff reductions that have been undertaken unilaterally, regionally, and multilaterally; and
3. The increasing role of transnational corporations brought about by liberalization and expansion of flows of foreign direct investment.

East Asian developing economies, in particular, have enjoyed a rising share of world trade, as income growth has been extremely rapid in recent decades (World Bank, 1993; Oshima, 1993; James et al., 1987). Between 1990 and 1996, the share in world merchandise trade of ten East Asian developing economies (China, Korea, Taiwan, Hong Kong, Philippines, Indonesia, Singapore, Malaysia, Vietnam, and Thailand) rose from 11% to 17%.[1] Unilateral liberalization measures have helped these economies to achieve such a phenomenal increase in world trade share. For example, large emerging economies in East Asia, including China and Indonesia,

Table 3.1
Growth Rates of World Output and Trade Volume, IMF Estimates

Variable	1988	1989	1990	1991	1992	1993	1994	1995	1996p	1997p	1988-95
World Output	4.6	3.7	2.6	1.5	2.4	2.4	3.7	3.5	3.8	4.3	2.9
Goods & services	8.2	7.4	5.3	3.7	4.7	3.9	8.8	8.9	6.7	7.2	6.2
Goods	8.8	6.9	4.7	3.8	6.0	3.9	9.5	9.1	6.4	7.1	6.4

Sources: IMF, *World Economic Outlook.* Washington, DC: IMF, May and October 1996.

have increasingly relied on market forces and have consequently boosted their share of world exports of non-oil manufactured goods. Indeed, the market share of East Asian economy exports in the total apparent consumption of manufactured goods in the OECD countries has risen sharply between 1980 and 1993 (Lloyd and Toguchi, 1996).[2]

In the future, long-term trend growth in East Asian developing economies' trade is likely to be more closely in line with expansion of world trade than in the recent past, when growth was much higher in East Asia. Short-term growth in international trade is subject to cyclical fluctuations that are influenced by exchange rates and other factors. However, domestic trade may become a strong future source of growth in these economies as they mature. Currently, in some East Asian economies expansion of domestic trade has been constrained by a combination of infrastructure bottlenecks, restrictions on foreign investment in retail trade and distribution, and a plethora of local and province-level trade restrictions and formal and informal levies. Easing these obstacles will accelerate growth in domestic trade. Both China and Indonesia can expect to depend more on the growth of the domestic market as a major impetus to economic growth rather than upon exports. It is likely that domestic trade growth rates will exceed those of international trade. Indeed, it would be realistic to accept medium-term to long-term forecasts of world trade and production as benchmarks for the future expansion of the real volume of international trade in the coming decade in the large East Asian economies.

Exports and imports of goods and services as a percentage of GDP are already quite high in East Asian developing economies compared with the United States and Japan (Table 3.2). It is still probable that the growth in the real value of international trade may exceed real income growth in East Asia. Hence, some expansion above the benchmarks is still plausible and, in some cases, is even likely (e.g., India, Indonesia, Philippines, and Vietnam). With the achievement of long-term liberalization of international trade through the Uruguay Round Agreement of 1994 and with the establishment of the World Trade Organization (WTO) with an ambitious future agenda, world trade is set to expand more rapidly than would have been the case otherwise.

MACROTRENDS AND MICROTRENDS IN EAST ASIAN TRADE

A pronounced slowing down in the growth of East Asian merchandise trade occurred beginning in the latter half of 1995 and continuing in 1996. This slowdown can be seen in the case of exports (Table 3.3) and imports (Table 3.4) comparing 1995 and 1996 growth rates. Macroeconomic causes of slower growth included, in some cases, real appreciation of the exchange rate that left some currencies overvalued and that led to a shift of investment and production from internationally traded goods and services to nontraded goods and services (i.e., real estate, property development, and construction). In other cases, more rapid growth in domestic consumption and demand than in production took place. Finally, the slowdown in

Table 3.2
Shares of Imports and Exports of Goods and Nonfactor Services in GDP (percentage)

Country	Exports				Imports			
	1990	1995	1996		1990	1995	1996	
China,P.R.: Mainland	14.8	21.1	21.1		12.0	19.4	18.9	
China,P.R.:Hong Kong	134.3	149.7	141.8		125.8	153.3	142.8	
Indonesia	26.6	26.3	25.8		26.0	27.6	26.7	
Korea	29.8	33.1	32.4		30.3	34.1	36.4	
Malaysia	76.3	95.5	NA		74.2	98.9	NA	
Philippines	27.5	36.4	42.0		33.3	44.2	51.7	
Singapore	180.2	173.7	165.9		173.4	157.0	151.5	
Taiwan	46.8	48.8	48.3		41.8	46.8	44.5	
Thailand	34.0	41.1	NA		41.5	48.0	NA	
Japan	10.7	9.4	8.9		10.0	7.9	9.4	
United States	9.7	11.3	11.4		10.9	12.4	12.6	

Sources: IMF, *International Financial Statistics*. Washington, DC: IMF, October 1997 CD-ROM; ADB, Key Indicators. 1997 Internet download.

Table 3.3
East Asia's Export Growth Slowdown, 1995–1996 IMF Estimates

Country/Territory	Exports (US $ mil.)		Growth Rate (% annual change)	
	1995	1996	1995	1996
China	148,755	151,093	23.1	1.6
Hong Kong	173,546	180,525	14.6	4
Taiwan	111,833	116,194	19.4	3.9
Indonesia (non-oil exports)	43,285 34,954	47,823 38,093	13.3 15.1	10.5 9
Japan	443,005	411,242	12.1	-7.2
Korea	125,365	127,592	30.5	1.8
Malaysia	73,990	77,001	25.9	4.1
Philippines	17,249	21,466	28.4	24.4
Singapore	118,172	125,118	22.6	5.9
Thailand	56,662	57151	23.1	0.9

Sources: IMF, *Direction of Trade Statistics Yearbook.* Washington, DC: IMF, 1996 and June 1997; Taiwan Ministry of Finance 1996; Indonesia Central Bureau of Statistics, for nonoil exports, Trade Statistics, March 1997.

Table 3.4
East Asia's Import Growth Slowdown, 1995–1996 IMF Estimates

Country/Territory	Imports (US $ mil.)		Growth Rate (% annual change)	
	1995	1996	1995	1996
China	132,007	138,822	14.2	5.2
Hong Kong	192,764	198,551	19.2	3
Taiwan	103,652	101,372	19.5	-2.2
Indonesia	43,285	42,830	13.3	-1.1
(non-oil imports)	37,718	39,333	27.4	4.3
Japan	335,871	349,508	22.6	4.1
Korea	135,153	147,375	32.1	9
Malaysia	77,662	77,001	30.4	-0.9
Philippines	28,419	40,038	26.1	40.9
Singapore	124,394	131,505	21.6	5.7
Thailand	73,959	74,616	35.2	0.9

Sources: IMF, Direction of Trade Statistics Yearbook. Washington, DC: IMF, 1996 and June 1997; Taiwan Ministry of Finance 1996; Indonesia Central Bureau of Statistics, for nonoil exports, Trade Statistics, March 1997.

the region's imports reinforces the slower growth of exports because a significant share of trade is intraregional.[3]

Microeconomic causes included the slump in worldwide electronics prices and demand (East Asian economies' exports and imports have a large electronics component). Infrastructure bottlenecks are another plausible reason at the microlevel for a slowdown. Moreover, some countries have implemented intervention policies that are unfavorable for expansion of trade by restricting certain imports in the name of reducing current account deficits (e.g., Korea's austerity program, China's nontransparent restrictions and procurement policies, and the rising use of antidumping as a new trade restriction in Southeast Asia).

The slowdown in the growth of international trade may be a precursor of slower real economic growth in select East Asian economies: Thailand, Malaysia, Korea, and Indonesia. The medium-term outlook is for continued growth of output and trade but at a more sustainable pace than before.

KEY ISSUES IN WORLD TRADE IN GOODS AND SERVICES

From the perspective of East Asian developing economies, key international trade policy issues are those that are likely to influence the market access of East Asian export-oriented manufacturing and service industries as well as those that impose adjustments upon domestic import-competing industries, including agriculture. These issues arise at the multilateral, regional, and bilateral levels.

Implementation of the Uruguay Round Agreement

At the multilateral level the first priority of East Asian developing countries (aside from China and Taiwan) is the implementation of the Uruguay Round Agreement of 1994.[4] The Uruguay Round Agreement offers East Asia improved market access for manufactured exports through the reduction of tariffs. It also means that agriculture and textiles will be brought under General Agreement on Tariffs and Trade (GATT)/WTO rules. A key concern is in the implementation of the textile agreement. Thus far, quotas have been relaxed on items that have little commercial impact. There are questions over whether developed countries in Europe and North America will be able to muster the political will necessary to abolish quotas in textiles and apparel, particularly when the time comes to do so in 2004. An added concern is whether certain East Asian textile and apparel manufacturers will be able to adjust to freer trade without the market distorting Multifibre Agreement (MFA)-quotas. Uncertainty over whether the quota markets will indeed implement fully the agreement may lead some East Asian producers to delay making necessary adjustments in a timely fashion.

Ongoing Services Negotiations

The satisfactory conclusion of negotiations in the area of commercial services remains to be achieved. The General Agreement on Trade in Services (GATS) provides a framework within which negotiations on service sectors may be conducted. Negotiations over telecommunications, financial services, maritime transportation, civil aviation, business and professional services, and the movement of natural persons are being carried out and are of strong interest to East Asia. Achievement of improved market access is one object. However, East Asian economies that are large net importers of commercial services should also recognize the economy-wide benefits that can be gained through greater openness and efficiency in traded services. The improved efficiency of services can come about through increased competition provided by foreign suppliers of services. Lower prices of such services can lower the costs of domestic firms in nonservice sectors, including manufacturing. In turn, the lower cost of services in the domestic economy will enhance exports by other sectors.

The WTO Work Agenda: Present and Ongoing

The following is a partial list of items that are in various stages of completion in the WTO:

1. Nonpreferential rules of origin;
2. Customs procedures and valuation;
3. Article 24 and regional trading arrangements;
4. Standards and product testing;
5. Functioning of the dispute settlement mechanism; and
6. The question of new members.

In each of these work agenda items, individual East Asian developing economies have particular interests. However, for some items (e.g., rules of origin) they have a common interest in seeing that these so-called technical matters are not turned to protective uses.[5] In the area of standards and testing the principle of mutual recognition may be agreeable to East Asian developing economies so that their exporters are not put at a disadvantage by adoption of only European or U.S. standards.

The Future Agenda: New Issues and the "Social Clause"

Another priority common to East Asian developing economies is that of the future work agenda of the WTO. Leaders of East Asian developing countries have voiced the concern that developed countries are attempting to influence the future work agenda to give priority to issues that are not directly related to international trade and investment. They object to attempts to establish "linkage" between trade and issues of labor standards and rights, environmental standards, and human rights. The European call for a so-called social clause covering various elements of a society's safety net may appear as an attempt to impose added protection against East Asian exports.

It will be difficult for East Asian leaders to block efforts to link trade with environmental issues, particularly when they are clearly linked, such as in transportation of petrochemicals or other potentially hazardous materials in international sea-lanes. Moreover, it may be better to accept discussion of these issues at the multilateral level of WTO rather than to be subject to direct bilateral pressure alone. East Asian leaders may also wish to take a proactive stance and set forth issues they believe have priority in future WTO work (i.e., tightening of antidumping regulations, market access for laborers from developing economies in developed economies, etc.).

KEY ISSUES IN REGIONAL TRADE AND ASEAN ECONOMIC COOPERATION: AFTA

The Association of Southeast Asian Nations (ASEAN) has steadily progressed in its efforts to deepen and broaden economic cooperation in the region. The following are some of the main issues facing ASEAN in regional trade.

The Enlargement Issue

ASEAN almost achieved its objective of broadening membership to all 10 countries in the region in 1997. Political turmoil created by the Hun Sen coup in Cambodia prevented the entry of that country into the group. However, Vietnam (1996), Laos (1997), and Myanmar (1997) did join ASEAN. The entry of Myanmar is controversial and has drawn criticism from Western democratic countries. Yet ASEAN has shown in its decision to delay the entry of Cambodia that the group maintains its interest in a stable and democratically elected government there. The position with regard to Myanmar may seem at odds with the group's resolute stand on Cambodia. However, ASEAN's approach of "constructive engagement" with Myanmar appears to be paying dividends. The democratic opposition has been allowed to openly hold a party convention. Understanding of ASEAN's varying approach must take into account the group's long-term commitment to a peaceful and stable Cambodia. Indeed the issue of Cambodia has been crucial in strengthening ASEAN as a cohesive grouping.

As these new members have much lower per capita GDP and are less developed than the other six members, there are concerns that ASEAN may turn into a two-tier organization. If they are to catch-up with the rest of East Asia, all three new members will have to undergo trade policy reforms and economic restructuring. Development of market-oriented policies is essential in meeting the requirements for full participation in ASEAN economic cooperation. It is not clear what effects the recent financial and exchange rate crisis will have on the willingness of these transitional economies to expedite economic reforms. Their ability to implement liberalization programs is still in doubt. Through the act of joining ASEAN they have indicated a willingness to proceed with serious reform efforts in the near future.

The AFTA Common Effective Preferential Tariff (CEPT) Scheme

The ASEAN Free Trade Agreement (AFTA) is being launched on an accelerated timetable as a result of the Bangkok Summit in 1995. Essentially by the year 2003 tariffs on almost all intra-ASEAN trade will be between 0% and 5%. In fact, much of the CEPT program will be implemented by the year 2000. Nearly all manufactured goods are included in the program. And although some items are on temporary or special exclusion lists (for a period of 10 years), few items are on the permanent exclusion list. The CEPT scheme will thus bring almost all merchandise trade within AFTA.

In addition to CEPT, the group has launched the ASEAN Industrial Cooperation (AICO) program, which will allow manufacturing firms meeting certain minimal criteria within member countries to benefit immediately from import duty relief. AICO could prove to be important in sectors where import duties are set to remain high (e.g., in autos, chemicals, and metals) because the items are temporarily excluded from CEPT or simply have high tariffs until 2003. Thailand and the Philippines have approved import duty relief for auto parts producers in the two countries. Though Indonesia and Malaysia have in principle agreed to AICO, they have not yet approved any specific cases of relief from tariffs under the scheme.

ASEAN members are also engaged in most-favored nation (MFN) tariff reductions. Unilateral trade liberalization is being undertaken by Indonesia, the Philippines, Thailand, and Malaysia. In the case of Indonesia, the simple unweighted average tariff has been reduced from 20% in 1992 to 12% in 1997. Further reductions according to a published schedule will reduce almost all tariffs to a maximum of 10% in 2003. Thus, the margin of preference given by Indonesia to other ASEAN members will be, at most, 10% and in many cases only 5% or 2.5% as of 2003. There will be little trade diversion in the case of Indonesia. Cuts in MFN tariffs by other members similarly will reduce the AFTA margin of preference and limit the amount of trade diversion.

The increased import competition will create pressures to improve efficiency in ASEAN industries, and the enlarged market will stimulate large-scale manufacturing facilities that can capture economies of scale and scope. However, there is bound to be some restructuring and painful adjustment for some firms in import-sensitive sectors. Without such adjustment, the gains from trade creation cannot be realized. There will be pressure on bureaucrats from formerly protected industries to implement safeguards or, even worse, antidumping measures.

Contingent Protection in ASEAN: The Rise of Antidumping

The experience of Europe, Australia, and North America indicates that contingent forms of protection, particularly the use of antidumping regulations, have proliferated as traditional nontariff and tariff protection has been progressively weakened through the several GATT rounds. Since the GATT system was established average tariffs in the industrial countries have fallen from around 30% to just about 5%. Import-competing industries that have problems meeting import competition in the absence of nontariff barriers (NTBs) and high tariffs have sought out and often received special protection through the antidumping mechanism. In Europe, Australia, Canada, and the United States, the antidumping mechanism has often been used against exports from Japan and East Asian developing countries, including Indonesia and other ASEAN members. For example, in 1996 and 1997, the EU imposed dumping duties on Indonesian exports of unbleached cotton fabric, plastic sacks, and bicycles. Unlike safeguards, which are clearly designed to provide import-competing industries with temporary relief from strong import competition, antidumping claims to check "unfair competition."

While Australia and New Zealand have eliminated the use of antidumping against one another through the harmonization of competition policies and laws, this is not the usual case in free trade areas. It is therefore unsurprising to observe the rise of antidumping within the ASEAN region as traditional barriers to imports are brought down.

In 1996 Malaysia imposed duties on two Indonesian paper products exporters accused of dumping their products. In 1997, Thailand opened an antidumping investigation against Indonesian exporters of tinted glass. Indonesia itself has imposed antidumping duties on stainless steel imports from a number of developing countries and has begun investigations on a number of other cases, including imports of carbon black from Thailand. The Philippines is probably the most prolific user of antidumping in ASEAN. There is no economic justification for the regulations on antidumping.[6] In fact, antidumping processes as practiced by the European Union (EU), Australia, Canada, and the United States have unduly restricted trade, raising prices and, often providing rents to producers at home and abroad. It would be unfortunate if ASEAN were to follow such a path as this could have a chilling effect on the expansion of trade within the region. The Uruguay Round Agreement brought a bit more discipline to the use of antidumping but still leaves much to be desired. ASEAN may wish to strengthen disciplines in the use of antidumping in order to prevent its widespread use and the attendant abuses and rent-seeking.

The ASEAN Services Framework

ASEAN leaders agreed to extend free trade to services in 1995 and placed priority on negotiations aimed at liberalization of telecommunications, transportation, tourism, and financial services scheduled for completion by the end of 1998.

The framework adopted is intended to be comprehensive; hence, a negative list approach is being taken. It would be unrealistic for ASEAN members to attempt to harmonize all their regulations in the services industries; thus, a form of mutual recognition of regulatory frameworks is likely to be adopted with certain minimal requirements. In this context, the principle of subsidiarity or decentralization of decision making so that appropriate levels of government are permitted to take initiatives to facilitate trade and investment in services has some relevance. This is particularly the case for the numerous sub-regional zones or growth triangles within ASEAN.

The extension of AFTA to the commercial services sectors is to be applauded, as it indicates ASEAN is intent on expanding economic cooperation to fast-growing tertiary sectors. Aside from the negative list approach and the mutual recognition principle, preferential liberalization of commercial service transactions should also seek to liberalize all modes of supply and to adopt a national treatment principle.[7] Such a comprehensive approach will ensure the maximum benefits from liberalization. The freeing of all modes of supply means that customers and producers of services can choose the mode that is most convenient and least costly. It also means that investment, right of establishment, and movement of natural persons are included in the framework. National treatment is defined as treatment of foreign services and services suppliers "as treatment no less favorable than that accorded to like domestic services and services suppliers."[8] However, it is sometimes difficult to interpret the meaning of national treatment in practice, as domestic regulatory requirements that appear to be nondiscriminatory may actually penalize foreign firms relative to domestic firms. Hence, flexibility in implementation of the principle is necessary.

APEC AND "EARLY LIBERALIZATION"

The Asia-Pacific Economic Cooperation (APEC) forum established a fairly long-term program for trade and investment liberalization in the region, with free trade targets of 2010 for developed economies and 2020 for developing economies. The vision offered at Bogor in 1994, however, did not establish modes for implementing the leaders' declaration. Consequently, in recent years APEC leaders and ministers have attempted to put teeth into the agreement through "down payments" (Osaka, 1995), "individual action plans" (Manila, 1996), and "early liberalization" (Vancouver, 1997).

APEC itself has thus far shunned attempts at a formal regional trading arrangement or free trade agreement for the group as a whole. However, there is a danger that a complex system of hub-and-spoke discriminatory regional trading arrangements may evolve that will leave some APEC members at a distinct disadvantage. For example, the attempt to establish a Western Hemisphere-wide Free Trade Area of the Americas (FTAA) will evolve in a hub-and-spoke fashion, with the United States or the North American Free Trade Area (NAFTA) as the main hub but with non-APEC spokes such as the members of the South American Customs Union

(MERCOSUR). Similarly, the enlargement of ASEAN to non-APEC members also presents an element of extra-APEC discriminatory treatment. There is also the Australia-New Zealand Closer Economic Relations (ANCERTA) pact, which may work out separate arrangements with the other regional groupings. The WTO does not cover preferential rules of origin in its work program. APEC members (particularly those that are non-members of regional trading arrangements) will favor a strengthened Article 24 of the GATT. At the same time, APEC itself might develop an approach to limit protectionist uses of rules of origin in the context of preferential trading arrangements.[9] The model for such an approach is likely to be based on WTO and World Customs Organization (WCO) decisions regarding non-preferential rules of origin.

FUTURE INTERNATIONAL TRADE TRENDS AND EAST ASIAN DEVELOPING ECONOMIES

The Rising Role of Services in International Trade

International trade in commercial services is rising as a share of international commercial transactions and this trend is likely to grow stronger as information-based activities become more important in global economic activity. Technological advances in telecommunications and the conclusion of negotiated agreements to expand market access in basic telecommunications, financial services, civil aviation and maritime transport, and business and professional services will reinforce the trend.

East Asian countries, particularly ASEAN members, have recently experienced financial crises and extreme exchange rate and stock market fluctuations. Large effective exchange rate depreciation has occurred in Thailand, Malaysia, Indonesia, and the Philippines. Among other East Asian economies, the Korean won has also depreciated sharply in 1997. WTO negotiations on financial services liberalization were set to conclude by the end of 1997, and the turmoil in financial markets has cast doubt on whether East Asian developing countries will be prepared to offer much in the negotiations. Japan, however, has adopted a "big bang" approach to open its financial services markets after April 1, 1998. Hence, it is setting a positive example in this regard. It may be argued that further opening of financial services will strengthen ASEAN financial markets and improve the standards upheld by financial institutions in the region. There is no question that serious restructuring in banking, real estate, and other types of financial services is going to take place. Hence, rather than pulling back from the negotiations, East Asian negotiators had better advance their own long-term interests by seeking to take advantage of opportunities to gain market access to the huge European, U.S., and Japanese markets for financial services.

Similarly, in transportation, tourism, and other services of interest to East Asia as exports, renewed efforts to make progress in negotiations are in order. In service industries where service providers and consumers cannot be separated, there are close links between investment, particularly foreign direct investment, and services trade. Liberalization of the temporary movement of natural persons is also a key to expanding trade in nonseparable services.

Globalization and East Asia

Several East Asian developing countries experienced large and increasing current account deficits in recent years. Initially the response was to blame the problem on "loss of competitiveness," resulting in a slowing of export growth and rising imports. In a number of cases governments have sought quick fixes. The implementation of special programs to "reduce imports and boost exports" in cases such as Indonesia, Malaysia, Korea, and Thailand is indicative of the lingering strength of mercantilism in the thinking of bureaucrats. Domestic firms and industries are perceived to be vulnerable to foreign competitors. Globalization is both inevitable and relentless in its impact. Some leaders have viewed globalization as an onslaught of competition for domestic firms from powerful multinational corporations in manufacturing, agriculture, and services. The impact of globalization in the real sector is partially deflected by restrictions on ownership and foreign investment and, of course, by trade barriers. However, in the financial sector, reliance on external finance has driven most East Asian economies to open up capital markets, though in an incomplete manner. Banking and stock market regulation has placed some limits on foreign ownership. However, the main purpose has been to influence credit allocation in favor of projects given priority by government. Prudential regulations have not been sufficiently developed, and investments have been funded through offshore borrowing, thus exposing these economies to exchange rate risk. The recent turbulence in the region's financial markets and currencies underscores the danger of excessive adverse investment selection.

In the era of globalization as before, international trade remains a positive-sum game with mutual benefits for participants. Fears of domination of domestic industry by transnational corporations are misplaced. The law of comparative advantage provides assurance that there will always be industries and services in which a country is relatively competitive in international markets. Indeed with large and growing domestic markets, including the ASEAN-wide market, competition among producers will ensure that in certain products and industries, world-class capabilities will emerge among the successful firms.

The recent financial problems experienced in Thailand and, more generally, in the region, in fact, result from internal inefficiencies and excessive debt-financed investments in non-viable projects and protected industries. Excessive investment in property and real estate development created a bubble that inevitably burst. Tightening government expenditures, floating of exchange rates, and allowing investment decisions to be driven by market forces rather than intervention will help stabilize the situation. With effective depreciation, export-oriented industries and projects will become more attractive. Further real sector deregulation and liberalization will be essential to putting these economies back on track. East Asian economies have widely varying practices in restricting foreign ownership and the free flow of funds. Hong Kong provides a free market model, while Taiwan and Korea have been reluctant to fully liberalize their financial markets. One reason for Hong Kong's success in weathering the recent turbulence is that it has refused to protect industry or to attempt to direct credit flows to favored interests.

The cancellation of several huge projects, cuts in overall expenditures by government, and increased efforts to enhance domestic savings demonstrate that leaders in Indonesia, Malaysia, and Thailand have grasped the fundamental issues underlying their current account deficits and what is necessary to restore a sustainable balance of payments. The task ahead is to follow through with further real and financial sector reforms.

The Future of Trade Deregulation

The agenda for trade policy reform in East Asia is in flux as traditional forms of protection are gradually reduced, and new issues and areas arise in the course of global negotiations and regional trading arrangements. Moreover, the extent of import barriers and investment restrictions varies across East Asia. For example, transitional economies in East Asia have a longer way to go to attain the objective of a freer and basically neutral trade regime than do the market economies. Services trade liberalization has already been discussed. Hence, the following discussion focuses on trade policy issues that influence goods and services in varying degrees.

Reducing Tariffs and Tariff Escalation

Tariff cuts under the Uruguay Round Agreement in North America, Japan, and Europe will benefit East Asian developing economies. Within East Asia, tariff rates vary from negligible (Hong Kong, Singapore), to modest (Indonesia, Malaysia), to high (China, Thailand). While tariff barriers are preferable to nontariff barriers, in the medium term, reducing the level and dispersion of tariffs is desirable. The "optimal tariff" literature suggests that some dispersion in tariff rates is desirable. Once one takes into account the role of politics and rent-seeking in setting tariffs as well as the dynamic effects on resource allocation and investment of such variance in protection, a different conclusion might be reached. Experience teaches that a simple system of low and equal tariff rates can be highly successful in promoting growth and efficiency in a country's international trade. Chile's success following adoption of a uniform and low tariff is a case in point.

While tariff levels in the OECD countries are quite low, tariff escalation—the practice of imposing higher tariffs based on the extent of processing—remains a serious problem for less developed exporters. Hence, East Asian trade negotiators might seek to reduce the escalation in tariff rates in more developed countries. They will, however, have to put their own houses in order in this regard (Safadi and Yeats, 1994).[10]

Nontariff Barriers (NTBs)

Quotas and import licensing systems have been greatly reduced in most East Asian economies that have used such restrictions in the past (Japan, Korea, Taiwan, Indonesia, Philippines). For example, in Indonesia as of 1996, fewer than 200 tariff lines had NTBs, down from thousands of such restrictions 10 years earlier. The Uruguay Round Agreement requires developing countries to phase out NTBs over a 10-year period and also puts a freeze on the introduction of new NTBs. Local content schemes that have been notified to the WTO are an example of an NTB that must be phased out. Many of the remaining NTBs are in agriculture and are to be replaced by tariffs. It would be wise to accelerate the phasing out of remaining NTBs, as they create monopolies and interfere with the proper functioning of market mechanisms. For example, local content schemes distort a firm's efforts to reduce costs away from domestic toward imported inputs.

Export Restrictions and Taxes

Export restrictions (aside from those involving hazardous or illegal items) have been employed by a number of East Asian economies. The export bans or taxes are designed to encourage the growth of processing industries. Often they have been justified as a counter to tariff escalation in trading partners or have been aimed at improving the terms of trade of an exporter considered to have market power. Prohibitive taxes or bans on exports of raw materials or lightly processed goods can, in the short run, provide assistance to processors and other downstream industries. However, such policies are likely to have damaging medium- to long-term effects, as they discourage investment in production of raw materials. This has been the case in Indonesian wood-based industries. It would be preferable to directly negotiate with trading partners to reduce tariff escalation harmful to processing industries than to adopt such restrictive policies.

There is also a terms of trade or large country argument for restricting certain exports. In the case of the terms of trade argument, this is likely to be fallacious, as substitutes can be found for almost any item. Hence, attempts to exploit market power may temporarily succeed in raising prices; however, this will induce consumers to seek substitutes and to reduce the volume of demand. Suppliers of possible substitutes will seek to capture a larger share of market demand and will most often succeed.

Domestic Trade Restrictions

Domestic trade restrictions have the effect of distorting markets, creating rents that can be captured by a monopolist or a cartel. Cartels or monopolies that control distribution of key commodities through collusive behavior have been created by government regulatory controls. This is a common practice in some East Asian cases (e.g., cement, cloves, fertilizer, and wheat in Indonesia). However, such restrictions raise costs and hinder the efficiency of industry by not allowing producers to freely compete. Restrictions on wholesale and retail trade in East Asian economies have resulted in inefficient distribution and marketing systems that raise costs to consumers and hamper producers of goods and services from fully developing potential markets. Arguments are made in support of restrictions on distribution by large-scale retail outlets and shopping malls, alleging these are harmful to small-scale vendors and hawkers. However, negative effects such as these are often exaggerated, as lower prices brought about by increased competition will benefit consumers, many of whom are from households with low incomes. It is likely that different types of retailers serve different market segments and can coexist by serving different niches in markets.

Domestic demand growth is important in sustaining economic growth nowadays in East Asia. Domestic trade is not only restricted by explicit regulatory controls but it is also subject to informal (and illegal) levies that are imposed by local authorities. These levies increase business costs and discourage investment. Hence, phasing out obsolete regulations limiting investment in domestic retail trade will be important in helping to sustain economic expansion.

Foreign Investment Regulations

East Asian economies are among the most open in the world when it comes to foreign direct investment in manufacturing. However, in services and agriculture, restrictions continue to be significant. Foreign ownership restrictions are common in financial services, transportation services, and telecommunications and in retail distribution and trade. In addition, foreign ownership shares of publicly listed companies are usually limited to a minority of shares. Restrictions on foreign ownership of land, property, and dwellings are also common. The latter may deter investment from abroad by increasing the costs of sending expatriate managers and skilled personnel to operate subsidiaries. Foreign ownership restrictions are being loosened gradually and will have to be reconsidered as services trade is liberalized.

Competition Policy

Business practices that are clearly anticompetitive have been tolerated and even encouraged in East Asia. In some cases, the government itself is the monopolist (typically in hard-wired basic telephone services). In others the government provides extraordinary exemptions from taxes and tariffs to a "national" producer, as in the "national car" programs of Malaysia and Indonesia.[11] These arrangements may be challenged by other governments and may require resolution through the WTO.

Developing East Asian economies often lack the legal and institutional basis for preventing anti-competitive behavior. They have offset this by opening their economies to foreign investment and import competition. However, in future they will have to do more to create a truly competitive market. By doing so they can dispel

pressures from powerful trading partners and lessen the disputes they will face in
WTO.

Antidumping and the Danger of Contingent Protection

Antidumping regulations are now in place throughout East Asia and are likely
to be used by governments under pressure from domestic firms that are encounter-
ing increased competition from imports. In the absence of harmonization of
business laws and practices, foreign business practices are likely to be viewed with
suspicion (this is typical in relations between Europe, Japan, and the United States).
Accusations of unfair business practices are often directed against pricing strategies
and antidumping serves as the weapon of choice in handling foreign competitors
who offer low prices.[12] The antidumping process has turned into a major growth
industry for lawyers, trade bureaucrats, and consultants in the U.S. case. As
experience shows, antidumping petitions alone usually generate less trade at higher
prices, oftentimes through "voluntary restraint agreements" between domestic
producers and foreign exporters or the local importer. Hence, the outcome of the
U.S. antidumping process itself is frequently anticompetitive. At a minimum, East
Asian developing economies should make sure their own antidumping regulations
are consistent with the WTO. It would be even better for East Asia to aim at limiting
use of antidumping procedures and of adopting open public hearings in alleged
cases of dumping.

Intellectual Property Protection

East Asian countries have begun to crack down on rampant piracy in the case of
intellectual property under heavy pressure from Europe and the United States.
However, in the long run it will be to East Asia economies' own advantage to
improve their intellectual property protection. Not only is this necessary to encourage development of indigenous talents, technologies, and research works, but it is
also essential in attracting higher-technology investors from abroad. If developing
East Asian economies expect foreign investors to bring in advanced technologies,
then the climate must be suitable and secure. Without strong enforcement of
intellectual property rights, only standard rather than advanced technologies will
be brought in by investors from abroad.

CONCLUSION

The topic of trends in international trade and trade policy reform in East Asia is
certainly one of global interest. In this chapter I have attempted to cover broadly
the issues that are of key importance from the standpoint of the developing
economies. Hence, the issues of linkages between trade and labor standards and
trade and environment have been only briefly mentioned. In the future, it is likely
that East Asia will have to consider these issues. A proactive approach to these new

issues at the multilateral level would in all likelihood be preferable to bilateral negotiations in serving the interests of the region's economies.

Currently, controversy is raging throughout the region regarding the merits and demerits of various approaches to financial liberalization and exchange rate management. The success of speculative attacks against ASEAN members' currencies and the problems in the region's financial markets have drawn attention away from the issues of trade policy reform. However, trade liberalization and further deregulation of foreign investment regulations should receive high priority once stabilization is achieved. Stable macroeconomic policies aimed at reducing excessive expenditures and controlling inflation will help to reduce budget and current account deficits. That should stimulate domestic savings, and, coupled with real sector reforms and liberalization, investment and financial markets would respond positively. Such a combination of policies would help restore investor confidence and would enhance credibility of economic policy-making in the region. The massive real exchange rate depreciation in these economies should spur a very strong surge in export growth in the next couple years. At the same time, trade reform will improve microeconomic performance and help to restore investor confidence in these economies. Trade policy reform is essential to more efficient investment and improving the quality of financial sector performance in the future.

NOTES

1. International Monetary Fund, *Direction of Trade Statistics Yearbook 1997* (Washington, DC: International Monetary Fund).

2. Lloyd and Toguchi show that increases in market share of East Asian developing economies and growth in apparent consumption of manufacturers in industrially advanced economies between 1980 and 1993.

3. It is sometimes claimed that East Asian developing economies' trade with one another is sufficiently large for the region to continue to grow even if developed economy markets cease to expand. It is estimated that about half of East Asia's merchandise trade is intraregional (including China, Hong Kong, Taiwan, Korea, Indonesia, Malaysia, the Philippines, Singapore, Thailand, and Vietnam). However, large elements of double counting result from inclusion of Singapore and Hong Kong, with large amounts of reexports. Self-sustained trade may be illusory, particularly if the region's economic growth declines.

4. For China and Taiwan, membership in the WTO is presently a high priority.

5. For example, the United States in 1996 changed its textiles and apparel nonpreferential rules of origin in a manner that potentially had rather severe consequences for East Asian exporters. See James (1997a).

6. See Deardorff (1992) for an exposition on the economics of antidumping.

7. For discussion see James (1997b).

8. UNCTAD and World Bank (1994), p. 143.

9. See James (1997a) for recommendations in this regard. The NAFTA rules of origin have led to massive diversion of textile trade from Asia to Mexico.

10. Safadi and Yeats (1994) show that East Asian economies' tariffs rise with the degree of processing of commodities. However, since import demand elasticities usually increase with processing, tariff escalation is not a necessary condition for trade bias against processed

goods. That is, equal tariffs on processed and unprocessed commodities may still impart a trade bias against processed goods.

11. Paradoxically, the Indonesian national car program has increased the degree of competition in the domestic market for sedans, leading to lower prices. The new policy states that any auto producer that reaches local content of 60% is entitled to national car program incentives. However, the private company now receiving national car incentives is required to reach only 20% local content and has three years to reach 60% local content. It is apparent that the government is putting pressure on banks to extend credits to the national car program operated by PT Timor and is also "encouraging" units of government to purchase Timor sedans.

12. *The Economist*, "Schools Brief" (November 8, 1997) pp. 101–2. It cites the WTO in estimating 900 antidumping measure that are now in place., with 206 new actions in 1996 alone.

REFERENCES

Deardorff, Alan. (1992). "Economic Perspectives on Antidumping Law." In John H. Jackson and Edwin A. Vermulst, eds. *Anti-dumping Law and Practice: A Comparative Study.* Ann Arbor: University of Michigan Press, pp. 23–40.

James, William E. (1998). "Trade and Financial Market Reforms in ASEAN: Putting the Cart before the Horse?" *ASEAN Economic Bulletin*, forthcoming.

———. (1997a). "APEC and Preferential Rules of Origin: Stumbling Blocks for Liberalization of Trade?" *Journal of World Trade* 31(3), June, pp. 113–34.

———. (1997b). "ASEAN Economic Cooperation and Commercial Services: Regulatory and Technical Issues in Expanded Liberalization." Draft chapter for *Challenges for Indonesia, ASEAN, and the Asia Pacific Region in the 21st Century: Essays in Honor of Professor Suhadi Mangkusuwondo*, ed. Mari Pangestu, Syahrir, and Srimulyani Indrawati.

James, William E., Seiji Naya, and Gerald M. Meier. (1987). *Asian Development.* Madison: University of Wisconsin Press.

Lloyd, Peter, and Hisako Toguchi. (1996)."East Asian Export Competitiveness." *Asia-Pacific Economic Literature* 10(2), November, pp. 1–15.

Oshima, Harry T. (1993). *Strategic Processes in Monsoon Asia's Economic Development.* Baltimore: Johns Hopkins University Press.

Safadi, Raed, and Alexander Yeats. (1994). "The Escalation of Asian Trade Barriers." *Asian Economic Journal* 8(2), July, pp. 147–79.

UNCTAD (United Nations Conference on Trade and Development) and World Bank. (1994). *Liberalizing International Transactions in Services: A Handbook.* New York and Geneva: United Nations.

World Bank. (1993). *The East Asian Miracle.* Oxford: Oxford University Press.

4

Sector-Specific Industrial Policies and Southeast Asian Economic Development

F. Gerard Adams and Heidi Vernon

The rapid economic growth of East Asia has inspired an extensive discussion on the policy strategies that lie behind successful development. There is little disagreement on such basic issues as free markets versus planning; macroeconomic stability; the need for infrastructure investment; or export promotion versus import substitution. There is much support for a "political economy" view of East Asian development (Stiglitz, 1996; Hill, 1996) that emphasizes the role of an appropriate blend of general economic policies, but there has been lively debate on targeted industry-specific development programs (Krueger, 1997).[1] Wade (1990) argues that interventionist policies advance growth, that they "led the market." Hughes (1995), on the other hand, takes the position that there is only a small role for sectoral intervention, so long as countries "get the basics right." This disagreement presented a considerable problem for the World Bank's[2] *East Asian Miracle* study (1993), which recognized the contribution of policy intervention but concluded that in most cases selective industrial policies did not and would not advance growth.

This chapter is a survey of Southeast Asian experience on this aspect of economic development policy. Are industry-specific initiatives important to the promotion of rapid modernization? Can one draw some conclusions that may be useful to developing countries' modernization policy?

In the 1960s, the development strategy of Japan's Ministry of International Trade and Industry (MITI) called first for building strategic industries like steel and chemicals (Adams and Ichimura, 1983). Similar, industrially targeted strategies were adopted by Korea and Taiwan in their "rush" to development. "The governments of Taiwan, Korea, and Japan have not so much picked the winners as made them" Wade (1990, 334).

The countries in Southeast Asia whose rapid growth came only a little later (Malaysia, Thailand, and Indonesia) were much less systematic and narrowly interventionist in their development policies (Terry, 1996). While protection of infant industries (and sometimes mature industries) has been widespread in Southeast Asia, these countries have placed less reliance than Japan and Korea on government planners' targeting of strategic industries. They drew most heavily on entrepreneurial decisions by the domestic private sector and by foreign investors and utilized broad, now largely nondiscriminatory investment promotion policies. In Hong Kong, economic development has been left largely to the market forces.[3] Even in China, the impetus for economic development comes not from the centrally directed, state-owned enterprises (SOEs) but from locally owned and controlled businesses, the so-called town and village enterprises (TVEs), and from the private sector.

In recent years, there has been some resurgence of industrial targeting. We see the Malaysian and Indonesian attempts to develop national auto industries[4] and the Indonesian commitment to an aircraft industry. Much emphasis, particularly in Taiwan and Singapore, has been on the promotion of high-tech industries.

We posit that sectoral industrial policy may have its time and place but is not a generic prescription for rapid economic development. When countries are at early stages of development, incentives for development of specific new industries may be helpful, so long as the dynamics of the sectors targeted make them consistent with long-run prospects for international competitiveness. But as countries advance up the development ladder and require more sophisticated choices, promotional efforts by the public sector are better of a general, non-industry-specific nature. These efforts include advancing education, science, and technology, building infrastructure, and promoting domestic saving and investment and foreign capital inflows. Specific choices about industrial structure and investments are best made by private decision makers.

DEVELOPMENT AND INDUSTRIAL POLICY

Policy measures that have been used to promote the development process in East Asia have ranged widely, from broad, macroeconomic initiatives aimed at increasing saving or expanding exports, to narrowly focused sector interventions like public investments in specific industrial projects or tariff protection for particular industries. Most countries have combined different approaches so that a discussion of industrial policy must be integrated into a more general view of development strategies. It is our objective, here, to distinguish "industrial policies" (IP) from more general approaches to development.

Defining the concept of IP is not a trivial problem. A difficulty is that most policies promoting development have sector-specific impacts, whether intended or unintended. Moreover, economic analysis must consider all the various sectors of the economy, including agriculture, mining, and services, in addition to industrial activities.

The immediate emphasis of industrial policies, as conventionally defined, is on the development of particular industrial sectors, but this may or may not call for policies that are industry-specific. IP can be viewed much more broadly than the industrial "targeting" concept that has frequently been attached to it. Alternatively, at the opposite extreme, IP might be said to include almost any development policy, particularly policy focused on the sources of a nation's productive power, productivity, and competitiveness. This would include all policies that might shift production functions, improve supply and quality of inputs, alter the composition of factor inputs, introduce new technology, and so on.

Our notion of IP is fairly broad but not all-encompassing. It is useful to think about industrial policies in the following way.

Industrial policies in general: This category includes all policies that have a deliberate industrial or sectoral impact. It excludes broad macro- and social policy initiatives intended to affect demand or income. The broad grouping may be divided into two types of policies[5]:

Sector-specific policies: These are policies directed at particular industries or sectors. They may be focused on an entire sector, microelectronics, for example, or they may be more narrowly targeted. In some cases in East Asia, they have involved establishment of specific national enterprises, such as the steel and petrochemical complexes in Taiwan. Their distinguishing characteristic is the need to select and to discriminate among economic alternatives. Government technicians make or influence choices that would ordinarily be business decisions. Typically, these industrial policies are seen as "picking the winners," the so-called sunrise industries, but an important function, particularly in Japan, has also been to provide a smooth transition for the losers, the "sunset" industries.

Activity-specific policies: These policies promote particular activities, like investment, research and development (R&D), and exports, but do not focus deliberately on a particular sector. The benefits of these policies may be available on a nondiscriminatory basis to all industries, but they have differential sectoral impacts. While these activities also involve government officials in determining economic priorities, they are less directly interventionist. Choices are not between industries but only between activities. Business decision makers may carry out a favored activity in the industrial setting and in the establishment where it is economically the most appropriate.

What are the merits of this classification scheme? On one hand, it includes a somewhat broader range of policies than have traditionally been considered "industrial policy." Much of the effort to promote industrialization has, after all, taken the form of favoring investment, infrastructure, transfer of technology, and so on, without narrowly specifying the industries where these activities are to be carried out. On the other hand, this classification excludes broader development policy initiatives concerned with income distribution, government expenditures, monetary policy, or exchange rate intervention.

A word should also be said about regional policies. Regional diversities have increased as the East Asian countries have become urbanized and industrialized. It is not surprising, then, that many countries have instituted policies that favor development of backward regions, providing promotional benefits to industries that locate in outlying industrial zones away from the most crowded urban centers. In recent years, for example, Indonesia has concentrated on encouraging companies to invest in the less developed eastern islands, and Thailand's Board of Investment (BoI) has offered its incentives primarily to investors in outlying areas. Such policies are a form of market intervention directed at industrial location. In most cases, however, they do not represent narrowly focused industry-specific policies. As a result of growing regional disparities, they are increasingly necessary, particularly in countries that have opened their political systems in the direction of popular democracy. While regional policies are not, strictly speaking, industrial policies, they are important to the following discussion.

Finally, the close linkages between industrial policy and trade policies must be noted.[6] Protectionism had been one of the underpinnings of import substitution and of efforts to support industries in some Southeast Asian countries. The turn toward export promotion called for exchange rates and promotion policies that favored actual or potential exporters. Trade within the East Asian region remained relatively modest but has begun to grow rapidly under the aegis of the Asian Free Trade Area (AFTA) and the Asia-Pacific Economic Cooperation forum (APEC).

These regional associations should greatly increase intraindustry competition in Southeast Asia. How far they will go toward opening Southeast Asian industries to competition from the rest of the world will depend on the external trade policies of these trade groupings. Considerable progress in lower trade barriers was being made in the first half of the 1990s. Unfortunately, the 1997 crisis may lead to some regression in the trade liberalization process.

THE EXPERIENCE OF THE SOUTHEAST ASIAN COUNTRIES

In many Southeast Asian countries, industrial policy is not easily separable from development policy. After it became apparent in the 1960s that import substitution policies would not enable these countries to make significant further progress, development strategy turned toward promoting exports. Exports were used to provide foreign exchange for infrastructure investments and industrialization. The competitiveness of export-oriented industries provided incentives for attracting foreign investment and technology transfer.

In the early phases of development, the Southeast Asian countries promoted certain basic industries like steel and cement, either as part of their policy of import substitution or as a part of a systematic development strategy, in Korea and Taiwan, for example. Some narrow industrial targeting of this kind is still part of the development strategy of most countries, but it is more prevalent in Malaysia and Indonesia than in Singapore or Thailand. However, the most important influences on the evolving industrial structure of Southeast Asia have been broader. Policies of export promotion, development of infrastructure, trade policies, attraction of foreign direct investment, expansion of education and training, institution building in finance and securities markets, and incentives for research and development have all had significant structural impact. In some cases, the sectoral changes occurred as a result of intentional, finely honed policy actions; in others they occurred as part of the broad restructuring of the economy that is economic development.

With the exception of Singapore, most East Asian countries retain substantial import restrictions and tariffs. Recently, there has been a significant trend toward liberalization and privatization. Some countries still have some interventions in private markets with respect to investment approvals, price controls, preferential interest rates, and state-owned companies. These interventions are sometimes part of industrial policy, but more often they are vestiges of past history, often in response to pressures from rent-seeking political and business groups.

Now, some of these countries are targeting their industrial structure and export promotion policies toward technically more advanced industries like motor vehicles, auto parts, and sophisticated electronics or to products like computer chips or disk drives, where they see some long-run advantage. They are moving away from primary or simple, labor-intensive products such as textiles, footwear, and consumer electronics, where there is much competition and where rising labor costs are making industries noncompetitive. With some striking exceptions, such policies have been consistent with a long-run perception of comparative advantage. In other words, most—but not all—industrial policies in this part of the world have been consistent with market trends.

In this section we review the experience of the principal Southeast Asian countries with regard to industrial policy. We recognize that some of these countries have overarching policy agendas, political and social as well as economic, that influence their policies and that have significant industrial impact. Examples include the ethnic and income distribution objectives of the government in Malaysia, the need for nation building in Indonesia, the call for broader and more equitable regional development in Thailand, and questions of space and urban amenities in Singapore.

Industrial and Development Policies in Thailand[7]

Thailand has long maintained a cooperative relationship between its private and public sectors. There is a tradition of indicative planning, but there has not been a systematic attempt to modify industrial structure. The private sector has been the principal development force.

Thailand was traditionally an economy with a good deal of government intervention. In recent years, efforts to reduce these interventions, to privatize public enterprises, and to use private capital to meet infrastructure needs have tended to liberalize the economy. Development policy has taken the form of incentive programs for investment, import substitution, and exports.

Until recently, decisions to grant promotional privileges were made on the basis of detailed discussions with the applicants and were subject to presentations of business plans for large projects. Proposed projects were assessed for their feasibility, their contribution to import substitution, and their impact on existing producers of competitive products. Many industries, meeting the requirements of a broad eligibility list, qualified for promotional tax privileges and other concessions. Industrial policy, as applied by the Board of Investment (BoI), was not so much an advance statement of certain sectoral preferences as a reaction to requests for promotional privileges. A range of activities was given preference consistent with Thailand's comparative advantage of low labor cost and a productive agricultural material base. Industrial development was a particular concern with focus on linkages between sectors, the development of agricultural processing industries, and the encouragement of investment for export production.

In response to declining export performance, the Thai Ministry of Industry has drafted a master plan for industrial development to the year 2012. The plan remains quite general, seeking promotion of a range of industries that can gain export market share, including:

—autos and auto parts

—electric and electronic appliances and machinery

—frozen food

—agricultural machinery

—services, including telecommunications and transportation

A more recent proposal provides special promotions for software production. In the last few years, BoI promotion regulations have placed primary emphasis on the location of industries away from the crowded Bangkok and eastern seaboard areas, rather than on specific industries, though some industrial preferences remain. It is more realistic to see Thai industrial policy in terms of an activity-specific set of policies that encourages investment, foreign capital inflows, exports, and, to some extent, import substitution, rather than industry-specific industrial policies.

The effects of rapid, uncoordinated growth and urbanization became glaringly apparent toward the end of the 1980s. Infrastructure bottlenecks, urban crowding without adequate public transportation, and shortages of electric power and water and sewer facilities became a barrier to foreign enterprises interested in operating in Thailand. Shortages of labor, particularly engineers and managers but also trained workers, caused labor costs to rise and caused Thailand to lose its competitive position as compared to other more populous Asian countries like Indonesia and China. The populist Thai governments of recent years have turned their attention toward social issues, including distribution of income, regional development, education, science and technology, and better natural resource utilization.

Only three sectors have been specifically targeted for development. As in many countries, special regulations cover imports of autos and auto parts. In Thailand development of a domestic auto industry was encouraged by high tariffs on assembled imported cars and lower duties on imported parts. Tariffs were lowered in 1991, and restrictions on imports were reduced, allowing lower prices and a rapid expansion of auto demand. Significant expansions of local assembly operations and of parts production ensued. Thailand is becoming a center for auto parts production to meet domestic requirements and to export to neighboring markets.

Petroleum, petrochemicals, and natural gas development has been encouraged. The Petroleum Authority of Thailand, a government-owned corporation recently partially privatized, is a major operator in the refining and distribution of petroleum products. The government also participates in fertilizer and petrochemical plants based on offshore natural gas reserves and has encouraged government–private partnerships.

Financial sector development has been another objective of public policy. The Bank of Thailand and the government have encouraged the development of the Stock Exchange of Thailand (SET) and the Bangkok International Banking Facility (BIBF). The aim, not so far accomplished, has been to set up a fully integrated financial sector for the domestic economy and to service financial needs in the neighboring countries of Southeast Asia. The developments that followed demonstrate the risks of such an approach. The framework of the BIBF served as a means for channeling large quantities of foreign capital into Thailand in 1994–1996, attracted by the differential between interest rates in Thailand and in world financial markets. When lenders lost confidence in Thailand and the baht depreciated, Thai financial institutions found themselves with large foreign debts denominated in U.S. dollars.

Industrial and Development Policies in Indonesia

Indonesia has long followed an industry-specific industrial policy, but it has not been along the systematic pattern emphasized by Japan and Korea. Perhaps because of Indonesia's government/business structure, in which most large industries are controlled by private conglomerates or government-private partnerships, industrial policy has been more industry- and enterprise-specific than investment or export promoting in general. Unlike many of the dynamic Asian developing economies, incentives to produce for the domestic market do not appear to be fully offset by incentives to produce for export.

Recent industry targeting seems to follow a strategy of reduced dependence on oil and gas exports combined with technological advancement in telecommunications and other technology-driven sectors. The underlying assumption appears to be that, in some fields, Indonesian industry can catch up with more advanced countries by leapfrogging to the latest technologies.

Industry-specific policy in Indonesia has actively promoted industries, largely through the process of setting up government corporations. These businesses are granted monopoly or near-monopoly status and protection from foreign competition through tariffs and non-tariff barriers as well as subsidies. Strategic industries have been selected largely on the strength of their high-technology component.

The industries selected include:

—aircraft, where Indonesia produces its own light planes

—automobiles, where Indonesia has granted special advantages to an affiliation with a Korean company to build a "national" car

—shipbuilding, a capital-intensive, non-high-technology industry

—steel

—telecommunications, including the production of telecommunication equipment

—machine tools and construction equipment, and

—military products

We note that some of these industries require high technology, much of which Indonesia has acquired abroad. Others are highly capital-intensive. The fit of these industries with Indonesia's comparative advantage as a resource-rich, labor-abundant country lacking capital and technological skills is not at all clear (Hill, 1996). Many of these industrial operations have been phased out with the crisis and the change from the Suharto regime.

Industrial and Development Policies in Malaysia

Malaysia's industrial and development policies have relied heavily on close cooperation between business and government institutions. While most investments have been private, the government has targeted certain industries to facilitate growth, technical change, and a national identity. In the 1980s, Malaysia promoted a number of heavy industry projects, usually in collaboration with private, often foreign investors (World Bank, 1993). An overarching objective for advancing the economic status of the ethnic Malay population has also influenced policy.

Malaysia has turned from being primarily an exporter of primary commodities toward export production of manufactures. Malaysia's Vision 2020 program seeks to advance growth, in large part by supporting strategic industries. Export manufacturing is supposed to grow rapidly and to diversify away from simple electronics and apparel. Malaysia's first stage of industrialization involved encouragement of resource-based goods, such as rubber, wood, and agricultural manufactures. More advanced industries, however, are now being promoted, and export industries are encouraged to develop backward linkages for their inputs from other domestic producers. Activity-specific industrial policies take the form of investment promotion tax allowances, free trade zones, and export credits. Activity-specific activities are being combined with specific industry objectives by offering special advantages for investment in high value-added and high-tech industries, which are granted "pioneer" status.

Sector-specific development began with the cement and steel industries. While these enterprises are now privately owned, they continue to require protection and to operate below capacity. Similar initial public financing and development protection were provided for the petroleum refining and industrial chemicals industries. Shipyards and, particularly, ship repair have also benefited from government support, but the competition from Singapore in this field has been hard to beat. The Proton automobile project has been the most important of the targeted projects. The national car was planned as a program to build Malaysian national pride. With Japanese technical support and massive protection, Malaysia's development of a domestic automobile industry is sometimes seen as a qualified success. A major proportion of the domestic market and exports of cars have provided a modest, but not unreasonable scale of production. Although a substantial share of the content of the vehicles is still imported, a sizable parts-producing industry should serve domestic needs and some export markets. It is not clear how much of this effort can be continued in view of Malaysia's difficulties since 1997 and Dr. Mahathir's new economic policies. On the other hand, efforts by Malaysia to stimulate its economic recovery behind the barriers of its newly enacted exchange controls continue to have important industry-specific focus.

Industrial and Development Policies in Singapore

Since Singapore is a small and, from the perspective of trade barriers, a virtually open economy, the emphasis has been on free trade and the attraction of direct foreign investment. In place of targeting specific industries, Singapore has sought to build an environment suited to investment with good infrastructure and a highly educated labor force.

Singapore's policy is largely of the activity-specific type designed particularly to attract foreign direct investment. The emphasis has been on high-level, indigenous technology, promoting innovation and entrepreneurship and increasing the supply of educated workers. This is reflected in Singapore's extremely ambitious plans for education and training.

Infrastructure and housing development has been prodigious. More than 90% of the population live in government-built housing. Even better transportation facilities are planned as well as a telecommunications system making Singapore an "intelligent island."

There has been little narrow targeting. Incentives have been concentrated on broad industries, particularly promotion of high-tech production. Emphasis on high technology and the suitability of local facilities and labor have made electronics, including computer parts, peripherals, and telecommunication equipment, a natural beneficiary of investment and R&D incentives.

Financial and service operations are protected and licensed. Financial incentives are provided for foreign companies to locate their regional headquarters in Singapore.

For the future, Singapore, whose area and population are very limited, is extending its activities to entrepreneurship into neighboring countries, providing tax exemptions and subsidies to domestic businesses willing to set up operations and to invest in nearby countries. For example, based on Singapore's service sector, which is the best in the region, Singapore has taken an active role in developing urban services in China and Vietnam.

Industrial and Development Policies in Taiwan

The relationship between government and the business in Taiwan has been seen as a paradigm for economic development policy, what Wade (1990) has called the developmental state. Beginning with policies directed toward development of export industries and protectionism, Taiwan found in the early 1980s that these fields were no longer fully competitive in world markets due to rising wages, an appreciating exchange rate, and increasing protectionism. In response, Taiwan embarked on a development strategy aiming at high-technology fields (Smith, 1997; Shive and Lee, chapter 7, this volume).

Import trade for labor-intensive manufacturers was liberalized and export incentive reduced. Encouragement of investment into strategic industries under the Statute for Encouragement of Investment (SEI) was phased out in 1990 to be replaced by the Statute for Upgrading Industry (SUI). The latter, as well as numerous other measures, focused on development and improvement of technology. The Taiwan government continues to play a supportive role to high-technology industries through provision of training, equity loans, research support, science parks, and technological education and research.

THINKING ABOUT INDUSTRIAL POLICY

The industrial policy experience of the Southeast Asian countries has some commonalities but also some significant differences. All have gone broadly to export promotion, encouragement of investment, and opening to direct foreign investment. Most of these countries have, at times, followed the policy path pioneered by Japan, Korea, and Taiwan and have built some basic strategic industries. In recent years, however, their policies have diverged considerably with regard to sectoral intervention, with Indonesia and Malaysia opting for some narrow interventions in favor of high-tech, capital-intensive industries. Thailand and Singapore, on the other hand, have allowed sectoral decisions to be done largely, but not exclusively, by market forces. It is difficult to correlate the practice of industrial policy with the outcome. In this section we evaluate the success or failure of the principal policy initiatives.

Economics of Activity-Specific Policy

There is no doubt that the moves toward export promotion and incentives to investment, foreign as well as domestic, have paid off in terms of growth. Many of the policies that advance education, science and technology, and infrastructure are aimed directly at the principal development bottlenecks faced in Southeast Asia. While support of this type does involve the public sector in economic choices, these are, after all, the kinds of broad choices faced by all governments in the performance of their public sector obligations. They are generally not activities suited to private, profit-making enterprises, though working with the private sector has turned out to be advantageous for raising capital and for maintaining efficiency.

The impact of openness is still under dispute. For that matter, it is not clear how open to competitive imports the Southeast Asian countries are even today, since, with the exception of Singapore, they have had fairly substantial protective tariffs, particularly for their strategic industries. Trade barriers are expected to decline under AFTA and APEC initiatives.

The Economics of Sector-Specific Policy

The process of economic development in East Asia has been largely one of structural change from primarily agricultural, to labor-intensive manufacturing, to more sophisticated manufacturing, and, in the smaller countries, to a high-tech service economy. Understandably, industrial policy has sought to advance industrial structure along such a path.

Strategic Industries and Industry-Specific Policy

The promotion of basic industries has been a common phenomenon in the East Asian countries early in the development process. In part, this reflects the construction industry's needs for basic materials, such as cement and steel reinforcement bars, that are relatively costly to ship and that can be produced locally. In Korea and Taiwan, the development of basic industries followed the pattern first established in Japan, seeing these industries as strategically necessary for deeper industrialization. The Southeast Asian countries have not, by and large, pursued this path as a principal means toward more advanced development.[8] It is not clear that promotion of basic industries would have served to advance industrialization, except in the earliest stages of development.

High-Tech and Industry-Specific Policy

Whether industry-specific policies are useful for the development of high-tech industry is debatable. On one hand, the presence of high-tech industries may encourage both technology transfer and research and development and may provide linkages to facilitate the introduction of more advanced industries. On the other hand, high-tech industries must have sufficient "fit" so that, ultimately, their operations will be consistent with the nation's comparative advantage, and the products will be competitive at home and abroad. The returns are not yet in on whether high-tech industries will pay off directly and/or in terms of external effects. The issue is whether government organizations can pick and choose among the available technological possibilities to find the promising technologies, to discard those that do not pan out, and to build the technological hierarchies that have future potential. Such decision making seems better placed among profit-making entrepreneurs than in the hands of government officials. If there is to be high-tech promoting activity, it is better left broadly defined, based on close consultations with business or allowing private entrepreneurs to make the ultimate decisions.

CONCLUSIONS

It is questionable whether sector-specific policies have paid off in Southeast Asia. So long as the sector-specific policies have been mostly of a general nature and consistent with the natural comparative advantage of the country, they have probably done no harm and possibly provided some activities with significant benefit. That means that promotion of agriculture-related industries in Thailand, Indonesia, and, early on, in Malaysia was probably beneficial. Promotion of intermediate manufactures utilizing labor was probably advantageous in Thailand, as has been the emphasis on high-tech electronics in present-day Singapore. More dubious is the promotion of high-tech and heavy industries in Malaysia and Indonesia. Prestigious products may contribute more to national identity and pride than to economics. While these industries may create linkages to domestic suppliers and tend to upgrade the level of technology, they are unlikely to achieve competitiveness in a world where other countries are far and away ahead on the technological ladder.

NOTES

1. "Perhaps the key issue on which there remains disagreement regarding appropriate trade policy is whether there is a role for the state in 'picking the winners,' or selectively in incentives confronting different industries" (p. 1).

2. "[V]ery rapid development of the type experienced by Japan, the Four Tigers, and, more recently, the East Asian NIEs has at times benefited from careful policy interventions [p. 24]. Our assessment . . . is that promotion of specific industries generally did not work . . . [p. 24] . . . the fact that interventions were an element of some East Asian economies' success does not mean that they should be attempted everywhere, nor should it be taken as an excuse to postpone needed market-oriented reform" (p. 26). The World Bank's statistical analysis shows that "industrial policy only marginally affected industrial structure" and "productivity change has not been higher in promoted sectors" (pp. 312, 315).

3. Haggard (1990) appropriately classifies Hong Kong and Singapore on an entrepôt trajectory.

4. As in Brazil during the 1970s (Adams and Davis, 1994).

5. An analogous classification is the distinction between functional and sectoral industrial policies (Wade, 1990).

6. Wade (1993) argues that interventionist trade policy was a significant ingredient of Taiwan's industrial strategy.

7. The next section draws on the WEFA Group (1994).

8. Such highly capital-intensive and technically complex industries would not attract local capital in the absence of government subsidies and protection. This would justify some aid only if, as in the infant industry argument, these industries would become efficient and competitive as they advance in learning and scale. In most cases in Southeast Asia, however, they have not done so.

REFERENCES

Adams, F. G., and C. A. Bollino. (1983). "The Meaning of Industrial Policy." In F. Gerard Adams and L. R. Klein, eds., *Industrial Policies for Growth and Competitiveness.* Lexington, MA: Heath-Lexington.

Adams, F. G., and I. M. Davis. (1994). "The Role of Policy in Economic Development: Comparisons of the East and Southeast Asian and Latin American Experience." *Asian Pacific Economic Literature* 8(1), (May), pp. 9–26.

Adams, F. G., and S. Ichimura. (1983). "Industrial Policy in Japan." In F. Gerard Adams and L. R. Klein, eds., *Industrial Policies for Growth and Competitiveness.* Lexington, MA: Heath-Lexington.

Arndt, Heinz. (1989). *Industrial Policy in East Asia.* Vienna: Unido.

Baldwin, R. E. (1969). "The Case against Infant Industry Protection." *Journal of Political Economy* 77(3), (May–June), pp. 295–305.

Haggard, S. (1990). *Pathways from the Periphery: The Politics of Growth in the Newly Industrializing Countries.* Ithaca, NY: Cornell University Press.

Hill, H. (1996a). *The Indonesian Economy since 1966.* Cambridge, MA: Cambridge University Press.

———. (1996b). "Toward a Political Economy Explanation of Rapid Growth in Southeast Asia." Paper presented at meeting of East Asian Economic Association, Bangkok.

Hughes, Helen. (1995). *Achieving Industrialisation in East Asia.* Cambridge: Cambridge University Press.

Krueger, Anne O. (1997). "Trade Policy and Economic Development: How We Learn." *American Economic Review* 87(1), pp. 1–22.

Pack, Howard, and Larry Westphal. (1986). "Industrial Strategy and Technological Change: Theory vs. Reality." *Journal of Development Economics* 22(1), pp. 82–128.

Smith, Heather. (1997). "Taiwan's Industrial Policy in the 1980s: An Appraisal." *Asian Economic Journal* 11(1), pp. 1–34.

Stiglitz, J. E. (1996). "Some Lessons from the East Asian Miracle." *The World Bank Research Observer* 11(2), pp. 151–77.

Terry, E. (1996). "An East Asian Paradigm?" *Atlantic Economic Journal* 24(3), (September), pp. 183–93.

Wade, R. (1990). *Governing the Market: Economic Theory and the Role of the Government in East Asian Industrialization.* Princeton, NJ: Princeton University Press.

———. (1993). "Managing Trade: Taiwan and Korea as Challenges to Economics and Political Science." *Comparative Politics* 25(2), (January), pp. 147–67.

The WEFA Group. (1994). *Industrial Policies in Southeast Asia.* Eddystone, PA: The WEFA Group.

World Bank (1993). *The East Asian Miracle: Economic Growth and Public Policy.* New York: Oxford University Press.

5

Industrialization and Environmental Policy in East Asia: A Comparative Study of Japan, Korea, and China

Hidefumi Imura and Takeshi Katsuhara

Economic development in East Asia took place in successive waves: Japan's high economic growth began in the mid-1950s, the economic leap forward of the Four Tigers started in the early 1970s, while the 1980s saw China and the ASEAN countries enjoying astounding economic expansion. A number of strains, however, are to be seen behind the phenomenal economic success of the region; one of the most significant among them is the worsening state of the environment.

Environmental developments and policy are of particular importance in East Asia because of rapid growth and industrialization, because of the relatively inefficient energy use and high pollution output of East Asian industries, and because of the large relative magnitude of some of the newcomer economies, China in particular. As East Asian industrialization proceeds apace, output of noxious pollutants such as particulates, sulfur oxides (SO_x) and carbon dioxide (CO_2) will be rising rapidly in the region, unless preventive measures are taken. The result is high levels of pollutants not only in the growing industrial countries themselves but also in their downwind neighbors, like Japan, and in the whole world (greenhouse effect). For this reason, it is important to evaluate the likely environmental consequences of East Asian growth and to visualize policies, domestic and international, that may help to ameliorate the growing pollution problem.

The process of economic development and the associated environmental consequences are similar among East Asian countries. The so-called flying geese pattern (Okita, 1993) model can be applied to environmental issues, arguing that the more recently growing countries are following a path established by the more advanced country (Japan). There are also significant differences, however, between the countries with respect to resources, type of industry, and economic organization that influence environmental considerations. Based on these ideas, this chapter presents a comparative study on environmental actions in three East Asian countries: Japan, Korea, and China.

ENERGY SUPPLY-DEMAND STRUCTURES AND ENVIRONMENTAL PROBLEMS

Economic growth and energy demand are closely related to each other. Energy consumption per person increases with economic growth in response to rising industrial production, increasing freight and passenger transport, the wider dissemination of home electric appliances, and so forth. Energy use, as long as its major source is fossil fuel, is accompanied by emission of air pollutants and CO_2. Thus, the economy, energy, and the environment are closely linked to each other. Decoupling of these three factions is very difficult: the trilemma of economy, energy, and environment.

Table 5.1 compares the growth of GNP (per capita) of Japan, South Korea, and China. We should note, however, that the critical consideration here is the larger population of China relative to Japan (about 10 times) and Korea. Moreover, the dollar comparison severely understates China's output, in purchasing power terms, with respect to the other two countries. The figures for the early 1990s show that China was approaching Japanese production of steel and paper and far exceeded production of Japan in the cement industry. Use of appliances and cars was, of course, still far behind in China.

Table 5.2 compares energy consumption and pollutants emissions for the three countries. China is far above Japan in energy consumption and far ahead, by an order of magnitude, in pollutant emissions.

When comparing primary energy consumption per capita in 1994, Japan stood at 3.89 toe (tons oil equivalent), Korea at 2.99 toe, and China at 0.66 toe. CO_2 emission per capita was 2.95 tons of carbon for Japan, 2.45 tons for Korea, and 0.68 tons for China (The Energy Data and Modelling Center, 1996). China, in particular, is ranked the world's third largest carbon dioxide-emitting country due mainly to its high total energy consumption and coal-dependent energy supply structure. If the Chinese economy keeps growing at its present pace, even a conservative forecast would cause this value to double by 2020, to the present level of the United States. This would have a sizable impact on global warming as well as on air pollution. Energy efficiency improvement therefore has a triple significance to China: economic efficiency, air pollution control, and stabilization of global warming.

Primary energy consumption per million U.S. dollars of GNP (1994) was 162 tons for Japan, 571 tons for Korea, and 1,638 tons for China, showing great differences among the countries. The gaps found in resources, energy inputs, and pollution loads per unit of production have significant implications when viewed from the perspective of international trade.

In Japan, a reduced energy intensity of the product mix contributed much to energy conservation in the 1970s, triggered particularly by the increased oil price caused by the first oil crisis. Then, after the second oil crisis in the early 1980s,

Table 5.1
Economic Development in Japan, South Korea, and China

	Japan			SKorea			China		
	1971	1980	1991	1971	1980	1991	1971	1980	1991
GNP per capita $	2,176	9,051	27,306	300	1,587	6,493	120	304	323
Raw Material Production (Million tons)									
Crude Steel	92.4	107.4	105.9	0.5	8.6	21.9	17.8	37.1	71.0
Cement	58.2	86.4	89.0	-	15.6	39.2	25.6	79.9	252.6
Ethylene	3.3	3.9	6.2	-	0.4	1.6	0.0	0.5	1.8
Paper	7.2	10.3	17.0	-	1.4	3.6	2.4	5.4	14.8
Motor Vehicles No. per 1000 persons	170	324	446	36	13	62	1	1	4
Production of Appliances per 100 persons									
Television	132	139	122	3.5	179	370	.01	2.5	23
Wash. Machines	25	37	44	-	5	50	-	0.2	5.9
Refrigerators	42	43	45	0.9	17	75	.00	.05	4.1

Sources: World Bank, World Tables; Korean Statistical Association, Korea Statistical Yearbook; Chinese Statistics, Chinese Statistical Yearbook.

Table 5.2
Energy Consumption and the Associated Emission of Pollutants in Japan, South Korea, and China

	Japan		SKorea			China		
	1975 (b)	1987 (b)	1975 (b)	1987 (b)	1991 (c)	1975 (b)	1987 (b)	1992 (d)
SOx Emissions (1000t)	2569	1141	1159	1292	1598	10168	19954	16848
per Capita (t/Capita)	.023	.009	.033	.031	.037	.011	.016	.014
per GNP (t/mill. $)	1.71	.047	24.1	10.0	8.7	85.4	65.6	34.3
Per Land Area (t/km2)	6.80	3.02	11.7	13.1	16.1	1.06	2.09	1.76
NOx Emissions (1000t)	2329	1935	220	555	878	3727	7371	
per Capita (t/Capita)	.021	.0160	.006	.013	.020	.004	.007	
per GNP (t/mill. $)	1.55	.80	4.58	4.30	4.80	31.3	24.2	
per Land Area (t/km2)	6.17	5.12	2.22	5.60	8.87	0.39	0.77	

	Japan			SKorea			China		
	1971	1980	1991	1971	1980	1991	1971	1980	1991
Primary Energy Demand									

(mill. TOE) (a)	268	346	438	17	41	102	236	412	665
Share/ Coal(%)	20.9	17.3	17.6	35.3	31.7	24.6	80.5	74.5	77.9
Gas	1.1	6.1	10.5	0.0	0.0	2.9	1.3	2.9	2.0
Nuclear	0.7	6.4	12.8	0.0	2.4	14.7	0.0	0.0	0.0
Hydro	2.6	2.3	1.8	0.0	0.0	0.0	1.3	1.2	1.7
per Capita (TOE/capita)	2.53	2.95	3.54	0.51	1.09	2.36	0.28	0.42	0.58
per GNP (TOE/mill. $)	213	184	148	490	613	557	2437	2611	1676
per Land Area (TOE/km2)	713	920	1164	141	340	847	26	45	72
Final Energy Consumption (mill TOE) (a)	213	248	305	14	34	79	193	325	496
CO_2 Emissions (mill tC) (a)	244	291	339	16	39	82	247	424	686
per Capita (tC/capita)	2.30	2.48	2.73	0.49	1.02	1.90	0.29	0.43	0.60
per GNP (tC/mill. $)	194	155	114	472	577	450	2548	2683	1731
per Land Area (tC/km2)	646	770	897	162	394	828	25.8	44.3	71.7

Note: GNP at constant 1987 price is used.

Sources: The Energy Data and Modeling Center, Energy and Economics Statistical Data Book '94, 1994; Science and Technology Agency of Japan, Energy Use and the Environment in Asia, 1993; Annual Report on the State of the Environment in Korea, 1992; and Chinese Environmental Yearbook, 1993.

efforts were focused on changing the industrial structure to expand the share of low energy-intensive products. Since the end of the 1980s, however, both the decline in international oil prices and the yen's appreciation until 1995 have tended to reduce the incentive for energy conservation.

In Korea and China, increased production has consistently been a major cause of increased energy demand. In both countries, no noticeable change in industrial structure has occurred to help reduce energy consumption (Imura and Katsuhara, 1995). In Korea, steel, shipbuilding, and other energy-intensive industries have contributed much to economic growth, as in Japan in the 1960s. In China, the elasticity of energy demand increase to GDP growth has been restrained to a relatively small value: its average from 1994 to 1993 was 0.52.[1] This may have been attributable, to a certain extent, to the government's policy to control energy supply to industries, but it may also reflect problems with measuring Chinese GDP growth. The traditional energy supply structure in China, which has relied heavily on coal, is likely to be a major constraint to China's future economic development, as a result of increasing production costs due to the depletion of coal reserves and the increased burden of transportation costs resulting from the uneven geographical distribution of coal-producing centers.

ENERGY AND ENVIRONMENT IN MAJOR INDUSTRIES

Large percentages of energy consumption are accounted for by basic materials industries such as steel, cement, petrochemicals, paper and pulp, and electric power. In China, the steel and electric power industries account for nearly 50% of the nation's primary energy consumption. A study of the industrial sectors highlights China's low efficiency in energy utilization (Table 5.3). Energy consumption per ton of crude steel in China is about twice the corresponding figure for Japan, and on-site thermal efficiency in Chinese power plants is 20% lower than in Japanese power plants.

In the Chinese steel industry, the existence of many small, old-fashioned facilities has posed a big obstacle to environmental protection measures. In Korea, on the contrary, the largest part of the steel production increase was achieved by the Pohang steelworks, which alone produced 23.4 billion tons of crude steel in 1995.

Growth of electric power consumption from 1971 to 1994 was about 2.5 times in Japan, while the corresponding figure was as high as 16.7 times in Korea and 6.3 times in China. China has devoted much effort to hydroelectric power generation, as represented by Sanxia Dam. Although China has a plan to expand nuclear power generation in the future, the present capacity of its coal-burning thermal power generation could be increased to a level equivalent to dozens of nuclear power plants merely by improving on-site thermal efficiency from the present level of 31.5% (1991) to the Japanese level of 38.8%. But this may be an insurmountable challenge in view of the antiquated state and small scale of many Chinese plants.

Table 5.3

Comparison of Japan with China with Respect to Production, Energy Intensity of Production, and SO$_x$ Emissions

		Steel		Electricity		Cement		Ceramic, Stone and Clay Products	
		Japan (1985)	China (1987)	Japan (1985)	China (1987)	Japan (1985)	China (1987)	Japan (1985)	China (1987)
	Production	Finished Products	Finished Products	(Million kWh)	(Million kWh)	(1000t)	(1000t)	Sheet Glass (1000 boxes)	Sheet Glass (1000 boxes)
		(1000t)	(1000t)	535,575	495,980	76,725	186,250	35,393	58,030
		97,524	43,860	(100)	(93)	(100)	(243)	(100)	(164)
		(100)	(45)						
Factors Contributing to SO$_x$ Emissions	Energy Consumption Per Unit Production	(Tcal/1000t)	(Tcal/1000t)	(Tcal/Mill kWh)	(Tcal/Mill kWh)	(Tcal/1000t)	(Tcal/1000t)	(Tcal/1000boxes)	(Tcal/1000boxes)
		4.928	12.596	1.910	3.520	1.279	1.365	1.842	8.905
		(100)	(256)	(100)	(184)	(100)	(107)	(100)	(483)
	SOx Emissions Per Unit Energy Consumption (SOx/Tcal)	0.277(t/Tcal)	3.586(t/Tcal)	0.182(t/Tcal)	1.769(t/Tcal)	0.102(t/Tcal)	1.472(t/Tcal)	0.627(t/Tcal)	3.275(t/Tcal)
		(100)	(1295)	(100)	(972)	(100)	(1443)	(100)	(522)

Source: The I-O Tables for the Analysis of Energy Consumption and Air Pollution with respect to China and Japan (Tokyo: MITI, 1995).

Environmental loads, such as air pollution, in steel and other industries generally manifest themselves as the synergistic effects of three factors: production volume, energy consumption per unit of production, and specific pollutant emission per unit of energy consumption. In countries like Korea and China, which experience rapid expansion of production, pollution loads will inevitably increase unless effective measures are taken against the second and third factors.

CHARACTERISTICS OF ENVIRONMENTAL PROBLEMS IN THE THREE COUNTRIES

In Japan, environmental policy priorities were gradually shifted as Japan ran into severe industrial pollution from the 1960s to the 1970s, urban and household pollution problems in the 1980s, and global environmental problems in the 1990s. Korea and China, on the other hand, still face major challenges in coping with industrial pollution.

Air pollution caused by sulfur oxides (SO_x) presents a good example to compare the state of environmental countermeasures in the three countries. In Japan, an estimated total of 4.8 million tons of SO_x was emitted in 1967, when air pollution was at its worst level. In the 1970s, however, the problem was largely solved, mainly thanks to the widespread use of flue-gas desulfurization technology. In Korea, where 1.6 million tons of SO_x was emitted in 1991, the increase in emissions from factories and power plants has been substantially stabilized thanks to reduced sulfur content in fuels since the 1980s, but the flue-gas desulfurization process has yet to be introduced, and the expansion of industrial production might offset the improvement to be achieved.

In China, which relies on coal for 75% of its energy use, the generally high sulfur content of coal reserves has resulted in the emission of 18 million tons a year of SO_x. The generation of SO_x in China has been increasing steadily year after year. If the current pace of coal-based energy consumption continues, China is likely to have 38 to 40 million tons a year of SO_x emissions by around 2020. In this respect, hopes are being pinned on the development of conventional and new, low-cost, but effective, flue-gas desulfurization technology.

There also are other environmental problems. In all three countries, control of urban and household pollution problems has become an important policy objective as the standard of living has risen. In large cities in each country, motor vehicles have become a major source of pollution in addition to industrial plants. Household heating equipment is also a major pollution source in the winter season in Chinese cities north of the Changjiang. The figures are high, but gradually declining.[2] The volume of domestic waste is constantly increasing, and citizens' complaints about their living environment are on the increase. Pollution of rivers, underground water, and seawater has become a major problem. In China, since it takes a long time for pollutants discharged into water systems in inland areas to reach the sea, a great number of people tend to be exposed to pollution risks of water. Moreover, control of the desertification of inland areas is a big challenge in China, where forests account for only 13.4% of the national land surface.

Establishment of Environmental Legal Systems and Institutions

Japan was the first in the region to face serious environmental problems. From the late 1960s to 1970s, Japan had to make a great effort to overcome them by instituting legal and administrative systems and introducing a number of advanced control technologies. The ongoing pollution problems in Korea and China can be better understood by examining them through Japanese experiences. Those Asian countries, being "late comers" in the industrialization race, are in a favorable position to take "advantage of backwardness." If they can learn from the experience of Japan and other industrialized countries, they might achieve economic growth while avoiding the environmental failures that occurred in Japan.

Table 5.4 summarizes the major environmental events in the three countries. The Environment Agency was formally set up in 1971 in Japan and in 1980 in Korea. In China, the State Environment Protection Bureau was set up in 1988 to undertake nationwide environmental administration. To keep up with developments, the three East Asian countries have been consolidating their basic environmental laws and regulations. The contents and frameworks of the environmental laws of the three countries, however, have both similarities and differences, closely linked to the political systems peculiar to the countries. The scope of Japan's environmental policy was restricted to pollution control and nature conservation until the Basic Environmental Law was enacted in 1993. Korea's environmental policy changed drastically in the first half of the 1990s in response to the greater public demand for a clean and healthy environment together with the trend of economic growth, democratization, and opening to international competition. The Ministry of Environment was established in 1990 as a Cabinet-level ministry with strengthened responsibilities in air and water quality, tap water supply, waste management, and nature conservation. Following the enactment of the Basic Environment Policy Act in 1990, virtually all environment-related laws were rewritten, and the environmental administration was rationalized. Korea's Green Vision 21 was approved by the government in 1995 to make the transition "from a model country of economic growth to a model country of environmental preservation." Korea has introduced advanced systems of environmental management, such as EIA (environmental impact assessment) and application of economic instruments, which Japan has not yet institutionalized.

China's environmental legal systems and environmental management systems are considerably different from those of Japan and Korea. China has devised and enforced a number of Chinese-specific policy tools, based on socialistic policy ideas and principles, such as the Pollutant Discharge Expense Burdening (Paiwufei) System, the Three Simultaneity (Santongshi) System, the Environment Impact Assessment System, and the Environmental Protection Target Responsibility Sys-

Table 5.4

Chronology of Major Environmental Movements in Japan, Korea, and China

	Japan	Korea	China
Major Characteristics of Environmental Problems	-1960s: Time of environmental turmoil: rapid economic growth and industrial pollution, health victims, anti-pollution movement of citizens, reluctant industrial attitudes, etc. -1970s: Systematic implementation of environmental control,industrial structure change triggered by oil crisis, etc. -1980s: Increased demand for the "quality of life," such as urban environmental amenities -1990s: Increasing public concerns about global environmental issues, and the public consensus based on the "sustainable development" concept	-1970s: Start of rapid economic growth with relatively little attention paid to the environment -1980s: Systematic start of environmental control measures -1990s: Increased public concerns about pollution incidents. Environmental problems became a subject on the political agenda. Reorientation of the growth policy is necessary, giving a priority to environmental protection	-1980s: "Four Modernization" policy: co-operation with the West and introduction of modern technologies. Rising standard of living and increasing resource consumption and pollutant emissions. Environmental actions led by government initiatives -1990s: Environmental problems became a major constraint to economic development: environmental degradation accelerated; transboundary problems with the neighboring countries; environmental measures have become a requisite for acquiring development aid from outside.
Legislative and Institutional Framework at National Level	-1967: Enactment of basic environmental laws ("Basic Law for Pollution Control", "Air Pollution Control Law," "Water Pollution Control Law", etc.) -1971: Establishment of the Environment Agency -1973: Enactment of the "Health Damage Compensation Law" -1987: Amendment of the "Health Damage Compensation Law" -1993: Enactment of "Basic Environment Law"	-1977: Enactment of "Environmental Preservation Law" -1990: Enactment of "Basic Law for Environmental Policies" -1990: Enactment of "Atmospheric Environment Conservation Law": strengthening of emission standard, introduction of an emission charge system -1991: Enactment of the "Law on the Cost Allocation and Liability for Environmental Improvement" -1993: Enactment of "Environmental Impact Assessment Law" -1993: Five-Year Program for Energy Saving -1995: Public election of heads of local governments	-1979: Provisional enforcement of "Environmental Protection Law" -1988: State Environmental Protection Bureau was set up subordinate to the State Council -1989: Enactment of "Air Pollution Control Law" -1989: Nation-wide Enforcement of "Environmental Protection Law" -1994: Adoption of China's Agenda 21

tem. China, however, lacks necessary funds and technology for pollution control and abatement despite its advanced policy ideas and objectives (Table 5.4).

ENVIRONMENTAL FINANCING

Today, the "polluter pays" principle (PPP) is widely adopted as a basic rule for allocating the cost of environmental measures. The PPP is important in international trade policies to avoid distortions that might be brought about by government subsidies to businesses. Compliance with the PPP is, therefore, an important obligation for a country like Korea, which seeks to grow on the basis of international trade. Environmental charges and taxes are means to put PPP into effect, and they are important tools to raise revenues for implementing environmental measures in public and private sectors.

In recent years, the view that economic instruments should be used more effectively in implementing environmental policies is widely shared, mainly among OECD member nations. In Japan, subsidy-type policy measures such as low interest rate financing and subsidies to businesses, particularly to medium-size and small businesses, and tax exemptions have been widely adopted for encouraging environmental measures in the private sector, but payment instruments such as environmental taxes, levies, and charges have seldom been employed. Korea, on the other hand, has introduced environmental charge systems, including the Pollutant Emission Surcharge and the Environmental Improvement Burden Charge, while China has widely adopted the Pollutant Discharge Expense Burdening (Paiwufei) System. These systems in the two countries are important financial sources for enforcing environmental control measures.

Although the PPP has generally been supported as the basic principle of environmental policy, it is not necessarily a rule to be strictly adhered to, especially for a country like China, in which the rapid implementation of stringent control measures is desirable. China's Paiwufei System is an economic system for promoting environmental control measures. Under the present circumstances in China, Paiwufei has fallen dreadfully short of the financial requirements for implementing more radical environmental measures. As a result, China has had to rely on assistance and investment from the outside for realizing any large-scale environmental projects. The government should allocate more budget for public projects for environmental improvement and create financial mechanisms to assist environmental investment in the private sector. Here, the "two-step loan" approach presented by a Japanese aid agency, OECF (Overseas Economic Cooperation Fund), may provide a hint for utilizing foreign aid to establish such financial mechanisms. In this approach, governments receive official development assistance (ODA) from foreign countries and can then utilize it to assist environmental activities in the private sector.

Energy saving by conventional technologies has been practiced extensively in Japan, and further possibilities are relatively limited. There remain possibilities to invest in special energy-saving technologies, but these are costly and would require longer payback times. Therefore, it might be more cost-effective to make the same expenditure in China rather than in Japan. This suggests the possibility of a cooperative reduction of CO_2 emissions, to stabilize global warming.

TECHNOLOGICAL POSSIBILITIES

The development of low-cost pollution control technologies is the key to successful environmental protection. Pollution control and energy-saving technologies have made rapid progress in Japan mainly because aggressive investment was made in new plant and equipment during the period of high economic growth, in addition to the synergic effects of tightened anti-pollution regulations and increased energy prices as incentives.

In the early stages of environmental measures, the end-of-pipe (EP) technology of retrofitting pollution control equipment to existing production facilities is frequently employed. It would often prove inefficient, however, to retrofit the EP technology to obsolete facilities. In such cases, it is more efficient, in terms of both environmental measures and cost-effectiveness, to replace the entire manufacturing process with the cleaner production (CP) technology taking advantage of the opportunity to replace obsolete equipment.

In Korea, production facilities are now being expanded vigorously. If advantage is taken of this opportunity, environmental protection will make considerable progress. In fact, it is reported that the first flue-gas desulfurization equipment in Korea was installed in three thermal power plants. In introducing antipollution technologies, Korea will have to accept the increased cost of such technologies. The problem here is that industry might be reluctant to adopt anti-pollution technologies on the grounds that they would hamper economic growth, as was often seen in Japan in the 1960s and the 1970s. If Korea, as a full-fledged industrial country that has joined the OECD, is to continue its economic development through international trade, it must avoid international criticism for "pollution dumping." Thus, implementing domestic environmental protection is a particularly important task for Korea, together with conforming to the PPP.

Reexamination of industrial production processes themselves is an important key to maintaining the balance between economic growth and environmental protection. In order to promote pollution control measures, it is essential to nurture pollution control industries, technological improvement consultants, and engineers specializing in environmental management. Especially under the present circumstances in China, simple and low-cost antipollution technologies would have great potential. Careful study is required to determine which is more desirable for China: traditional, labor-intensive methods; less efficient, but lower-cost, domestic technologies; or the most advanced modern technologies to be imported from outside.

The headache to China is the existence of many small-size, old-fashioned facilities. Both modern facilities incorporating the most advanced technologies and obsolete facilities more than 50 years old are scattered on its vast territory and are in operation. There is a large gap between the well-equipped factories of national priority enterprises or foreign-owned enterprises and those of rural and township enterprises. Underdeveloped environmental industry in China, that is, the immature state of domestic technologies capable of supplying low-cost antipollution equipment, also poses an obstacle to the implementation of environment protection.

APPLICABILITY OF JAPAN'S EXPERIENCE

Japan's role and initiatives will be increasingly important for the protection of the environment in East Asia. Japan's environmental protection measures, particularly its experience in overcoming pollution, will offer a number of helpful suggestions to various countries, including Korea and China. Japanese policies or technologies cannot be readily applied or transferred, as such, to other countries because of differences in economic, social, and cultural conditions. In this respect, a World Bank report entitled "Japan's Experience in Urban Environmental Management" provided a penetrating insight into the matter (World Bank, 1994).

Economic, social, and cultural factors unique to Japan lie behind the fact that serious environmental problems occurred, and, at the same time, effective countermeasures were successfully taken there. The high rate of growth of the Japanese economy, which caused the environmental disasters, enabled the country to make adequate investment in anti-pollution technologies: Japan has taken advantage of new industrial processes, which are economically and financially justified in themselves, to bring about environmental improvements. The unique relationship that exists between government and industry, the ability of industry to be self-reliant in technology development, and the introduction of mass transport systems all proved effective in environmental protection. Local governments also played a significant role. While the central government instituted overall environment-related laws and regulations and extended financial assistance, local governments played a leading role in environmental protection at the local level. These developments occurred since freedom of speech and political discussion, guaranteed in Japan, allowed media campaigns and local protest movements, and antipollution public opinion forced government and industry to take control measures.

By comparing underlying conditions in Korea and China with those in Japan, one can obtain useful suggestions as to the factors essential for the success of environmental protection in those countries and the conditions that need to be established. Freedom of political discussion and speech, in particular, is an important factor for environmental protection. It is especially important to provide local people with proper opportunities to participate in the process of addressing environmental problems. Understanding and cooperation of businesses and local people, promotion of environmental education, establishment of a pollution victim relief system, and monitoring of pollution sources are also essential.

In Korea, which has long been preoccupied with the cult of rapid economic growth, and in China, now speeding its way toward the so-called socialist market economy, knowledge of how to foster environmental awareness, promote understanding, and establish norms about the social responsibility of enterprises and their relations with the general public in coping with pollution will have a strong bearing on environmental protection.

JAPAN'S ENVIRONMENTAL INITIATIVES

Environmental cooperation between Japan and China is being promoted based on the Japan–China Agreement on the Cooperation for Environmental Protection, which was concluded in 1994. Japan and Korea also have cooperation projects based on the Science Cooperation Agreement. Furthermore, regional cooperation, such as the project on the monitoring of acid rain in East Asia, started with participation of experts from Japan, Korea, and China.

Japan is the largest donor country to China among member countries of the OECD Development Assistance Committee. The Japanese government set five priority areas in economic cooperation with China: economic infrastructures, agriculture, environment, health and medical service, and human capacity building. In addition, in 1992, Japan and China reached an agreement that Japan's ODA to China will give special priority to environmental protection. The outcome of Japan's environmental aid to China includes the Japan–China Friendship Environmental Protection Center, built in Beijing, and a number of other projects being undertaken. MITI (Ministry of International Trade and Industry), in particular, started its "green aid plan," focusing on the transfer of Japanese technologies. For China, model projects for energy-saving and coal-burning technologies are being implemented.

East Asia, including China, is potentially a great market for environmental technologies. In addition to Japan, the United States and European countries have shown great interest in this market for their technologies. They must not, however, forget that their technologies alone may not provide a practical solution to the problems in countries like China that lack the necessary funds and skills.

LOCAL INITIATIVES FOR INTERNATIONAL
ENVIRONMENTAL COOPERATION

Japanese industrial cities such as Kitakyushu, Osaka, and Kawasaki played an important role during the rapid economic growth period of Japan in supplying basic materials necessary for capital formation and improvement of infrastructure. In Korea and China, a large quantity of basic materials, such as steel, chemical products, and cement, is required to sustain economic growth, and demand will be even stronger in the future. Given that Korea and China will need huge industrial cities as supply centers of basic materials, experience in environmental protection in Japanese industrial cities is highly applicable to similar cities in Korea and China.

Efforts to strengthen international environmental cooperation are actively being made by the environmental authorities of local Japanese governments, particularly in the Kyushu district, which is geographically close to Korea, China, and other East Asian nations. In the industrial city of Kitakyushu, in particular, there is an accumulation of industrial pollution control technologies developed by the steel, chemical, and other industries located there. The municipal authorities there have administrative know-how in local environmental management practices, such as regulation of pollution sources, environmental inspection and monitoring, environmental planning, pollution control agreements, and encouragement of concerted action of private businesses and citizens.

Based on these accumulated resources, the city of Kitakyushu is now vigorously promoting environmental cooperation with Dalian, a seaport city in the Liaoning Province in northeast China, in working on the "Dalian Special Environment Protection Zone" project, which was formally endorsed by the Chinese government in 1994. It is hoped that the project will serve as a successful model of urban environmental management based on international environmental cooperation at the local level.

FOR SUSTAINABLE DEVELOPMENT OF EAST ASIA

Although the East Asian countries, except Japan, are still collectively classified as developing countries, their economic situation is entirely different from that of the least developed countries. The standard of living of people in these countries has materially improved, with household appliances, automobiles, and other durable consumer goods rapidly proliferating in daily life. Rising living standards, however, will be accompanied by expanded consumption of resources and emission of pollutants. The industrialization of China, in particular, will have profound implications for the global environment due to its rapid pace of economic growth and its tremendous population. Economic growth in Korea has been outstanding: its real GDP has increased by a factor of more than 12 since 1963, and it became the 29th member of the OECD in December 1996. It is the seventh largest OECD economy in terms of GDP. Although Korea has been a recipient of foreign aid, this situation is changing in line with its economic development. The amount of Korean ODA was 0.03% of its GDP in 1995, or a mere one-tenth of the average for OECD Developmental Assistance Committee member countries. Korea will be required to increase the environmental components of its development.

Japan, Korea, and China have had close historical relations, having common cultural backgrounds. They have both similarities and differences, however, in the principles and practices of environmental policies, depending on their economic, social, and cultural conditions. Nonetheless, their cooperation is being strengthened, and Japan's initiatives to transfer its experiences to the other countries have become increasingly important.

Economic links among countries in East Asia are being tightened, allowing us to envisage the creation of a common economic region in the next century. There has been a significant movement for Japanese enterprises to relocate their production facilities to Korea and China, where wage and other production costs are relatively cheaper. Although there is a large gap of environmental regulation between Japan and the other countries, most Japanese enterprises abroad as well as at home observe Japanese standards. This will have a favorable impact on the dissemination of environmental technologies and practices in the region. Moreover, there is a new movement in environmental cooperation between local governments. The unique Japanese methods of local environmental management might be transferred to other countries. This will contribute to the strengthening of their local capability to solve environmental problems.

NOTES

1. It may, however, also reflect problems of measurement, perhaps overstatement of output since coal production is probably measured fairly accurately (Adams and Chen, 1996).

2. The much lower level of pollution in Kitakyushu, Japan, a steel producer, is notable.

REFERENCES

Adams, F. G., and YiMin Chen. (1996). "Skepticism about Chinese GDP Growth—Comparison of Chinese GDP Elasticity of Energy Consumption with Other Countries." *Journal of Economic and Social Measurement* 22, pp. 231–40.

The Energy Data and Modelling Center. (1996). *Energy and Economic Statistical Data Book 1996.* Tokyo: Energy Conservation Center.

Imura, H., T. Futawatari, and R. Fujikura. (1995). "Economic Development, Energy, and Environment in East Asia: A Comparative Study of Japan, South Korea, and China." *Journal of Global Environmental Engineering* 1, pp. 79–100.

Imura, H., and T. Katsuhara (1995). *Environmental Problems in China* (in Japanese). Tokyo: Toyo-Keizai.

Ministry of Environment. (1996). *State of the Environment in Korea.* Seoul: Ministry of Environment.

OECD. (1991). *Recommendation of the Council on the Use of Economic Instruments in Environmental Protection.* Paris: OECD.

Okita, S. (1993). "Steps to the 21st Century." *Japan Times.*

World Bank. (1994). *Japan's Experience in Urban Environmental Management.* Washington, DC: World Bank.

II

Country Experience

This part of the volume is concerned with the experience on the country level. We begin with a discussion of Japan's policy toward the East Asian countries. Then we turn in Chapter 7 to public policies in each of the economies in the area. First we consider the so-called Tigers, Taiwan, South Korea, Singapore, and Hong Kong. Chapters 11 to 13 are concerned with ASEAN. Chapters 14 to 16 are concerned with China and Vietnam. In each case the authors discuss policies that have particular relevance to the economies involved, so that a wide coverage of various aspects of policy, macropolicy, industrial policy, trade policy, and, in some instances, social policy is obtained.

6

Japanese Economic Policy toward East Asia

Toru Yanagihara

East Asia is an important geographical focus of Japanese external economic policy. It might be said that East Asia is the only region for which Japan has formulated a systematic regional approach to its external economic policy. The purpose of this chapter is to highlight some features of Japanese economic policy toward East Asia. The discussion is organized around three interrelated questions. First, the overall thrusts of the Japanese economic policy agenda are reviewed to provide a backdrop for Japanese external economic policy. Second, the main concerns of Japan's economic policy toward East Asia are reviewed. Here we cover bilateral, regional, and multilateral approaches. Particular attention will be paid to a newly emphasized approach to international economic relations, a "rule-based" approach. Third, Japan's role in the response to the recent turmoil in the East Asian economies is reviewed.

POLICY AGENDA FOR THE JAPANESE ECONOMY

The central themes of the policy agenda in Japan are summarized as several interrelated aspects of structural reform. The recognition of the need for reform derives from the poor growth performance of the economy all through the 1990s following the bursting of the asset price bubble in the late 1980s. It has been further prompted by perceived needs to improve the fiscal and financial situation, which have taken on added urgency as a result of continued sluggish economic conditions. The Economic Planning Agency (EPA) has estimated that real annual growth rate of GDP will be higher by 0.9% for fiscal years (FY) 1998–2003 if structural reforms are implemented as contemplated by the government.

There are more fundamental, long-term factors as well. The Economic Council, an official advisory body to the prime minister, issued a report entitled "Economic and Social Plan for Structural Reform" in 1995. This document represents an official consensus by the economic bureaucracy in the government on the conditions and challenges the economy faces over the medium and long term. The perspective presented there is mostly inward-looking, with concerns about domestic conditions commanding principal attention. Anticipated aging and shrinking of the population constitute one of the central concerns. Another domestic issue of import is a fundamental change in economic management philosophy and practice from the one suited to the postwar catch-up to another more appropriate for an advanced and mature socioeconomy.

External conditions and tasks are considered as well. Globalization of the world economy is emphasized, ushering in an age of increasingly integrated markets and "megacompetition" on a global scope. *De jure* and *de facto* global rules and standards are being established to govern business operations and governmental actions. Increasingly, enterprises choose the countries in which to locate, not vice versa. A domestic economy can no longer survive, much less prosper, without being fully and effectively integrated with the global economy.

The Japanese policy outlook and reform agenda are essentially liberal and internationalist. This is reflected in expressions such as "aiming at an economy and society open both internally and externally," "pursuit of international harmonization of economic institutions and practices," and "active participation in the rule-making in international arenas." This emphasis on rules and institutions represents a new and important thrust in Japan's external economic policy. The central focus of this new emphasis is on the promotion of liberal frameworks for trade and investment in both multilateral (WTO) and regional (APEC) levels.

There remain elements of traditional developmentalist perspectives in the basic approach of Japan's external economic policy. Official development assistance continues to serve as an instrument for contributing to the betterment of economic, social, and environmental conditions in the developing world. Global and regional perspectives are given prominence in addressing telecommunications infrastructure, environment, food, population, and health.

With regard to manufacturing and services, there are concerns about the "hollowing out" of Japanese industries in the rapidly changing context of increasingly global competition. In such assembly industries as automobile and electronics, Japanese corporations have been expanding their production overseas at a rapid rate over the past decade, oftentimes relocating their domestic operations to sites overseas. On the other hand, inward flows of foreign direct investment (FDI) remain much smaller than outward flows. Apparently, the business environment in Japan is not attractive to either Japanese or foreign enterprises. This recognition constitutes one important spur to the political decision in favor of overhauling the whole economic and social system of postwar Japan.

This sentiment is elaborated in a document entitled *Future Issues Concerning International Trade and Industry Policies*, prepared by the Ministry of International

Trade and Industry (MITI) in June 1997, in which the ministry's view of the domestic and international situation and its proposal for future policy actions are presented.

In the initial part of the document, entitled "Basic Perception on Domestic and Foreign Economic Environments Surrounding Japan," two fundamental sources of concern are identified as "megacompetition and a rapidly graying society." On megacompetition and the situation of Japan the document states:

The remarkable progress of information technology and the spread of free trade, among other factors, have induced vigorous movement of business resources on the global scale. . . . Coming into full force today is megacompetition where businesses choose the countries in which they wish to operate. . . . In this megacompetition, many countries have made it a national agenda to develop a business environment that facilitates robust economic activity. Due to a high cost structure, Japan faces an increasing danger of industry drain, where even industries that are inherently cost competitive in Japan flee the country to set up operations abroad.

On the aging of population the document presents a rather gloomy outlook as summarized in the following paragraph:

Japan is now experiencing what no other industrialized country has ever experienced. The shrinkage of productive-aged population accompanying the rapid graying and decline of savings rate have dampened the country's economic strength. At the same time, the increase in such public burdens as social security threaten to strike another blow to the Japanese economy.

Similar sentiments of concern are being expressed with regard to the efficiency and international competitiveness of the Japanese financial sector, prompting a push for financial system reform, dubbed as the Japanese version of the Big Bang.

There are positive messages as well. The MITI document just quoted defines the overall objective of its policy as "to conquer the issues described above and to form a vital and resilient economic system." On the direction of a policy on the international front the document contains a section entitled "Strategic Formation of a Global Economic Environment," in which the following paragraph is included:

In order to improve access to regional markets for Japanese industry in the age of megacompetition, it is necessary for our country, with the cooperation of the private sector, to take the initiative in setting international rules on such economic matters as trade, investment, competition, intellectual property, and electronic commerce in manners that are as advantageous as possible for the Japanese economy. To this end, Japan should play an active role in the development of regional markets by using bilateral routes, such regional forums as APEC (Asia-Pacific Economic Cooperation) and ASEM (Asia-Europe Meeting), and such multi forums as WTO and OECD. . . . In particular, Japan should introduce private-sector capability and offer the Asian region, with whom our country is highly interdependent, effective and efficient cooperation in solving a number of problems that have surfaced. These problems include the surge in the demand for infrastructure that supports economic growth, the deterioration in environment due to the rapid economic growth, and the lack of fundamental systems such as intellectual property rights, standards, and statistics.

This reference to, and emphasis on, Asia represents a recurring theme in this document. The following paragraph reveals MITI's thinking in a straightforward manner:

Asia is a growth center of the world and Japan has an intimate economic relationship with this region. Japan should build a solid industrial network with regions such as Asia and expand the Japanese economic frontier based on this network. For this purpose, Japan should cultivate the needs for business development by each industry, eliminate trade and investment barriers, improve social capital, establish an orderly framework for intellectual asset protection, develop industrial cooperation, and eliminate such growth restraints as environmental and energy problems. To this end, it would be in the interest of Japan to advance comprehensive and strategic approaches through bilateral discussions and APEC.

JAPAN'S APPROACH TO ECONOMIC RELATIONS WITH EAST ASIA

Traditionally, the Japanese approach to economic relations with East Asia has been characterized by its sympathy and support for the developmental aspirations of neighboring nations. Japan took upon itself the role of a benign elder brother, showing the path of development for latecomer nations and providing assistance as requested. The dominant perspective here was bilateral, and the dominant notion informing economic assistance was that of "states of development." Japanese policymakers viewed each East Asian economy separately and designed assistance programs according to its stage of development, typically defined by the level of industrialization attained. This apparently sympathetic and supportive approach was not altogether based on altruistic motivations. On the contrary, it was, no doubt, also an expression of enlightened self-interest on the part of Japan. Japan has relied on East Asia for food, energy, raw materials, and sea lanes (for petroleum from the Gulf, in particular); securing access to these has constituted, and continues to constitute, an important concern for Japan's economic security.

Since the mid-1980s, Japanese manufacturing firms have developed extensive networks of cross-border production arrangements across the region, helping to forge a much closer integration of the East Asian economies. These arrangements have been formed and multiplied through a series of waves of direct investments by Japanese corporations in East Asia. This development has been most marked in the leading industries of Japan, that is, electronics and electric machinery and automobiles. East Asia represents both cost-effective production sites for an increasingly diversified array of industrial products and, with high and sustained rates of economic growth, rapidly expanding markets for a variety of goods and services. In the 1990s, Japanese commercial banks have expanded their presence in East Asia rapidly, facing reduced demand from their domestic corporate clients. All in all, East Asian operations have become crucial elements for Japanese business.

This development has prompted policymakers to articulate Japan's approach to economic relations with East Asia. Two partly overlapping thrusts emerged. The first is the extension and systematization of the developmentalist perspective to the regional level. This might be called a regionwide industrial policy approach. The most notable manifestation of this approach has been the New Asian Industrial Development Plan (New AID Plan), announced by MITI in 1987. The main aim of the plan was to promote industrial developments in East Asian economies, ASEAN countries in particular, in a mutually compatible and complementary manner. This plan was overtaken by the rapid deployment of Japanese business activities in ASEAN countries in the late 1980s. This approach remains one important thrust of Japan's economic policy toward the ASEAN countries.

The second thrust of Japan's approach to East Asia that emerged in the late 1980s was a desire to form a regionwide scheme for consultation and coordination in the management of regional economic affairs. The motivation behind this initiative seems to have been multifaceted. First, there was perceived need to establish policy dialogues among the regional's policymakers to provide a favorable policy environment for the promotion of intraregional economic relations. Second, there was concern about the nature and degree of adjustment needed on the part of East Asian economies in the wake of the Plaza Accord and an expected slowdown of economic growth in the United States. Third, there was rising concern about the attitude of the United States toward East Asia as it experienced expanding trade deficits with the region. Fourth, there were also concerns about the trend of regionalization in Europe and the Americas and corresponding concern with a possible breakdown of the multilateral trading regime. These intra- and extraregional considerations led to the formation of APEC.

APEC was initially conceived by Japanese policymakers as a geographical extension of economic relations between Japan and ASEAN. This reflected the recognition of emerging, regionwide networks of production and distribution arrangements. On one hand, not only Japan but Asian NIEs emerged as important sources of FDI in the new 1980s. Another important development was the emergence of China as a market, investment destination, and exporter. These changes prompted the Japanese to adopt a comprehensive perspective on economic relations within the region. In their view, APEC represented a regional scheme for the promotion of economic development through increased flows in trade and investment, technology transfer, human resource development, and development of infrastructure. There was clear recognition of the asymmetric nature of relationships between the more and less developed economies within the region, the former providing development assistance to the latter.

In early 1990s APEC adopted liberalization of trade and investment as its major goal under the strong leadership of the United States. The Japanese were initially rather concerned about the "rule-based" liberalization approach proposed by the United States. For one thing they were afraid that "Asian characteristics" of APEC as a consensus-based cooperative scheme with Japanese style of leadership might be lost in the process of negotiations over terms and conditions of liberalization. In essence, the Japanese wanted to see APEC as a scheme owned by its developing country members, with the developed country members engaging in consultation and providing assistance as necessary. In the event, as liberalization of trade and investment came to be accepted by many members, Japan also endorsed liberalization as a major goal of APEC. As it turned out, Japan was about to embrace a "rule-based" approach to trade and investment relations as a new thrust of its external economic policy.

One important recent feature of Japanese external economic policy is the emphasis on the "rule-based" approach to international economic relations. This emphasis arose in the wake of a series of acrimonious trade disputes with the United States since the 1980s, in which the U.S. side repeatedly resorted to unilateral or result-oriented measures. With the establishment of the World Trade Organization (WTO), there have been systematic extension and intensification of the "rule-based" approach as the central thrust of Japanese external economic policy.

This new thrust of Japanese external policy is put forward most elaborately in the *Report on the WTO Consistency of Trade Policies by Major Trading Partners*, published annually by the Subcommittee on Unfair Trade Policies and Measures of the Industrial Structure Council, an official advisory body to the Ministry of International Trade and Industry. The main purpose of the report is to identify and analyze the trade policies and measures of Japan's 10 major trade partners (namely, the United States, the European Union, Korea, Thailand, Singapore, Hong Kong, Australia, Malaysia, Indonesia, and Canada). This report seeks to examine the consistency with WTO Agreements of trade policies and measures taken by these countries. The report emphasizes the importance of using multilateral dispute settlement procedures of the WTO to address unfair trade policies and measures.

As is evident in the "top 10" list, many economies in East Asia are important partners for Japan in trade (and even in investment). (China and Taiwan rank high among Japan's 10 major trading partners, but they are not covered in this document since they are not WTO members. Japan supports early accession to WTO for both of them.) Japanese external economic policy seems to be increasingly informed by the most-favored-nation and nondiscriminatory rules of WTO in dealing with these East Asian economies. Let us quote some summary statements for individual East Asian economies:

Korea: The number of items under the Source Diversification System for Specific Imports was reduced and Korea plans to eliminate the measure by 1999. We believe, however, that Korea violates most-favored-nation treatment by erecting quantitative restrictions against Japan and that the system violates GATT Article XI and is also inconsistent with GATT Article XII, and should be eliminated as quickly as possible. We appreciate the relaxation of regulations in services. In areas such as safeguards, anti-dumping legislation, local content requirements and rules of origin, monitoring is necessary.

Indonesia: We appreciate the elimination of import restrictions and relaxation of regulations in services. But some measures concerning automobiles such as the National Car Program violate the WTO Agreement and prompt conformance with the WTO Agreement is required. (More on this later.)

Thailand: Import restrictions under the Export and Import Act could constitute a violation of the WTO Agreement and should be eliminated as quickly as possible. We hope local content requirements will be terminated. We appreciate Thailand's deregulation in financial services, and its improvements in the protection of intellectual property.

Malaysia: We appreciate that Malaysia is improving the protection of intellectual property.

Singapore: No substantial issues were pointed out except for intellectual property protection, but we also note that Singapore is committed to full implementation of the TRIPs Agreement by the end of 1998.

Hong Kong: No substantial issues were pointed out except for intellectual property protection, and we note that Hong Kong has stepped up its efforts to eliminate counterfeit goods.

The National Car Program in Indonesia is an important and symbolic case in this regard. Japan believes that it violates most-favored-nation treatment by providing special treatment to imports from a specified country (Korea) in the form of waivers of tariffs when finished cars are imported and luxury taxes when they are sold. Japan initially sought reconsideration from Indonesia through bilateral discussions but later decided, in parallel with the EC and the United States, to request consultations with the government of Indonesia under GATT Article 22 in light of the fact that sales of the "national car" started in October 1996.

This case, along with a similar case in Brazil and negotiations over China's accession to WTO, is significant in clearly revealing Japan's current position to the effect that the conduct of industrial policy must be in conformity with the WTO Agreement and its obligations. The following statement is worth quoting in full:

Indonesia, Thailand, and Malaysia all impose quantitative import restrictions which are incompatible with the GATT and which should be phased out. Developing countries may be concerned that, by abolishing import restrictions, they will be causing short-term negative effects for domestic industries. The fact is, however, that such restrictions, if maintained over long periods of time, not only hurt the interests of consumers and user-industries at home, but, by discouraging efforts to build competitiveness, obstruct the development of the very industries they were designed to assist. Ultimately, the elimination of import restrictions in accordance with WTO rules will improve these countries' own economic well-being. Japan strongly expects these countries to plan and systematically eliminate import restrictions with the help of sound industrial and economic policies. Japan should assist the process by providing policy support based on its own experience in promoting industry and eliminating border measures. In that regard, the on-going Industrial Policy Dialogues and other forms of exchange can be useful. Furthermore, Japan should request Indonesia and Malaysia to revise their export restrictions on logs and other measures to comply with WTO rules.

To sum up, at present, the Japanese approach to economic relations with East Asia comprises three levels: bilateral, regional, and multilateral.

At the bilateral level, Japan continues to provide financial and technical assistance for the promotion of economic development. There are three important new elements in this traditional approach. First, there is emphasis on industrial structural adjustment, for which Japan extends assistance aimed at upgrading human resources and technical and managerial capabilities of local businesses. It also engages in industrial policy dialogues as part of its intellectual assistance. Second, there is increased attention to special development with a view to alleviating income disparities generated in the course of rapid development. Third, a more conscious and systematic approach is adopted for the protection and restoration of the environment. The first of these elements might be viewed as uniquely Japanese in content and style. The other two were initially adopted in part in response to criticisms directed at Japan for its lack of concern with social and environmental conditions in the East Asian countries. By now, however, these concerns seem to have been fully internalized and established as the important pillars of Japanese assistance policy.

At the regional level, the dominant focus continues to be ASEAN. Here the central attention continues to be placed on promotion and possible coordination of industrial development. This may be viewed as an exercise in regional industrial policy with a view to realizing economies of scale and specialization. Liberalization of trade and investment rules within ASEAN are favored in the context of region-wide industrial development. Japanese interests in APEC also center around its effects on ASEAN. APEC addresses much broader issues and provides a useful background for Japan–ASEAN relations.

At the multilateral level, Japan has adopted a "rule-based" approach as the central thrust of its external economic policy with the establishment of the WTO. This general policy stance has come to be applied to its relations with East Asian economies in an increasingly more vigorous and systematic manner. With this new emphasis on multilateral rules, that is, WTO compatibility, traditional Japanese views on the need for, and effectiveness of, industrial protection-cum-promotion policy are being expressed in a more circumscribed manner.

RESPONSE TO ECONOMIC CRISIS IN EAST ASIA

The unfolding financial turmoil in East Asia has confronted Japan with an urgent task of crisis management on a regional scope. Japanese attitudes have not been clear-cut regarding the leadership role it is willing to exert. Initially, when Thai officials sounded out the possibility of arranging a rescue package outside an IMF accord, Japanese financial authorities urged them to seek an agreement with the fund. Then Japan co-sponsored, with IMF, a support group meeting for Thailand in Tokyo and called upon other Asian countries to participate. Japan took an essentially identical stance when Indonesia and South Korea later flirted with an idea of putting together a financial package for the stabilization of their economies relying solely on contributions from Asian nations.

At the same time, however, Japanese financial authorities were quite forthcoming in responding to the proposal, initially made by Thailand and seconded by other ASEAN member countries, to establish an Asian Monetary Fund (AMF) to cope with currency instabilities in the region. In fact, Japan took initiatives toward its founding, calling on China and Korea to participate and sounding out the reactions of the United States and the IMF. In the event, faced with the opposition of the United States and the IMF, Japan dropped its espousal of AMF.

Japanese financial authorities have traditionally maintained a softer attitude toward macroeconomic and structural adjustments in developing countries compared with the Anglo–American orthodoxy represented by the IMF and the World Bank. The underlying concerns are two-fold. First, the Japanese tend to take a longer-term developmental perspective in their approach to adjustment issues. They pay more attention to the need for developing economies to strengthen technological and managerial capabilities of the real sector of the economy over the long term. This contrasts sharply with lopsided emphasis placed by the IMF on macroeconomic balance and financial stabilization. It also differs critically from the World Bank emphasis on liberalization, deregulation, and privatization as key directions of structural adjustment. Second, the Japanese tend to pay more attention to living conditions of people and to possible sociopolitical disruptions as a result of strict adjustment measures. They are temperamentally averse to adversities and uncertainties engendered by drastic reform measures and habitually prefer kinder, gentler approaches to economic problems.

In relation to the present economic crisis in East Asia, there has emerged a renewed sense of discomfort among Japanese policymakers with the IMF programs designed for Thailand, South Korea, and Indonesia. Japanese criticisms of IMF programs are typically not well articulated or coherent. They relate to one or another of the following aspects of stabilization and reform measures prescribed by the IMF. First, the Japanese criticize the imposition of high interest rates for the stabilization of exchange rates in view of adverse impacts high interest rates generate on real sector activities. Second, they are critical of liberalization of short-term capital flows. They see short-term flows of capital as an intrinsically disruptive factor complicating macroeconomic management and are in favor of controlling those cross-border flows. Third, the Japanese find fault with what they see as the sociopolitical disruptions caused by too hasty imposition of IMF-prescribed reform measures in Indonesia.

In spite of these reservations and criticisms toward the IMF, the Japanese had no choice but to settle for a compromise that was reached at the Manila Meeting of Finance and Central Bank Deputies on 18-19 November, 1997. The compromise consisted of (1) recognition of the central role of the IMF in the international monetary system and (2) agreement on a new framework for regional cooperation for the stabilization of currency and financial conditions. The framework (Manila Framework) consists of a mechanism for regional surveillance and dialogue on the economic situation and a concerted financing arrangement (CFA) to supplement IMF resources in supporting foreign exchange reserves.

The Manila Framework differed from the proposed AMF in the following two ways. First, while the AMF was conceived as an alternative to the IMF, the role of the Manila Framework is subordinate and supplementary to the existing IMF operation both in policy matters and in the provision of financial resources. Second, the financial arrangement, CFA, is *ad hoc* and does not entail the establishment of permanent funds as in the case of IMF.

As it turned out, Japan appears to have settled for a modest role of supporter for the IMF-orchestrated rescue and restructuring programs for the crisis-ridden East Asian economies. There seem to be a number of partly overlapping factors responsible for this decision on the part of Japanese authorities. First, as the East Asian crisis spread and lingered, the solution increasingly looked far more complicated and the needed financial support more large-scale than initially expected. Under such circumstances, Japan was simply unwilling to take on the responsibility of offering an alternative to the IMF approach and financing. Second, as a background to the preceding point, Japan lacked the policy-oriented analysis of the East Asian economies needed to be able to devise alternative policy to the standard IMF approach. Third, Japan never developed "soft power" diplomatic skills for setting agendas and managing negotiating processes. Such capabilities would have been needed if Japan ever seriously desired to have its own way in face of opposition from the United States. Fourth, with Japanese economy in a sorry state and no clear vision of its future course, the Japanese were not in a position to suggest alternative proposals to resolve the East Asian economic crisis. In fact, Japan has been cast in a rather negative light in relation to the East Asian situation. If anything, with its economy stagnating and its financial sector retrenching, Japan was viewed as part of the problem. The response Japanese policymakers took to the collapse of the bubble economy throughout the 1990s is often referred to as what other East Asian economies should not do if they desire to avoid falling into a prolonged stagnation (as in Japan). Japanese policymakers and opinion leaders no longer have the self-confidence that they exhibited at the height of their nation's economic success.

This latest episode of attempted "East Asian regionalism" is reminiscent of another surrounding the formation of the East Asian Economic Group, initially proposed by Prime Minster Mahathir of Malaysia. On that occasion as well, Japanese authorities exhibited an ambivalent attitude, trying to strike a delicate diplomatic balance between their sympathy with East Asian regionalism and their concern over antagonizing the United States.

Japan will continue to face a dilemma in dealing with financial affairs in East Asia. As a global economic power, Japan endorses the principle of opening and liberalizing of domestic financial markets. At the same time, however, it is much more sympathetic, compared with the United States and the EU, with the concerns held by Asian nations regarding possible adverse effects of premature financial opening and liberalization on the long-term development of their economies. Japan will have to continue to engage in a delicate balancing act.

7

Public Policies in the Taiwan Economy: The Nurturing of a Market Economy

Chi Shive and Hsien-Feng Lee

Taiwan's rapid and smooth development of its economy over the last four decades is well documented.[1] However, there seems to be a lack of serious discussion on how policies were formed. What are the crucial factors affecting each important policy in relationship to the process of development? What were the pros and cons in the policy debate? This chapter searches for some missing links to fill the void. Taiwan is the only developing economy that has risen to the level of an industrial country by the IMF classification and is classed as a free market economy according to the Heritage Foundation.[2] How that market was nurtured deserves attention not only among scholars, but among public policymakers as well.

POLICY REFORM DURING 1950–1960

Export orientation or outward-looking is always mentioned first when discussing the attributes of Taiwan's economic development success. However, this was not what policymakers had in mind in the late 1950s. Rather, it was inward-looking import substitution, the concurrent popular development strategy of overvalued domestic currency and high tariffs and strict quantitative import control. After considerable debates and a critical pull from outside, the switch from inward-looking to outward-looking was made to pave the way for rapid economic development in the following four decades.

The argument for export promotion was based on comparative advantage and the fact that Taiwan has few natural resources apart from high population density. The longer-term comparative advantage, therefore, did not lie with such agricultural raw materials as rice and sugar but with products requiring labor-intensive production. However, given inward-looking policies, industrialization was limited to the development of industries producing for a highly protected domestic market. Industries facing measures that favored import substitution found it very difficult to export and thus to expand. At the same time, it was almost impossible for industries producing import substitutes to enjoy the economies of scale and efficiency of production with low purchasing power and per capita income, though the rural sector did expand at the time. Qualitative and quantitative restrictions on imports were equivalent to denying the economy the benefits of specialization on the basis of comparative advantage.

However, when the proposal to promote exports and to adopt relevant measures such as devaluation of domestic currency and trade liberalization was made, industrialists and official decision makers were hesitant. The concern was not from vested interests but from lack of confidence for the economy. There were fears that Taiwan-made products could not compete with foreign goods. There were also fears that devaluation would worsen the economy's terms of trade and cause imported inflation.

As debates were carried on, the situation in the late 1950s had become very clear. The domestic market was saturated with light industrial products, manifested by low-capacity utilization (Liang and Liang-Hou, 1988; Lin, 1979). The market was characterized by increasing domestic competition and a depressed price trend in textiles, leather, rubber, wood and paper products, and cement. Some factories reduced both price and quality, while others used foreign trademarks or even deceptive market gimmicks to expand sales. The intensifying competition caused some bankruptcies. Total exports in 1958 fell due to a contraction of sugar exports, despite increases in most other exported products. Sugar comprised 51.5% of total exports, and its fall sent a strong signal to policymakers.

At the same time, some well-known Chinese economists, like S. C. Tsiang and T. C. Liu, were trying to persuade the government that export promotion could earn the country more foreign exchanges, while devaluation would not cause inflation if it was coupled with trade liberalization. They explained that if imports were expanded with exports after devaluation and liberalization, trade would continue to balance, and there would be no unmatched expansion in aggregate demand resulting from the devaluation. Thus, if no monetary expansion was allowed, the price level was more likely to fall than to rise because of more efficient reallocation of resources.

The debate at the time related to the structure of further developments. Some advocated embarking on a second phase of import substitution and developing heavy industry, based on the belief that only with a well-developed industrial base could Taiwan find economic and military independence. A comparison of Taiwan with other small countries with a heavy industrial sector and a sophisticated defense industry, such as Belgium and Switzerland, was made to show good prospects for Taiwan in this regard. Most policymakers, however, believed that the development of heavy industry was beyond Taiwan's capabilities, given the shortages in capital and manufacturing ability, including skilled workers.

At this stage, the debates and circumstances caused the government to reevaluate existing policies. Government officials came to recognize that there had to be a market for industries suffering from inadequate domestic demand while at the same time there was need to solve foreign exchange difficulties. Two additional concerns helped to solidify export-promotion thinking. First, some devaluations and tax rebates on exports were started in 1955 and brought a recovery in exports from a low point in 1954. However, the devaluations were not yet linked with import liberalizing measures, and the growth of industrial exports during the 1950s was still minimal. Second, inflation then was a political and economic taboo that prohibited the use of expansionary monetary policy to boost domestic demand.

At this stage, U.S. assistance (U.S. AID) came to play a decisive role in the policy switch (Jacoby, 1973).[3] In 1959, the AID Mission set out "an accelerated economic development program" for Taiwan, which projected the attainment of self-generated growth within five years. Director Wesley C. Haraldson proposed an eight-point program of action by the government, including noninflationary fiscal and monetary policy, tax reform, unification of foreign exchange rates, liberalized exchange controls, establishment of a utilities commission and of investment banking machinery, and the privatization of government enterprises. In his speech, Haraldson also mentioned more aid being available provided military expenditure was reduced, and other conditions were met (Jacoby, 1973).

The speech received wide coverage and sparked considerable debate. The business community generally supported his proposal as being appropriate measures to correct Taiwan's economic problem but disagreed on receiving more U.S. aid. Economic agencies agreed that Taiwan's industries should become more independent of aid. They believed that, unless black market interest rates fell, and the industrial profit ratio went above 6%, industry would not be able to attract investment. The Foreign Exchange and Trade Commission, constantly under pressure from strong demand for more foreign exchange, commented that in order to promote production, exports had to be promoted, and only through stimulating exports would production increase.

High-ranking officials understood the implication of Haraldson's message. A major "weapon" of AID to influence the Taiwan government was a promise to increase or a threat to reduce the level of aid. Officials were convinced that the aid not only was limited but also would be terminated sooner or later. Subsequent discussions between the Mission and the government and the intention to attract more capital led to the elaboration of the eight-point proposal into Taiwan's own 19-Point Program in 1959–1960. The additional points included actions to improve the environment for both private and foreign investment, the encouragement of savings and private investment, full utilization of government production facilities, elimination of subsidies, increasing public utility rates, liberalization of trade regulation, and keeping military expenses at the 1960 level.

Following the announcement of the 19-Point Program, a series of market-friendly steps was taken. Much progress was made toward reducing red tape in general and industrial land acquisition in particular through the Statute for Encouragement of Investment, promulgated in 1960. Others included adjusting prices toward a market-determined level, simplifying the foreign exchange system from multiple to dual and then to unitary, offering tax and other incentives to investors, establishing the Stock Exchange, liberalizing foreign exchange controls, and so on. After the exchange rate was devaluated to a more realistic level, and trade liberalization was implemented, exports really took off. In the 1960s, annual average growth of exports was 21.7%, and in the 1970s, 32.6%.

In sum, the industrial stagnation in the late 1950s demonstrates the limits of inward-looking development strategies, which usually are accompanied by a shortage of foreign exchange and inefficiency. Taiwan's reform in the late 1950s and early 1960s represented a far-reaching liberalization. Although the direction seemed right, there was caution within the government. The decision-making process for the switch was not smooth and was not based on clear-cut calculations of the policy alternatives. Foreign influence and pressure did provide a stimulus.

INDUSTRIAL POLICY IN RETROSPECT

Taiwan's successful industrial development over the past four decades has been due to many factors, beginning with a strong and growing agricultural sector. The pattern of growth in Taiwan lends substantial support to the view that accelerated growth in the agricultural sector can promote development in the nonagricultural sector and therefore should be of considerable interest to other countries seeking to promote development. Agriculture is the largest sector in the underdeveloped economies and can provide savings as well as labor for nonagricultural development. Part of the agricultural surplus can be exported to finance the import of much needed foreign capital goods. Such exports can help alleviate the foreign exchange constraint. In addition, an expanding agricultural sector, accompanied by rising farm family income, can represent a major market for consumer goods produced by domestic manufacturers. The agricultural sector would share in the heavy protection costs related to the import-substitution strategy widely pursued in the developing world. By providing an adequate food supply, agricultural growth can help stabilize general prices and therefore mobilize and reallocate domestic resources more effectively.

However, the contribution of agriculture cannot be achieved without the strong support of public policy, particularly in the area of physical investment, technological upgrading, and institutional arrangements for distribution and credit. Moreover, Taiwan's structural transformation stresses the important role of spillover effects from intersectoral demand linkages and human capital development in economic growth. In addition, sound macroeconomic policies that do not overly distort relative factor prices help promote small industries (Mao and Schive, 1995).

SECONDARY IMPORT SUBSTITUTION

Import substitution is an important and frequently applied development strategy among developing countries. Import substitution loosely refers to the argument of domestic production to replace imports. To define it more strictly, import substitution occurs in an industry only when the import share of that industry decreases; this, in turn, contributes to the industry's growth. As to the scope and the sequence of import substitutive industries, two stages of development of such industries can be defined, namely, the ordinary import substitution (OIS) and secondary import substitution (SIS) industries. The former refers to consumer durables as well as nondurables, while the latter refers to capital goods and intermediates, such as parts, materials, and semifinished products. The OIS industries are labor-intensive, if the car industry is excluded, while the SIS industries are capital- and technology-intensive in general. SIS are also the upstream industries of OIS. Therefore, the development of OIS is usually ahead of that of SIS. Moreover, the linkage argument asserts that the backward linkages are more important than the forward ones. If so, there is theoretical support about the sequence of the development of these two types of industries. However, SIS industries may often have been pursued prematurely thinking that these industries are more productive, promote foreign exchange savings, or are necessary for security domestic supply.

During the period 1966–1971, three industries—rubber and products, artificial fibers, and miscellaneous manufactures—showed a significant drop (defined as greater than 10%) of their imported intermediate inputs. During 1971–1976, the artificial fibers industry continued to replace imports for intermediate use; however, the rubber and products and miscellaneous manufacturing industries showed a negative trend; that is, greater imports were made by these industries for further processing. The three remaining industries—artificial fabrics, miscellaneous chemical manufactures, and iron and steel—started processed import substitution for intermediate use. With respect to capital goods industries, the machinery industry did well in replacing imports for final use during 1966–1977 and 1976–1981. The electrical equipment and apparatus and the transportation equipment industries, which cover both consumer durables and capital goods, also did well during 1966–1976, but not during 1976–1981. Thus, the export promotion stage preceded the secondary import-substitutions stage by about one and one-half decades in Taiwan.

In the case of Taiwan, conditions facilitating the development of the second import-substitution industries can be due to change of factor endowment and scale economies of capital-intensive industries. First, export-led industrialization may quickly dry up surplus labor in a small economy, particularly if the economy has turned its comparative advantage to trade, and capital can be accumulated from a high savings rate as well as from a trade surplus. Thus, the factor endowment can be changed. In addition, capital-intensive industries are usually large-scale and involve more complicated technologies. The scale problem can be alleviated by the growth of downstream industries, and the technology unfamiliarity problem may be solved from experience, learned and accumulated. A question is raised whether Taiwan needed second import-substitution policies.

Two policies aim at developing second import-substitution industries: local content requirements and target-industry promotion policies. The first one was adopted in Taiwan in 1962, when Japanese companies came to the highly protected domestic markets of Taiwan and concentrated on final assembly. A minimum 40% local content rate was set up for nine products for foreign firms first, then to all producers. This policy helped certain domestic parts and component industries, but the overall effect is in serious doubt for two reasons: (1) official figures for local content may deviate from reality because of the difficulty of defining and measuring "locally made" parts, and (2) the requirements were not applied to exports. That is, exports could use imported materials or parts whenever needed. The second factor also implies that if the local supply of parts and material was available and actually used for exports, the price of these local supplies must have been competitive. Under these circumstances, the rise of local intermediate goods industries has nothing to do with protective policy and only little to do with local content requirements.

INDUSTRIAL POLICY

A target industry policy can be pursued in three ways: public enterprises, preferential loans, and tax incentives. The most effective of these is public enterprises. In Taiwan, the Chinese Petroleum Company built its first naphtha cracker in 1968 and has added four more since then. In 1977, the Chinese Steel Corporation went into operation. Both companies are state-owned and reduce imports by downstream industries. However, other public enterprises, one in copper refining and the other in aluminum refining, were dissolved because of bad management, high energy prices, and strong competition from abroad. The Taiwan Semiconductor Manufacturing Company, the first major producer of very-large-scale-integrated circuits (VLSI) in Taiwan, jointly owned by government, Philips, and private investors, received no favorable treatment from the government except capital and some experienced, skilled manpower. However, the success of a target industry policy depends on three conditions: (1) no protection incentive is offered; (2) there is no guarantee that wrongdoing by a public enterprise will be pardoned; and (3) subsidies through low-cost loans and sharing R&D and labor training costs are the main supports to those second import-substitution industries. Moreover, the government did not move to promote second import-substitution industries immediately after the first phase of import substitution, and that was critical in explaining Taiwan's success. However, the success of the second half of the 1970s led a trade surplus in Taiwan's economy in the 1980s (Schive, 1994, 1997b). Preferential credit policies are discussed later.

THE ROLE OF SMALL AND MEDIUM ENTERPRISES (SMES)

In Taiwan SMEs (firms hiring fewer than 100 people) dominate the manufacturing sector in number, especially in the export market. The establishment of the Small and Medium Business Bureau under the Ministry of Economic Affairs in 1967 encouraged people to think that policies encouraging SMEs had worked in

Taiwan. SMEs account for more than 96% of total manufacturing firms. SMEs contributed about 70% of Taiwan's total exports in the late 1970s, and this figure fell to 52.56% of Taiwan's total exports in 1994. SMEs exported nearly 70% of their total output during the same period.

SMEs were frequently found to concentrate on labor-intensive operations because of low-wage incentives and the cost-down pressure from competition. In Taiwan, SMEs tended to be export-oriented and to rely on original-equipment-manufacturing (OEM) because marketing both in foreign and domestic markets involves a large amount of working capital.

The well-proven price competitiveness of Taiwan's products in the international markets indicates that the quality of the products must have been acceptable given the price charged abroad. Moreover, some concerns about SMEs being shortsighted and not taking a long-term approach to investment in R&D, providing training programs, and so on are wishful thinking. It has also been argued that there are too many domestic exporters so that competition became cutthroat. However, the same competition drove out inefficient local competitors and foreign ones as well. Most of the time, local producers survived, but foreign ones faded away. That was how Taiwan achieved so many laurels as a leading exporter in the international market.

With regard to policy links, the first SME policy, "The Rule for Promotion of Small and Medium Enterprises," was promulgated in 1967. The criterion for selecting SMEs was subsequently revised several times. One major change in the law was the assurance of equal treatment for SMEs whenever an incentive is granted to a large business. The law was aimed at providing a wide range of assistance to SMEs, including market promotion, upgrading technology, labor training, management rationalization, cooperation, and forming strategic alliances. In spite of these ambitious policy goals, the impact was either small, as judged by the number of recipients, or generally unclear (see Ministry of Economic Affairs, 1991). The only exception might be the credit insurance fraud fund for SMEs. By the end of 1991, a total of 79,700 applicants had been approved, with a total amount of NT$144 billion distributed. The fund has been operating quite successfully, judged by the low percentage of bad loans reported.

It may not be easy to answer the question whether SMEs in Taiwan did benefit from government policies. However, most of the industrial policies in favor of large companies have not worked seriously against SMEs. The export-promotion scheme adopted in the 1960s, one of the major industrial development policies, did not discriminate between firms of different sizes. The most effective policies to influence resource allocation are tax incentives, credit control, and the setting up of public enterprises in certain industries. The Taiwan government has applied all three of these policies with a high degree of self-restraint. For instance, stable prices ever since 1960 have reflected a conservative monetary policy being consistently pursued. The operation and expansion of public enterprises were limited to basic industries or to those with significant economies of scale, such as power, refining, and petrochemicals. Thus, a favorable macroeconomic environment and self-restrained industrial policies were keys to fostering Taiwan's SMEs (Schive, 1995, 1997a).

FINANCIAL POLICY

Financial Market in Transition and Financial Liberalization

Due to deeply rooted fear of runaway inflation, the government had been very conservative in fiscal and monetary policies. Budget balance was always emphasized until the late 1980s. Until the 1980s, the financial market was still heavily regulated in Taiwan, and the calls for financial liberalization had been years old. However, for fear that the economy would be stagnant without new input from the financial sector and concern for the proper use of accumulated large foreign exchange reserves, the liberalization and the sequence of liberalization of that sector were much debated. Moreover, the government was more hesitant in financial liberalization than that of other markets. At that time the banking market was dominated by a small number of public banks. When interest rate liberalization was suggested, there was great opposition from the alliance of banks because in a period of tremendous excess liquidity, interest rate liberalization meant more competition and a narrower interest rate spread. The introduction of the reform was expected to face strong resistance. Finally, in the late 1970s and early 1980s, there were several major defaults and bankruptcies due to outright frauds, bad management, or economic recession. That gave another incentive for the monetary authorities to embark on the road toward financial liberalization.

The macroeconomic situation in the 1980s in Taiwan is a relevant issue. The excess of domestic savings over domestic investment in the 1980s, accompanied by a huge trade surplus and rapid expansion of the money supply, led to a serious excess liquidity problem. The limited variety of financial assets and investment channels could no longer satisfy asset demand. The excess liquidity created dramatic rises in the prices of stocks and real estate. Financial investment companies collecting funds by paying monthly interest rates as high as 9% expanded very quickly. This not only threatened financial stability but also caused unequal income and wealth distribution and facilitated speculation. Although in the mid-1980s some foreign banks had set up branches in Taiwan, their operations were mostly restricted. They were not allowed to receive term deposits with a maturity over six months. They were excluded from the call-loan markets, and they could not get rediscounted loans from the Central Bank. Domestic banks were under no competitive pressure from their foreign counterparts, and, hence, without pressure to improve their efficiency. In addition, the huge trade surplus in the 1980s invited pressures from the foreign countries to open the domestic financial market, to lessen exchange rate intervention, and to deregulate exchange controls (Chiu, 1992; Shea, 1994; Schive, 1997a).

The authorities proposed several measures to deregulate—interest rate decontrol, market entry deregulation, and privatization of major banks—but with the major effort focused on interest rate decontrol. In 1976, a formal money market was established, and its unregulated rates were used as an indicator for the adjustment of regulated bank rates. In November 1980, the Central Bank promulgated the "Essentials of Interest Rate Adjustment," which allowed banks to set their own interest rates on negotiable certificates of deposit (CDs) and debentures, as well as on bill discounts, and enlarged the spread between the maximum and minimum regulated lending rates. Since March 1985, under the prime rate system, the range of lending rates was further expanded. Banks were also allowed to set their own rates on foreign currency deposits in September 1985, and the difference of interbank call rates was gradually allowed to enlarge. The regulations prohibiting the maximum deposit rate from exceeding the minimum loan rate were also abolished in September 1985. Moreover, the Banking Law was revised, effective on July 20, 1989, to abolish the control of maximum deposit rates and the maximum and minimum loan rates. Thus, the rates on loans, deposits, and other financial instruments principally are determined in the market.

Several measures were adopted to decrease entry barriers to markets of financial institutions. In 1984, regulations governing branching by existing banks were relaxed. The 1989 revised Banking Law liberalized the setup of new private banks and granted the Ministry of Finance power to authorize new banking products. The Ministry of Finance intends to open the market to new banks gradually by limiting the number of licenses in each round.

The Securities and Exchange Law was amended in January 1988 to lift restrictions on setup of new securities companies. It also permits qualified integrated securities firms to offer margin financing directly to customers. Stock market disclosure requirements have been strengthened, and tighter insider trading regulations were introduced, although these regulations are still far from satisfactory and have not been implemented effectively.

In addition, state-owned banks are scheduled to be privatized in order to enhance efficiency and survival to compete with private banks. However, this privatization plan was strongly opposed by the Taiwan Provincial Assembly. In December 1996, the National Development Conference called for the privatization program of all public enterprises, including government-owned financial institutions, within a five-year span from 1997 to 2002.

Financial reform in Taiwan came to stage only in the late 1980s, when the control of the interest rate and foreign exchange rate was removed, as were the entrance barriers for nationals first, then for foreigners as well. Deregulation in the capital market has been effective only in the 1990s and is an ongoing process. A totally free capital market will be established by the end of the year 2000. Although the sequence of reform seems correct, the privatization of major state-owned banks is seriously behind schedule and does not match the performance of financial liberalization in other areas.

PREFERENTIAL CREDIT POLICY

In Taiwan, preferential credit policy has long been adopted to help promote new industries. In the 1980s, the scope of the industry and the terms of subsidy were redefined in the Strategic Industry Promotion Program. The Committee for Evaluating and Promoting Strategic Industries was set up under the Council for Economic Planning and Development in 1982. There were in total 145 manufactured products to be selected and promoted, according to six criteria—high industrial linkage effect, high potential market share, high-technology intensity, high value-added, a low energy coefficient, and low level of pollution emissions. Most of the items selected were in the machinery and information electronics industries. Biochemical and material industries were also promoted after 1986. In addition, 10 newly emerging industries and eight key technologies were chosen in the "Six-Year-National-Development Plan." The "strategic" industries receive two measures of favorable treatment: preferential cheap credit and technology and management advisory assistance. To the former a preferential low interest rate, which was 0.5% to 1.75% lower than the middle- to long-term loan rate, was available.

However, an investigation assessing the effect of this preferential loan policy (Yang, 1993) showed that preferential loan policy for strategic industries had not significantly improved the investment, financial situation, and operational performance of firms.

FISCAL POLICY AND CAPITAL FORMATION

The ratio of domestic gross investment to gross national product (GNP) had been very high until 1980 (i.e., 33.8%) and fell steadily thereafter to 23.8% in 1994. Public investment accounted for almost one-half of domestic gross capital formation. Investment in social infrastructure appears to have taken the place of investment by public enterprises.

The Statute for the Upgrading Industries was promulgated in 1990 for replacing the Investment Law, which was more industry-specific. The new law offers tax benefits to all industries for certain types of investment, like R&D, manpower training, pollution-protection measures, and so on. Under the Statute for Upgrading Industries, the following incentives are provided: (1) industries using selective technologies are eligible for the accelerated depreciation and tax credits of 5% to 20% relating to R&D, manpower training, pollution control, new industrial equipment, energy saving, and international marketing; (2) a company is exempted from stamp tax and deed tax, in the case of merger or acquisition; (3) tax credits are available for acquisition of land for industrial use; (4) tax exemption is permitted from comprehensive (personal) income tax for royalties derived from patents or computer software; (5) companies that invest abroad may set aside a tax-free reserve of up to 20% of their total outward investment to cover investment losses; and (6) tax benefits are provided for the encouragement of purchasing machinery and equipment for energy saving. In addition to business income tax provisions, individual income tax, custom duties, commodity taxes, business (value-added) taxes, and property-related taxes, and so on, are also used to stimulate private investment.

A complicated question is whether and to what extent private investment was influenced by these tax incentives. An empirical study showed that tax holidays and accelerated depreciation had only a marginal effect on business investment in Taiwan (Hsu and Chen, 1989).

FISCAL POLICY

The government implemented a conservative fiscal policy until about 1989. The ratio of total tax revenue to GNP decreased from 20.1% in 1990 to 16.5% in 1996. Since 1990, the rate of increase of government net revenues declined gradually. Since 1989, there has been a decrease because of, in part, significantly expanding expenditures on social welfare and public infrastructure in recent years.

On the tax side, the government has implemented tax reform and provided tax benefits to attract foreign direct investment. Generally speaking, Taiwan provides more tax benefits, including tax exemption or saving of income tax, business tax and stamp tax, and so on, to offshore banking units (OBUs) than do Singapore and Malaysia. However, the tax authorities do not provide tax benefits to the operational centers of multinational enterprises in Taiwan.

HUMAN CAPITAL AND SCIENCE AND TECHNOLOGY

In Taiwan, most educational services are supplied directly or indirectly by the public sector, because it is generally thought that education will yield benefits to the society. Public educational expenses are financed by tax revenue. Education will increase knowledge and skills, enhance productivity, and thus will contribute to economic growth. In Taiwan, the nine-year primary and secondary education is provided completely free of charge, and publicly funded senior high schools, colleges, and universities are widespread. Even private schools and colleges receive large subsidies or grants from the government. Public expenditures on education, sciences, and cultural services have increased from 13.7% of total government expenditures in the fiscal years 1957–1960 to 18.6% in 1994–1996.

Human Capital

Changing the labor force was a great challenge to economic development in the last four decades in Taiwan. In the 1950s, a serious problem of unemployment arose due to the limited supply of arable land and water. However, the pool of surplus labor permitted the government to pursue policies that promoted labor-intensive technology until 1975, that is, in the primary import-substitution (1953–1961) and export expansion period (round from 1961–1970s), in the transition process.

However, the pool of surplus labor became gradually exhausted by 1968. This led to an underutilization and educational mismatch in the 1970s (Liu, 1992). Moreover, rapid export growth and low rate of increase of population and labor force combined to lead to rising wages and demand for well-educated workers. Thus, a higher-quality labor force was needed by upgrading technologies. This replacement process was slow because of decline of fertility and the need of young people to obtain education and training, delaying their entry into the workforce.

Prior to 1967, about 60% of pupils were enrolled in the senior high academic schools, and only 40% in senior vocational and technical schools. However, the government modified this ratio to meet the need for workers. By 1989, the senior high academic schools represented 30%, while senior vocational and technical schools were 70%. During this period, university students shifted from humanities and agriculture toward engineering, medical sciences, and social sciences. The growth of educational opportunities has improved the level of educational attainment of the labor force. Education of 18–21 years, that is, for those attending colleges or universities, increased significantly from 11.47% in 1981 to 27.79% in 1995. The significant improvement in the quality of human resources acquired through increased investment in education has built human capital.

Moreover, prior to 1966, most training programs were provided by public and large private enterprises, because government did not deal with such programs in this period. During 1966–1976, several public training centers were set up to facilitate vocational training. In 1972, the Vocational Training Fund Statute was implemented and trainees in the private sector surged. Employers with 40 or more employees had to appropriate an amount to 1.5% of their total wage bill to an on-the-job training fund for training their employees. Due to the oil shock in 1973–1974, this statute was suspended in 1974. However, the Employment and Vocational Training Administration of the Council of Labor Affairs was established to coordinate employment services, vocational training, and trade-skill examinations. During July–December 1995, the appropriation for worker education amounted to NT$469 million, and 67% was financed by enterprises (industrial unions), 8.7% came from general federators of labor unions and craft unions, and 24.3% from public labor administrative agencies.

Science and Technology

Science and technological development contributes to the sustained economic growth. Because most of the businesses are small and medium enterprises lacking R&D capability, the role of government in promoting technology progress for industry is crucial to economic growth. In Taiwan, the government has played a dominant role in promoting science and technology development. In 1959, the government took the initiative to undertake research and development. At earlier stages, the policies were oriented toward basic science research and manpower training, because Taiwan's economy met with problems such as brain drain, and shortage of research and development funds and facilities. In 1967, the Council for

National Long-Term Development Science was reorganized as the National Science Council, which has been a leading governmental institution to design and promote basic research, manpower training, and technology research. In addition, Academia Sinica, directly under the State President's Office, is the leading academic research institution in several fields. In the Cabinet, the Committee of Advisors on Science and Technology, the Committee of Applied Research and Development, the Council for Atomic Energy, the Council for Agricultural Development, the Ministry of Economic Affairs, the Ministry of Transportation and Communications, the Ministry of Education, the Agency of Public Health, the Ministry of Defense, the Taiwan Provincial Government, and others, carry on research and/or contract out research and development projects in various fields.

In 1982, the Second National Conference on Science and Technology Development recommended eight "strategic" areas for technology development: energy, materials, automation, information, electro-optics, biotechnology, food, and hepatitis control. The third conference in 1984 recommended priorities in the long-term plan concerned not only with economic growth but also with improvement in the quality of life such as environmental protection. The government intends to provide a kind of public good of technology and to assist predominantly small and medium enterprises by establishing a public research infrastructure like the Industrial Technology Research Institute (ITRI) and the Information Industry Institute (III). These institutions transfer and diffuse newly developed technologies to private firms, so-called blue-collar R&D (Ranis, 1996).

In 1994, total R&D outlays amounted to 4,371 million U.S.$ and, 1.8% of the GNP, which is still less than the planned target—2% of the GNP. This ratio has been less than that of Japan (2.68% in 1993), the United States (2.61% in 1994), Germany (2.48% in 1993), France (2.48% in 1993), United Kingdom (2.19% in 1993), and South Korea (2.33% in 1993). By 2000, total R&D expenditures will be targeted at 2.5% of the GNP, and the R&D funded by the government will be 45%. R&D spending for basic research will be 15%, while that of technology development will be more than 50%.

Since 1980, Taiwan has allocated increasingly more resources to science and technology. The government's efforts in promoting science and technology development can be revealed in the rapid increase in the exports of the electronic and information products, which has exceeded that of labor-intensive products.

Labor Markets

In Taiwan, the government established labor market policies to improve labor market opportunities and the smooth functioning of the labor market. These policies also have been used to facilitate full employment. The unemployment rate has been lower than 3% since the late 1960s, with an exception during August–October 1996. The bulk of inequality of household incomes was accounted for by labor income inequality until the mid-1980s in Taiwan (Kuo, 1997, 1983; Fields, 1992). The Gini coefficients showed that the income distribution in Taiwan deteriorated since then, from 0.277 in 1980 to 0.317 in 1995.

In 1984, the Basic Labor Standards Law was promulgated. Its purpose was to provide minimum standards of working conditions, protect workers' rights and interests, strengthen labor–management relationships, and promote social and economic development. These goals are laudable; however, there are still many serious problems to be solved. The most serious problem was whether the law would be effectively enforced. Labor was covered by the Basic Labor Standards Law in the following industries: agriculture; mining and quarrying; manufacturing; electricity, gas, and water; construction; transportation; storage; communication; mass media; and other businesses. In May 1997, only a few industries, that is, banking, motion picture product and distribution, repair of motor vehicles, cleaning and dyeing, environmental sanitary and pollution control services, and so on, were newly covered by the law. In May 1997, 39.9% of all employed laborers were covered by the Basic Labor Standards Law.

Empirical studies showed that the Basic Labor Standards Law had no effect on wages or working hours in the period 1980–1988 in Taiwan, and the law made little difference to labor market conditions (Fields, 1992, 418–419). Until the late 1980s, labor unions in Taiwan were weak because of the suppression of the labor movement by the government, the impassiveness of workers toward unionization, the prevalence of small and medium enterprises, the high rate of labor turnover, and the competitiveness of the labor market, and so on (San, 1989, cited from Fields, 1992, 418). However, the labor movement has become more militant recently. Since 1990s, the labor unions in public utilities or public enterprises and private businesses and "nonregistered" labor unions have played active roles in the bargaining for wages and improvement of worker rights. Overall, the 1984 Basic Labor Standards Law has met with severe critics, not only from managers/owners but also from workers.

In summary, the appropriate role of the government in economic development attracted more attention and has been under dispute over many years. In Taiwan, the government has coordinated and encouraged private and public investment with intersectoral linkages, which helped remove coordination failures. Taiwan had special initial conditions—relatively skilled and educated workforce and relatively equal distribution of resources—that helped the takeoff process. Export-led development policies, including exchange rate policies, were also important to facilitate imports of capital goods (Rodrik, 1994, 1996, 1997).

The government's intervention in Taiwan's economic development is interesting to other developing countries. Both markets and the state play important roles in economic development. The macroeconomic aspects of development policies should also be taken into account as determinants of economic development in addition to those listed by Wade (1990). Along with the rapid growth over past years, Taiwan has gone toward a relatively decentralized society, where the complementarity between markets and the state should become clearer as economic development looks to the future.

CONCLUDING REMARKS

The contribution of policymakers to Taiwan's economic success is not from their farsightedness or smart intervention. Rather, it comes from the government's cautious steps in remedying market distortions and its restraint in imposing changes that may lead to more distortions. In the beginning, when the market was heavily restricted, piecemeal, but continuous, reform was taken to avoid sharp interruption in the market. Good examples can be found in the reform of industrial policy and financial liberalization. Yet market reinforcement efforts grew with time in scope and in pace. That is, no government is smart enough to replace the market, but the government can always nurture the market.

NOTES

1. Numerous studies have been devoted to exploring the success story, ranging from the agriculture sector (Lee, 1971), trade (Liang and Liang-Hou, 1988), money and financial market (Chiu, 1992), and foreign investment (Schive, 1990), to more specific ones such as labor market (Liu, 1992), small and medium-sized enterprises (Hu and Schive, 1997a, 1997b), and foreign exchange policy (Yotopoulos, 1996, 1997). All these empirical studies touched upon policy issues in relevant areas. Several recent books focus on policy issues solely: Li (1995); Kuo (1997); Wade (1990).

2. IMF (1997). Other countries or economies reclassified as industrial: Singapore, South Korea, Hong Kong, and Israel ("The Heritage Foundation/Wall Street Journal Index of Economic Freedom, 1997," Heritage Foundation, Washington, DC).

3. The U.S. AID Mission had a strong, persistent, and generally beneficent influence on the formation of Taiwan's economic policies. Though some of the mission's advice was not immediately agreed to, most of it was regarded as beneficial in the long run. International bodies such as the International Monetary Fund (IMF) also had important influence on Taiwan with regard to a specific sector by means of member obligation.

REFERENCES

Chiu, Paul C. H. (1992). "Money and Financial Markets: The Domestic Perspective." In Gustav Ranis, ed., *Taiwan: From Developing to Mature Economy*. Boulder, CO: Westview Press, 121–193.

Fields, Gary S. (1992). "Living Standards, Labor Markets and Human Resources in Taiwan." In Gustav Ranis, ed., *Taiwan: From Developing to Mature Economy*. Boulder, CO: Westview Press, 295–433.

Hsu, Song-ken, and Y. L. Chen. (1989). "The Status of Encouraging Investment and Fixed Capital Formulation." *Taiwan Economic Review* 17, 77–120.

Hu, Ming-Wen, and Chi Schive. (1997a). "The Changing Competitiveness of Taiwan's Manufacturing SMEs." Taipei, mimeo.

———. (1997b). "A Study on the Productivity and Efficiency of SMEs in Taiwan Manufacturers." *Taiwan Economic Review* 25, 1–26 (in Chinese).

IMF. (1997). *World Development Report*. Washington, DC: IMF.

Jacoby, Neil H. (1973). *U.S. Aid to Taiwan: A Study of Foreign Aid, Self-Help, and Development*. New York: Praeger.

Kuo, Shirley W. Y. (1997). *Economic Policies: The Taiwan Experience, 1945–1995.* Taipei: Hwa-Tai Publishing Company.

———. (1983). *Taiwan: Economy in Transition.* Boulder, CO: Westview Press.

Lee, T. H. (1971). *Intersectoral Capital Flows in Economic Development of Taiwan, 1895–1960.* Ithaca, NY: Cornell University Press.

Li, Kuo-Ting. (1995). *The Evolution of Policy behind Taiwan's Development Success.* 2d ed. Singapore: World Scientific.

Liang, K. S., and C. I. Liang-Hou. (1988). "Development Policy Formation and Future Policy Priorities in the Republic of China." *Economic Development and Cultural Change* 36(3), Supplement.

Lin, Ching-Yuan. (1979). *Industrialization in Taiwan, 1946–1972.* New York: Praeger.

Liu, Paul K. C. (1992). "Science, Technology and Human Capital Formation." In Gustav Ranis, ed., *Taiwan: From Developing to Mature Economy.* Boulder, CO: Westview Press, 357–393.

Mao, Yu-Kang, and Chi Schive (1995). "Agricultural and Industrial Development in Taiwan." In John W. Mellor, ed., *Agriculture on the Road to Industrialization.* Baltimore: Johns Hopkins University Press, 23–66.

Ministry of Economic Affairs. *White Paper on Taiwan's SMEs.* Taipei: Ministry of Economic Affairs.

Ranis, Gustav. (1996). "The Trade-Growth Nexus in Taiwan's Development." Prepared for the May 3–4, 1996, Cornell Conference on Government and Market: The Relevance of the Taiwanese Performance (1945–1995) to Development Theory and Policy.

Rodrik, Dani. (1997). "The 'Paradoxes' of the Successful State." *European Economic Review* 41, 411–442.

———. (1996). "Coordination Failures and Government Policy: A Model with Applications to East Asia and Eastern Europe." *Journal of International Economics* 40, 1–22.

———. (1994). "Getting Interventions Right: How South Korea and Taiwan Grew Rich." NBER Working Paper no. 4964.

Schive, Chi. (1997a). "How Was Taiwan's Economy Opened?—the Foreign Factors in Appraisal." Paper presented in the *Economics and Political Economy of Development at the Turn of the Century: Conference in Memory of John C. H. Fei*, Taipei, Academia Sinica, August 1–2, 1977.

———. (1997b). "Industrial Policies in Retrospect—with a Special Reference to Taiwan's Manufacturing Sector." Taipei, mimeo.

———. (1995). "Industrial Policies in a Maturing Economy." *Journal of Industrial Studies* 2, 5–26.

———. (1994). "Quality Upgrading of Taiwan's Experts: 1986–91." Paper presented at the fourth Biannual Meeting of East Asian Economic Association in Taipei, August.

———. (1990). *The Foreign Factor: The Multinational Corporation's Contribution to the Economic Modernization of the Republic of China.* Chicago: University of Chicago Press.

Shea, Jia-Dong. (1994). "Taiwan: Development and Structural Change of the Financial System." In Hugh T. Patrick and Yung Chul Park, eds., *The Financial Development of Japan, Korea and Taiwan.* New York: Oxford University Press, 222–287.

Wade, Robert. (1990). *Governing the Market Economic Theory and the Role of Government in East Asian Industrialization.* Princeton: Princeton University Press.

Yang, Ya-Hwei. (1993). "Government Policy and Strategic Industries: The Case of Taiwan." In Takatoshi Ito and Anne O. Krueger, eds., *Trade and Protectionism*. Chicago: University of Chicago Press, 387–408.

Yotopoulos, Pan A. (1997). "Incomplete Currency Markets and Growth: Some Evidence from Southeast Asia and the Lessons from Japan and Taiwan." Presented in the *Economics and Political Economy of Development at the Turn of the Century: Conference in Memory of John C. H. Fei*, Taipei Academia Sinica, August 1–2.

———. (1996). *Exchange Rate Parity for Trade and Development: Theory, Tests and Case Studies*. Cambridge: Cambridge University Press.

8

Public Policies in the Korean Economy

Kyu Uck Lee

INTRODUCTION

Despite the recent financial crisis set in motion at the end of 1997, Korea's record of rapid economic development over the past three decades remains very good. It is widely accepted that the Korean government has been largely responsible for the economic performance of the country because it has set the targets for economic growth, toward which it has implemented forceful policies and directed private economic activities.

During the Korean War, the Korean economy, which had already long suffered from Japanese colonialism, was reduced to almost nothing. The economic basis of the country was so devastated that the market practically did not exist. Under these initial conditions, strong government intervention succeeded in mobilizing the national spirit and energy and igniting economic dynamism. The Korean government took the initiative to rev up the engine of growth, which induced Korea's early economic takeoff.

As the size of the Korean economy grew, and its industrial structure was upgraded, Korea increasingly needed a new modus operandi, that is, a shift from government intervention to the market mechanism and from a closed economy to an open economy. However, long accustomed to direct government control, Korean business could not easily or readily execute such a shift. Though all economic agents appeared to agree on the need for fundamental change, the natural inertia governing their mind and the vested interests lining their pockets prevented them *in toto* from making the right decision at the right time. Moreover, the Korean government did not fully gear up its economy for global competition. In particular, it failed to educate the people about what is really meant by globalization and did not sufficiently implement institutional reforms required to create a full-fledged open economy. This lack of general awareness and preparedness on the part of government in instituting reforms may be the primary domestic cause of current economic difficulties.

In a way, the past success of the Korean economy planted the seed of its present debacle. The economic paradigm assigning the central role of economic management to the government has run its full course. It is high time for Korea to replace this paradigm with the principles of competitive market mechanisms. The future of the Korean economy hinges on whether it successfully accomplishes the task of structural adjustment. Fortunately, the new Korean government seems to be orienting its policies toward such an imperative.

In this chapter, we discuss how the Korean government has evolved its policies—with successes and failures—to cope with a changing economic environment. The focus is on the early development stage up to the 1990s. We briefly review the trajectory of the Korean economy since the 1960s and some major policies, namely, industrial policy, competition policy, deregulation, and *chaebol* (big business groups) policy. Finally, we offer some concluding remarks.

A BRIEF OVERVIEW OF THE RECENT HISTORY OF THE KOREAN ECONOMY

Before the first overall economic development plan was implemented in 1962, Korea was largely a traditional, closed agrarian economy, with about two-thirds of the working population engaged in agriculture. In this period, economic policy centered around rehabilitation of the war-torn economy through what may be loosely characterized as a policy of import-substitution of nondurable consumer goods behind a protective wall of high tariffs and stringent quotas. However, this import-substitution development strategy soon reached its natural limits, especially because of the small size of the domestic market and its large capital requirements.

After many years of economic stagnation and undaunted efforts to rebuild the country, a new government led by a former army general, President Park Chung Hee, came to power in 1961. Park and his administration were committed to economic development and enforced a series of Five-Year Economic Development Plans that set the targets for important macroeconomic indicators, such as the growth rate, exports, and the price level, and specified goals and incentives for selected strategic industries. In view of Korea's limited natural and technological resources and small domestic market, the government adopted an outward-looking development strategy. The essence of this strategy was the promotion of labor-intensive manufacturing exports in which Korea had a comparative advantage, while inducing foreign capital and technology into export industries. During the 1960s, the growth rate and exports overshot their targets. Major policy tools that brought about this result were selective financial support and tax breaks and entry regulations such as business licensing and permission. On the other hand, the expansion-oriented growth policy gave rise to high inflation, which was then countered by direct price regulation.

It is almost inevitable that all kinds of undesirable effects such as labor unrest, inequitable distribution of income, and environmental degradation arise in the course of economic development. In Korea, such problems became quite acute through the 1960s and 1970s because rapid economic growth was the primary national goal. However, these problems did not come to the surface under the heavy-handed authoritarian regime. For example, labor unrest was dormant until it erupted violently toward the end of the 1980s, when the authoritarian regime was ebbing. The point emphasized here is that economic development was not accompanied by political democratization until 1987. This fact has raised the question whether the latter is the prerequisite for the former.

The government-led high growth policy continued into the 1970s with only minor subtle changes and shifts in policy, made in response to a changing set of internal and external socioeconomic conditions. The policy for strategic industries became more pronounced, while government intervention became more visible in picking the entrants in key industries. This policy culminated in the Heavy and Chemical Industry Development Plan of 1973, which provided preferential incentives to industries such as shipbuilding, automobiles, steel products, nonferrous metals, and petrochemicals. To achieve economies of scale in a limited domestic market, the government often permitted monopolistic production in these industries.

By the latter half of the 1970s, the Korean economy began to show signs of strain, which was aggravated by the two oil shocks. The first oil shock of 1974 was rather easily overcome in terms of GDP growth; the growth rate showed only a modest decline. Corporate reorganization and industrial restructuring, started in 1972, helped to cope with the first oil shock. Nevertheless, the government enforced widespread price controls to cope with the ensuing inflationary spiral. The second oil shock of 1979, in contrast to the first one, left a deep scar in the Korean economy, exposing its weaknesses resulting from the malfunctioning of market mechanisms and the expansion-first growth strategy.

Recognizing that a major shift in policy orientation was in order, in mid-1979, the government announced a comprehensive stabilization program based on conservative fiscal and monetary policies. Unfortunately, these efforts were hampered by the impact of the second oil shock, the ongoing world recession, and a disastrous crop failure in 1980. Nevertheless, this stabilization program cannot be considered a total failure. Although it did not completely solve the mounting problems in 1980, it did establish a firm basis for the reform efforts of the new government inaugurated in September of that year.

The new government headed by another former army general, President Chun Doo Hwan, took several important steps in the mid-1980s toward deregulation and internationalization of the economy. First, to open domestic markets and to stimulate competition in the economy, it lowered import barriers to a considerable extent by reducing tariff rates and increasing the number of importable items. Next, financial incentives given to heavy and chemical industries were curtailed dramatically to enhance their competitiveness. Liberalization of the financial sector was initiated through privatization of the five commercial banks and the lowering of barriers set against foreign banks' entry into Korean financial markets.

Another important change in macroeconomic policies in the mid-1980s was to emphasize stabilization of the economy, in contrast to the previous policy in the 1960s and 1970s, which had stressed economic growth. As a result of tight monetary and fiscal policy, inflation subsided from a double-digit rate to less than 5% from 1983 onward. The structural adjustment and stabilization efforts in the 1980s are thought to have been successful. Since the mid-1980s, the Korean economy had demonstrated price stability and huge surpluses in the current account, while maintaining high-growth momentum. In view of the decades-long experience in the opposite direction, this record was indeed important and remarkable. Economic stability, thus created, laid the foundation for the Korean economy's decade-long high growth occurring from the latter half of the 1980s to 1995. This phenomenal growth was also aided by the "three low" phenomenon: low interest rates, low exchange rates, and low prices.

Economic stabilization policies in the early 1980s were quite a hardship to the Korean people. This policy approach could have been maintained by authoritarian-ism. However, such a policy could not persist under democratic regimes, as President Roh Tae Woo, a military academy classmate of his predecessor, was democratically elected in 1988 and was succeeded in 1993 by a civilian political leader, Kim Young Sam (commonly called YS) through democratic elections. In the course of democratization, every segment of Korean society manifested its discon-tent and demands without reservation. This social milieu made it difficult to maintain the stabilization policy, and, consequently, expansionary policy has been adopted since the latter half of the 1980s.

Whereas stabilization represented the changing tenet of macroeconomic policy, competition defined the basis of microeconomic policy in the 1980s. The most important in this context was "The Act for Monopoly Regulation and Fair Trade" (hereafter, the Fair Trade Act) enacted in 1981. This act replaced the Price Stabili-zation Act of 1975, removing its power of price regulation while strengthening its competition-promoting functions. The second pillar of competition policy was deregulation. Since the end of the 1980s, the Korean government has set out to dismantle economic regulations that hamper and even injure free and creative economic activities. However, despite these institutional reforms, actual policy administration has largely followed the same old authoritarian and interventionist pattern.

With initial strong popular support, the YS government energetically reactivated the move to vitalize market mechanisms and to deregulate, liberalize, and globalize the Korean economy. At the same time, it launched a reform policy to normalize the economic modus operandi that had been distorted in the past. Unfortunately, these efforts turned out to be substantially futile owing to the lack of leadership and the emergence of various bottlenecks.

First, government regulations that have lasted for three decades have formed a community of interests between the government and the parties regulated. Those who have benefited from regulations opposed changes and reforms that would wipe out their vested interests. Second, bureaucrats, businessmen, and consumers have long been tamed by government regulations, and hence they do not have a value system commensurate with the free market economy. Consequently, the evolution of economic institutions was not supported by the economic mind of the people. Third, the vacuum of the balancing and coordinating power left by the government's reducing its regulations had to be filled by market mechanisms. However, emaciated market mechanisms could not perform this function, which has led to inefficiencies and mismanagement in financial and business entities. Fourth, after the decades of rapid growth, the Korean economy was ripe for structural adjustment appropriate to the size of its economy and the stage of its development. Structural adjustment may entail bankruptcies and unemployment, which are difficult for the Korean people to swallow. The amendment and reamendment of the labor law early in 1997 were the most striking example. Finally, unlike previous authoritarian regimes, the YS government did not have recourse to coercion in dealing with social discontent. Instead, it had to rely upon suasion, coordination, or consistency. YS lacked the strong leadership required to overcome difficulties in the process of political and economic transformation.

All these factors had accumulated and finally exploded, wreaking havoc on the Korean economy toward the end of 1997. The 1997 financial meltdown was a sort of coup de grace to the legacy of rapid growth of the Korean economy. It was not the result of negligence by a few prominent persons but rather symbolized what has been left by past economic successes and failures. In March 1998, another civilian leader Kim Dae Jung (usually referred to as DJ), became president. Immediately after he became the president-elect and prior to his inauguration, he set out to mend the "suddenly" collapsed Korean economy tending to the demands of the IMF. The Korean government and the IMF have agreed on a macroeconomic policy mix featuring high interest rates and low growth rates along with other rather severe structural policies. The new President has tried to convince foreign investors of his firm stance on structural reform of the Korean economy. In his initial effort for economic rehabilitation, he successfully obtained a tripartite consensus among government, labor, and business on introducing flexibility in the labor market. The DJ government has also stressed, *inter alia*, sweeping financial reform, the fundamental reorganization of *chaebols*, which should ultimately lead to their de facto dissolution, the transparency of corporate governance, and the bold deregulation of inward foreign investment, including the permission for hostile mergers and acquisitions. These measures must be more carefully formulated before they are implemented. Should they take effect, Korea will emerge from the current economic crisis in better shape than if everything had gone on as usual. Paradoxically, the current economic crisis in Korea can serve as a cure for the economy's maladies if the appropriate policies are well executed.

THE EVOLUTION OF MAJOR ECONOMIC POLICIES

Industrial Policy

The strategy of industrialization shifted from import-substitution to export promotion during the first half of the 1960s. Why did this transition occur? First, a growth strategy based on import-substitution was found to be inappropriate due to the small domestic market and the large capital requirements of such ventures. Second, Korea's natural resource endowment was so poor that a development strategy based on domestic resource utilization was inconceivable. Third, Korean policymakers had to find a source of foreign exchange in order to meet balance-of-payments difficulties that were arising as the U.S. financial assistance programs were being phased out. Fourth, the availability of a well-motivated, low-wage labor force with a high educational level provided the country with a comparative advantage in high-quality, labor-intensive exports. Last, the political leadership was determined to attain a high rate of growth. In the transition to an export-oriented strategy, the devaluation of the Korean currency, the won, in 1964 provided an important turning point. In the 1950s, direct government subsidies had been given to promote exports of selected primary products. In the early 1960s, attempts were made to increase exports through exchange rate devaluations. But these export promotion measures, taken prior to the 1964 devaluation, were generally short-lived and were in many cases offset by other economic policies. Beginning with the devaluation in 1964, however, the government undertook a series of policy reforms in order to establish a system of incentives consistent with the export-oriented industrialization strategy. During the transitional period from 1961 to 1965, the export incentive system was greatly expanded. Preferential export credit became an important incentive for exports, since the interest rate reform of 1965 had widened substantially the interest rate differential between export credit and ordinary bank loans. Among the other export incentives provided during this period were (1) tariff exemptions on imports of raw materials for export production (drawback system); (2) indirect domestic tax exemptions on intermediate inputs used for export production and export sales; (3) direct tax deductions on income earned from exports and other foreign-exchange-earning activities; (4) wastage allowances for raw materials imported for export production; (5) a system of linking import businesses to export performance; (6) tariff and indirect domestic tax exemptions for domestic suppliers of intermediate goods used in export production; and (7) accelerated depreciation allowances for fixed assets of major export industries.

It should be noted that these measures were designed mainly to ensure that Korean exporters, who needed to sell their products at world market prices, could purchase intermediate goods for export production at world market prices. In other words, the major incentives served mainly to offset the disincentive effect on exports that the trade regime would otherwise have created. It should also be noted that these incentives applied to all exporters on a nondiscriminatory basis. In addition to these measures, the export targeting system was established in 1962 to further promote the export drive.

Some adjustments of the export incentive system were made after 1965 to accommodate changing economic conditions; these adjustments did not, however, change the system significantly. The government did gradually relax the quantitative restrictions on imports and reduced tariffs through several reforms after 1965. What was particularly important was that the government was able to maintain roughly the same real exchange rate through the 1966–1985 period; this was achieved by making periodic adjustments in the exchange rate and in major export incentive schemes. One study shows that, for most of the time before the mid-1980s, the Korean won had been overvalued in light of relative inflation between Korea and its major trading partners. This implies, if it is true, that the disadvantageous effect on exports of the persistently overvalued exchange rate was partly or completely offset by two kinds of government support for exporters: (1) an *ad hoc* export promotion system and (2) encouragement by the government.

Rapid economic growth required a tremendous amount of financial resources and consequently, among industrial policy tools, financial support was the most potent one. The small domestic capital market could not slake the thirst of voracious industrialists, leaving the financial market perennially with excess demand. The Korean government was the majority shareholder in most commercial banks, as well as special-purpose banks. Therefore, the authorities could influence the appointment of high-ranking bank officials in one way or another. Through this power, the government could allocate financial resources according to its policy goals. This practice naturally gave rise to political influence-peddling and unethical behavior among interested parties. Though the government privatized four commercial banks in 1984, this practice has not significantly dwindled. In the past, Korea maintained relatively low interest rates. Nominal rates were higher than those in advanced countries, but real rates remained at a relatively low level. Moreover, considering the chronic excess demand for money, the "official" interest rates were considerably lower than "curb market" rates. Under these circumstances, access to financial institutions itself was a special favor granted only to selected "customers." Enterprises that successfully obtained huge bank loans could easily accumulate profits without worrying about competition in monopolistic, protected domestic markets. On top of this, creeping inflation lessened the borrowers' burden of debt service.

A typical example of the public financial incentive system could be found in the Heavy and Chemical Industry Development Plan launched in 1973. Under this plan, the government established the National Investment Fund to provide capital at lower interest rates to meet the enormous investment requirements of these industries. This fund was created by contributions from banks, insurance companies, national savings associations, public employee pension funds, and postal savings. The magnitude of the fund increased almost 10 times over the 1974–1981 period. Nevertheless, the financial requirements of these industries could not be fully met by the fund alone. The shortage was filled by commercial bank loans, but with very favorable maturities and interest rates. In this process, banks were reduced to a window dishing out funds for heavy and chemical industries as dictated by the government, and the so-called government-directed banking firmly took root in the Korean economy. As a result of this preferential banking practice, the share of heavy and chemical industries in total investment increased from 57% in the early 1970s to 64% toward the end of the same decade. These industries further benefited from tax breaks provided by the Act for Regulating Tax Exemptions and Reductions of 1975.

In addition to financial support, the other mainstay of industrial policy was direct intervention of the government through economic regulations. Originally, regulations, especially in the form of selective entry, were introduced on the grounds that excessive competition could thereby be prevented, and hence scarce domestic resources could be efficiently allocated. For example, when an investment project drawn up by the government was to be carried out, usually only one enterprise was selected to undertake it. In the early phase of heavy and chemical industrialization, private enterprises were somewhat reluctant to participate in the drive. As preferential incentives were provided, and monopolistic positions were practically guaranteed, however, they vied with one another for entry into new industrial areas. The struggle among enterprises for entry was not exactly "competition" in the true sense of the word but rather "scrambling" for guaranteed monopoly profits.

To facilitate industrial support and regulations, the government introduced a number of laws specifically designed for seven individual industries covering machinery, shipbuilding, electronics, iron and steel, nonferrous metals, petrochemicals, and synthetic fibers. In addition, a large number of trade associations were established as the receiving end and intermediary of government regulations. A sizable portion of these associations came into being through the initiative of the government that delegated some of its regulatory functions to them. Trade associations served the regulatory purpose of the government, but they also fomented collusive practices among enterprises engaging in the same business areas. This undesirable effect has lingered for a long time after the Fair Trade Act prohibited such practices.

In response to the serious recession brought about by the second oil shock of 1979, the government enforced wide-ranging rationalization measures in the heavy and chemical industries. During the 1970–1980 period, investment projects in these industries were rearranged and readjusted three times in an attempt to solve the excess capacity problem and to realize economies of scale through specialization. Consequently, large-scale corporate amalgamations and the realignment of business areas were carried out in a number of industries such as autos, electrical machinery, and shipbuilding. Government-led structural adjustment continued into the 1980s in a slightly changed manner. The Industrial Development Act was introduced in 1986 as a legal device for industrial support, replacing previous individual laws for seven specific industries. Under this Act, any industry could be designated as a "sunrise" or a "sunset" industry to justify various kinds of financial support and industrial rationalization. Until the Industrial Development Act was amended in 1994 to induce industrial restructuring rather than industrial rationalization in tune with the spirit of the WTO, quite a number of firms, mostly in nonferrous metals, such as ferroalloy, electrolytic copper, and aluminum and in footwear, textiles, and dyeing, enjoyed support through this act. However, the Industrial Development Act gave rise to many problems, such as the survival of marginal firms and the inefficient allocation of financial resources.

Industrial policy market intervention by the government contributed significantly to the upgrading of the Korean industrial structure. On the other hand, it caused undesirable effects in the long run. First, as private enterprises were regulated by government guidelines, not by market principles, their independent viability and creativity were substantially injured. Second, when entry into industries was allowed on the basis of market analysis in the planning stage, incorrect demand forecasting resulted either in supply shortages or in excess capacity. Third, enterprises that complied with the government's directives or obtained business licenses could achieve rapid growth compared to other companies that operate independently. Therefore, the growth of an enterprise was determined by government discretion rather than by its own rational judgment. More fundamentally, the government–business relationship or the division of labor between government and market that was created through industrial policy became a structural characteristic of the Korean economy. In other words, the omnipotent government, on one side, and docile private enterprises, on the other, became the basic feature of the economic order in Korea. Such a relationship, extremely abnormal from the point of view of the free market economy, came to be accepted as the "norm." This state persists today, even though the government itself has long proclaimed its return to market principles.

Competition Policy

Although Korean market structure has generally been noncompetitive, related policy issues came to be discussed only after the country was hit by the first oil crisis in 1974. The severely distorted market mechanism and a sharp increase in the prices of imported raw materials caused inflation and demand–supply imbalances in many product markets. In dealing with this problem, the government emphasized microeconomic policy, in addition to traditional macroeconomic policy. In essence, the government attempted to monitor selected individual product markets and to apply appropriate policy measures. The Price Stabilization Act of 1975 was the legal foundation for this new economic policy.

The Price Stabilization Act applied to pricing of government monopolies, namely, cigarettes and public utilities such as electricity, railway transportation, and telecommunications. This act also set ceilings on basic daily necessities, including coal briquettes, and directly regulated the prices of monopoly and oligopoly products whose total domestic sales exceeded a prescribed amount. The producers subject to price regulation are as follows: (1) monopolists whose market share is 50% or more and (2) oligopolists whose combined market share is 60% or more and whose individual shares are 30% or more. These producers were required to file applications before they raised their prices. This act also stipulated against restraint of competition such as cartels, with exceptions of recession and rationalization cartels, and against unfair trade practices such as price discrimination, refusals to deal, tying arrangements, hoarding and cornering, and false and exaggerated advertising. This act purported to secure stable prices and fair trade. In actual implementation, however, far more attention was paid to price regulation than the prohibition of noncompetitive and unfair business practices.

Extensive price regulation, initially covering 148 products of 247 producers and gradually tapering off, was carried out until 1979. This price control system was gradually relaxed, and by 1979 only coal briquettes were still regulated. On the fair trade front, 100 cases of unfair trade practices were investigated between 1976 and 1979. However, almost all of the 85 cases actually prosecuted were related to the hoarding and cornering of staple food products, including rice. In contrast not a single case of undue restriction of competition was prosecuted. The only competition-related case that was examined under this law was the approval of collective activities in the cement industry on four consecutive occasions under the rubric of recession or rationalization cartels.

The Price Stabilization Act entailed various unexpected side effects, since it placed emphasis on the regulation of prices. It was preoccupied with the performance, rather than the structural, aspects of the market. Direct price controls on a wide range of commodities went beyond the limits of administrative capacity and led to a series of problems. Long-lasting price controls severely distorted the price mechanism and gave rise to phenomena such as dual pricing and deterioration of product quality, as well as chronic excess demand. Furthermore, most regulated firms lost interest in increasing the production of regulated products, which further weakened their ability to weather business cycles. Because prices rose unpredictably in a stop-and-go pattern, consumers neither had reasonable expectations about prices nor were able to plan their consumption rationally.

This experience, coupled with the aftermath of the second oil crisis, prompted a reappraisal of the past performance of the Korean economy and led to the general consensus that the market mechanism should play a greater role in the economy in the coming decades. The first major effort in this direction was the Fair Trade Act enacted in April 1981, which nullified direct price regulation under the Price Stabilization Act and set comprehensive new "rules of the game" for the market economy, namely, free and fair competition. This new act signified a fundamental change in government–business relations and was regarded as the economic constitution for a new era.

The Fair Trade Act is a comprehensive competition act. First of all, it forbids the abuse of a market-dominating position. An enterprise or a group of enterprises is deemed to have a market-dominating position if it meets the following conditions: the largest firm has more than 50%, or the three largest firms have more than 75%, of sales in a market with total annual domestic sales exceeding a prescribed amount.

The Fair Trade Commission (hereafter, the FTC) annually designates "market-dominating firms" according to these criteria.

Market-dominating firms are prohibited by the act from the following abusive activities: unreasonably determining, maintaining, or altering the price of a commodity or service rendered; unreasonably controlling the sale of commodities or services; unreasonably interfering with the business activities of other business concerns; unfairly hindering the entry of new competitors; and disrupting the marketplace by substantially restricting competition or harming consumers' interests.

The number of market-dominating enterprises increased sharply from 102 in 1981, to 386 in 1997. One of the reasons for this increase is that the criterion of market size in terms of total domestic sales remained unaltered. Of 166 markets with market-dominating firms in 1997, 29 were monopolistic, 62 duopolistic, and 75 oligopolistic. In spite of the increasing number of market-dominating firms, however, only 24 firms were found to have abused their market-dominating positions: 17 of them in hampering the business activities of other firms through false allegations and tying arrangements and 7 in below-cost pricing.

The act restricts mergers by firms exceeding a specified size if the firm could cause substantial injury to competition in any line of commerce. Given anticompetitive effects, exceptions can be made for mergers aimed at rationalization or strengthening the international competitiveness of an industry. A unique characteristic of the act is that, in addition to typical methods of business integration such as stock or asset acquisition, mergers, or interlocking directorates, it designates equity participation in new enterprises (including joint ventures) as a method of business integration. This is in response to the fact that more firms were newly established than were merged in the rapidly growing Korean economy. A meaningful and effective competition policy should take this finding into consideration. The FTC blocked only 3 out of the 3,342 cases of business mergers reported up until 1996. This low rate of enforcement was due to the fact that most of the cases involved mergers between subsidiaries of the same business group, whose anticompetitive effects were judged to be negligible, and because conglomerate integration was not controlled in practice.

The Fair Trade Act prohibits concerted activities by firms or cartels, which would substantially restrict competition in any line of commerce. The types of prohibited collective activities include cartels on prices, agreements on sales conditions, production and sales quotas, customers and market areas, production facilities and equipment, specialization, and joint ventures for collective management. However, the commission can permit cartels deemed necessary for achieving industrial rationalization, overcoming cyclical recessions, facilitating industrial restructuring, enhancing the competitive strength of small and mediim-sized firms, or rationalizing the terms of transactions. Until 1996, 188 undesired collective activities were remedied, with 116 of these on prices.

The act prohibits unfair business practices, including undue refusal to deal, or undue price discrimination, undue inducement or coercion of competitors' customers, abuse of a superior bargaining position, unreasonable restrictions on terms and conditions of transactions, and false, deceptive, or misleading representations or advertisements. The FTC rectified 2,522 cases of unfair trade practices during the 1981–1996 period: 750 on advertising and 720 on undue inducement of customers, among others.

The Fair Trade Act prohibits resale price maintenance as a special type of unfair business practice or vertical restraint. However, the act allows resale price maintenance to a certain category of publications designated by the FTC and also to commodities that meet the following conditions: (1) their qualities can be easily recognized as identical; (2) they are for daily use by general consumers; and (3) free competition prevails in their markets. Up until 1996, 103 cases were corrected for resale price maintenance.

The act expands the same set of restrictions on undue concerted activities and unfair business practices to trade associations and their member firms. In addition, trade associations are prohibited from restricting the present or future number of members, unreasonably restricting members' business activities, or forcing members to commit unfair business practices or resale price maintenance. Trade associations engaged rather extensively in various types of anticompetitive and unfair business practices. As of the end of 1996, there were 6,185 trade associations. Of these, 700 were organized by the Act for Small and Medium-Sized Firms and 3,433 by other special laws. In the 1981–1996 period, a total of 416 violations of the act by trade associations were recorded, with 260 on the restraint of competition among members.

The Fair Trade Act also has jurisdiction over international agreements or contracts between Korean firms and their foreign counterparts with regard to undue collaborative activities, unfair business practices, and resale price maintenance. The types of international contracts subject to approval by the Fair Trade Commission were initially those concerning (1) technological licensing, (2) loans, (3) joint ventures, (4) import agencies, (5) copyrights, (6) long-term imports, and (7) technological consulting services. However, to facilitate the inflow of foreign capital and technology, the act was amended in 1994, introducing a review system based on voluntary requests, while reducing the scope of its jurisdiction to those for intangible property rights, import agencies, and joint ventures. The FTC corrected 2,338 contracts, or 19.9% of the 11,763 it examined during the 1981–1996 period. Technological licensing accounted for 60.8% of all contracts examined and 67.3% of the all contracts amended.

The FTC was made a fully independent organization of the government by the 1994 amendment to the Fair Trade Act, whereas the commission had previously been under the Economic Planning Board. The commission plays a unique role in enhancing the efficacy of competition policies. The Fair Trade Act requires other government authorities to consult with the commission if they wish to introduce, amend, or enact any laws, decrees, or administrative measures that may restrain competition. During the 1981–1996 period, there were 1,612 cases of prior consultation on laws and decrees, of which 288 were rectified, and there were 162 cases of consultation on administrative measures, of which 51 were rectified.

In addition to the Fair Trade Act, the FTC has jurisdiction on the Act for Fair Subcontracting Transactions. Many small and medium-sized enterprises conduct their business in vertical relationships with larger ones. This act was legislated in 1984 to protect small and medium-sized enterprises against unfair practices committed by larger firms in subcontracting relationships. Between 1983 and 1994, the FTC corrected a total of 1,275 subcontracting transactions, 552 of which were in manufacturing and 727 in construction. The FTC also enforces the Act for Regulating Stipulations in Contracts. This act, legislated in 1984, covers contracts containing predetermined stipulations concluded by one side with a large number of parties on the other side. For example, tenants renting apartments are required to sign a contract whose detailed stipulations are predetermined by the landowner. The act declares that unfair stipulations in violation of the principle of good faith and sincerity are null and void. Since the act was introduced, the FTC has reviewed 454 cases, of which 160 have been corrected

Competition policy administered by the FTC has played an important role in nurturing the free market economy in Korea. The Fair Trade Act was introduced when the Korean government wielded almost unlimited power in industrial regulations, protection, and support. From its genesis, this act has clashed with other interventionist government policies and customs and was sometimes constrained in its effects. This limitation notwithstanding, the Act has accomplished a monumental result in that it has challenged noncompetitive market structures and behavior. The most significant contribution that the Fair Trade Act has made is that it has slowly, but steadily, awakened the Korean people and their government to the quintessential function of the market mechanism, working freely and fairly.

Competition policy must be coordinated with other policies. Insofar as this policy provides the most fundamental framework for market order and also contains elements of general industrial policy, other industrial laws such as the Industrial Development Act, the Copyright, and the Patent Act must be recast and enforced within the boundary set by the Fair Trade Act. Currently, activities "justified" by such laws are exempted. In a similar vein, external trade policy must be harmonized with domestic competition policy. Attempts to discriminate between the two types of policies will be futile in an open economy.

Deregulation Reforms

In addition to fair trade policy, deregulation constitutes the other key aspect of competition policy. In pushing for rapid economic growth, the Korean government imposed regulations on industry mainly to prevent "excessive" competition. Government regulation served its purposes quite well in the early stages of economic development when the economy was small, and the capabilities of the private sector had not yet matured. Continued on a wider scale, however, regulations became detrimental to efficient business activities. As government-led economic management centering on the regulation of the market revealed its limits, the government began to emphasize the role of the market mechanism. Launched in the mid-1980, economic liberalization was pushed ahead through the Sixth and Seventh Five-Year Economic and Social Development Plan periods. The New Economy Five-Year Plan presented by the YS regime also set the promotion of a market economy as the basic tenet of economic policy. Accordingly, the argument for deregulation gained momentum, and deregulation has been executed in earnest. During the past four years about 3,000 odd regulations were detected and dismantled.

Initially, deregulation was executed in a fragmented way as the need arose. In 1995 and 1996, however, the government placed the focus on a few regulations that have had relatively more significant and far-reaching impacts on the economy: foreign direct investment, finance, land use and development, establishment of factories, logistics and transportation, import and export procedures, customs clearance, construction, distribution, energy, environment, food, sanitation and health, employment and training, and laws and decrees in restraint of competition.

The Fair Trade Commission has also made efforts toward improving regulations on entry and market competition, though not necessarily from the angle of deregulation. In October 1995, the FTC selected for close scrutiny 20 monopolistic or oligopolistic products and requested other ministries to revise 54 laws and decrees that contain anticompetitive regulations. It also asked 17 government bodies to rewrite the articles and internal rules of 69 trade associations that restrain competition in their respective industries. Further, in January 1996, the FTC requested 15 government bodies to do the same thing for 149 trade associations. Subsequently, it reviewed laws and decrees related to finance, telecommunications, energy, transportation, sanitation, construction, distribution, agriculture and fisheries, professional services (e.g., lawyers, pharmacists, medical doctors), and alcoholic beverages and detected clauses that tend to restrain competition or cause inconveniences to business activities.

The new ministerial team in charge of economic policy, installed in March 1997, decided to launch a "regulatory reform to promote competition." To this end, it transferred the task of deregulation from the Ministry of Finance and Economy to the FTC. In the new reorganized administration comprehensive deregulatory reforms will be undertaken directly by the prime minister's office. The government has decided to legislate "a Basic Act for Regulatory Reform" upon reflection that deregulation has not been undertaken in a systematic manner in the past. This act is supposed to include a sunset provision, appraisal of the effects of new regulations, and the notification of regulation, among other provisions.

A notable feature of the deregulatory process in Korea is that the need for regulatory reform has been advocated practically unanimously. Such a consensus underlies the fact that virtually every Cabinet in the recent past has always put deregulation high on its reform agenda. Nevertheless, each group or segment of the society has its own differing view on deregulation. Private firms demand that restrictions on their pricing decisions and business transactions be removed while various entry barriers erected earlier be kept intact. Moreover, businesses claim that ever-tightening social regulations should be relaxed to a considerable degree. They want more freedom from government interference with their vested interests untouched. In other words, they want to "have their cake and eat it too."

Government officials generally subscribe to the basic goal of a free market mechanism while attempting to preserve their controlling power on industries and areas still under their jurisdiction. They assume an attitude of "supporting the general while opposing the particulars." On the other hand, the majority of the constituents who do not have a keen interest in particular economic regulations, those in academe who do not have relevant information on the regulations, and the politicians who are supposed to represent the public interest merely raise their voice in support of the basic principle of deregulation without presenting concrete alternatives and solutions to specific regulations. As a consequence, deregulation has been enforced mostly in areas in which the government and business have no acutely conflicting interests, for example, regulation on prices and transactions and social regulations. Even then, efforts have been devoted to curtailing red tape while putting aside essential elements required to control the relevant market. Institutional barriers to entry and exit, the most potent form of regulation hindering free competition, have not been attacked in full-scale.

What is required, then, is to review all existing regulations from the point of view of enhancing overall economic efficiency without respect to political considerations. Even if a well-specified regulatory program is prepared, its successful enforcement does not necessarily follow. It is imperative to overcome the obstacle of organized opposition by summoning the support of the general public to counterbalance the boisterous voice of the interest groups concerned.

One more point is pertinent here. If all socially undesirable regulations cannot be eliminated at once, the second-best solution may be selective deregulation. Hence, what and how much to deregulate become an issue of paramount importance. In this world of global competition, the most profitable way of deregulation for Korea may be to execute it in such a way as to contribute most to raising the international competitiveness of its industry.

Ultimately, deregulation leads to changes in the role of the government and, hence, inevitably requires the corresponding rearrangement of its manpower and organization. It must be reorganized on the principle of "a small but strong government." With this view in mind, the current government set up an administrative body that is expected to review the whole range of public services and related organizations.

The Control of Big Conglomerate Business Groups

Economic policies in Korea cannot be discussed in any meaningful way without taking into account big conglomerate business groups, or *chaebols* as they are commonly called. Since economic development plans were launched in full scale in the 1960s, the *chaebols* have always been in the center stage of the history of industrialization, characterized successively by "export drive," "heavy and chemical industrialization," and "upgrading of industrial structure." The *chaebols* have a number of characteristics similar to those of the pre–World War II Japanese *zaibatsu*. (In fact, they are written in the same Chinese characters.) In Korea, the Fair Trade Act defines a business group as "a group of companies, whose business activities are controlled by an identical person." Business groups embrace multidimensional problems intertwining overall concentration, monopoly, and diversification in addition to the concentration of corporate ownership, making possible the *de facto* control of a large number of subsidiaries by a particular individual and his or her family members.

As of 1996, the 30 largest business groups had a total of 669 subsidiaries, a considerable increase from 604 in 1993. This number was 509 when the Fair Trade Commission compiled the data for 32 business groups. In the mining and manufacturing industries, the size of the top five groups is substantially larger than that of the rest, and, furthermore, their share is generally on the increase. This observation tells us that to cut to the bone, the whole issue of economic power in Korea can be reduced to the issue of the top five *chaebols*.

The 30 business groups naturally account for a large share in heavy and chemical industries that require huge investment. But there is a distinct difference in major lines of business, in terms of two-digit industry, between the upper-ranking and lower-ranking among the chaebols. The top five have a dominant position in machinery, automobiles, and electrical and electronic products, which have grown to be the most vigorous among all industries in Korea. In contrast, other groups have a large share in capital-intensive industries such as refined petroleum products, chemicals and chemical products, and nonmetallic mineral products.

One prominent characteristic of the *chaebols* is the diversification of their business lines. In terms of the number of commodities, the top five business groups participate in 142 markets on the average. The higher the ranking of a chaebol, the larger becomes its number of commodities produced and the wider its extent of diversification. For example, the degree of specialization measured by the share of the largest three-digit industry in total shipments of a business group is about 55% for the top five whereas it is around 72% for the bottom five of the 30 largest business groups.

The *chaebols* have been the central feature of industrial organization in Korea. They have both positive and negative effects on the Korean economy. Therefore, the *chaebol* policy must aim at eliminating their adverse effects while encouraging their productive role. The most comprehensive assemblage of *chaebol* policy so far is the Fair Trade Act. The history of *chaebol* policy can be traced back to several decades ago, but it has been implemented mostly as a piecemeal shock treatment, not as a systematic approach. Furthermore, it has been implemented largely as an ancillary part of policies designed for other purposes.

The Fair Trade Act specifically intends to control the chaebols to a certain extent, forming the backbone of *chaebol* policy in Korea today. This act includes the restraint of "excessive concentration of economic power" as one of its goals, but concrete measures for such a purpose were first written in the 1986 amendment and have been amended several times. Before the latest amendment of February 1998, the act provided for (1) the prohibition of holding companies and transforming existing companies into holding companies, (2) the prohibition of cross-investment among subsidiaries of the same large business group and the restriction of the investment of a subsidiary in other domestic companies to 25% of its equity, (3) the restriction on debt guarantees of a subsidiary to 200% of its equity, (4) the restriction on the voting rights on stocks of subsidiary companies owned by financial and insurance companies belonging to the same large business group, and (5) the regulation of undue internal transactions within the same large business group.

The current DJ government has stressed that *chaebols* must trim their size by curtailing diversified business areas, sever intercompany linkages among their subsidiaries, and make their management more transparent. In this vein, the Fair Trade Act was amended recently to abolish the ceiling on the amount of total investment by subsidiaries of the 30 largest business groups. At the same time, debt guarantees were totally banned, while the existing guarantees are required to be terminated by 2000. However, the abolition of the regulation limiting total investment of *chaebols'* subsidiaries may contradict the policy of deconcentration of economic power. Debt guarantees are demanded by lending banks as collateral. Unless they resort to lending by credit appraisal, this practice may not be easily discarded. Therefore, the new amendment is only partially effective in checking the excessive expansion of business groups. In a similar context, the government urged banks to conclude recapitalization agreements with major borrowing companies that require these companies to reduce their debt-equity ratios to 200%. In view of very high debt-equity ratios of most of business groups this requirement is unrealistic. It remains to be seen how it will be met.

In formulating *chaebol* policy, the government must regard the chaebol issue not as a short-run problem but as a structural problem in Korea. It will take a fair amount of time before the policy gradually takes effect. Therefore, once a rational policy is formulated, it must be consistently implemented without being swayed by changes in the economic environment, short-run economic difficulties, and volatile public opinion. Taking the current IMF regime as a turning point, policy changes have been introduced to set corporate reorganization in motion. The ongoing reform is eradicating the vestiges of the government-controlled financial mechanism. Business groups themselves fully acknowledge the need for restructuring, though they do not welcome the speed of policy changes. If they succeed in realigning and reinforcing their business capabilities, they will be able to lead the strong growth of the Korean economy once again.

CONCLUDING REMARKS

The development process of the Korean economy for the last 35 years gives other developing countries a lesson on the successes and failures of development policies, especially in changing the roles of government and the market and in evolving appropriate institutions. While the performance of the Korean economy up to the

1970s showed the efficiency of a government-led development strategy, the subsequent period has demonstrated what kind of repercussions and costs such a strategy can generate and how difficult it is to correct these undesirable effects. Since the early 1980s, the Korean economy has attempted to address this problem by gradually adopting the principles of competition. However, Korea has made rather tepid efforts toward the goal of a full-fledged market economy.

The economic crisis starting at the end of 1997 was superficially attributed to a financial meltdown, but it was deeply rooted in distorted government–market relations in important economic areas including corporate management, the financial market, the capital market, and the labor market. Therefore, the task facing Korea is to reform institutional devices and to alter the mind of its business managers and government officials so that the market principles can work unfettered throughout the entire economy. Paradoxically, in this respect, the current economic crisis offers the Korean economy a long-awaited opportunity to reorganize itself and to arm itself with a new paradigm before it becomes a mature market economy.

9

Public Policies in the Singapore Economy

Kong Yam Tan

Since 1965, Singapore has achieved remarkable economic progress, averaging 8.9% per year. Rapid economic growth has been accompanied by substantial structural transformation from a regional *entrepôt* of raw materials and manufactured products into a high value-added manufacturing as well as financial and business services hub in the dynamic Asia-Pacific region. By 1997, despite the regional currency crisis, the economy is characterized by full employment, high savings and investment rates, a strong fiscal position, a healthy balance of payments, growing external reserves, a strong currency, and a low inflation rate.

The Singapore economy is characterized by small territorial size (630 sq. km.) and population (3 million), poor resource endowment, specialized production structure, and heavy dependence on foreign direct investment and international trade, as well as high economic vulnerability. These special characteristics dictated Singapore's development strategy in the past three decades, particularly the highly interventionist social and economic policies. They also shaped the objective of developing Singapore as a global city and the recent drive in regionalization and the export of surplus capital to tap into the growth of the Asia-Pacific economies.

In the 10 years since 1987, growth has averaged 8.7% per year. By the end of 1990, Singapore had evolved into a major regional business and financial hub in the dynamic Asia-Pacific region. The end of 1990 also saw the transition of political leadership from Lee Kuan Yew to a new and younger generation of political leaders headed by Goh Chok Tong. The new leadership crystallized the formulation of a comprehensive vision of the long-term strategic development direction of Singapore. Called the "Next Lap," this vision is for Singapore to attain the status and characteristics of a first-league developed country within the next 20–30 years. The specific industrial strategies were fleshed out in the Strategic Economic Plan (SEP) prepared by the Ministry of Trade and Industry (MTI).[1] The key elements in the SEP include positioning Singapore as a global city or "total business hub" in the Asia-Pacific region at par with other leading global cities in the world; emphasis on attracting high-tech, knowledge-intensive industries and promoting high-value, innovative, and creative activities; intensified investment infrastructure and enhancing human resources; promoting teamwork and cooperation between labor, business, and government; and internationalization of local firms as a means to transcend the constraints of small physical size and to achieve better access to overseas markets and technology.

This chapter concerns the public policies being instituted in Singapore to create competitive advantage by fostering high technology. First we consider public policies in Singapore in the context of the theory of the *developmental state*. Then we discuss Singaporean efforts to build an unexcelled regional information and telecommunications infrastructure. Finally, we outline the National Technology Plan and its objectives for the first years of the next century.

DEVELOPMENTAL STATE—CONCEPTUAL ISSUES

The traditional explanation for the success of the East Asian capitalist economies has been the efficient resource allocation effect of the free market, economic openness, the provision of a stable macroeconomic environment and a reliable legal framework, "getting the prices right," and the limited role of the government. Adherents of this neoclassical view include Chen (1979), Patrick (1977), Friedman (1980), and Fei (1983). Over the past decade or so, however, a new stream of literature has increasingly emphasized the directive and developmental role of the state in the economic success of East Asia. This revisionist view emphasized the significance of the government–business relationship, resulting in the governments' not merely being a referee and setting the broad rules of the game but often acting as a major participant with determining influence on business decisions through direct manipulation of incentives and disincentives in promoting industrial development (Mason et al., 1980; Johnson, 1981, 1982).

This literature emphasized that international competitive advantage in specific products and industries could be deliberately and purposefully created and nurtured by a process of skill, technology, and product upgrading. While from a short-run and static perspective, these intervention policies in the factor and product markets appeared to conflict with the operation of the free market and economic rationalism, interventions that nurture industries of rapid technological progress, rising labor productivity, and high income elasticity of demand could be dynamically efficient from a long-term perspective (Johnson, 1982; White, 1988). This view also emphasized the significance of the numerous formal and informal institutions and channels for consultation and coordination between the elite economic bureaucracy and the private sector in the process of policy formulation, implementation, and modification.

Government interventions using fiscal incentives, socializing of risk, and direct credit control mechanism could result in investment in specific key industries far higher than would have occurred in the free market situation (Amsden, 1989). Efficiency was maintained either through competition among protected domestic firms or through exposure to international competition. The supporting institutional and organizational arrangements in making such interventionist structure possible were soft authoritarianism and corporatist political structure which allow for market guidance (Johnson, 1982; Wade, 1992).

In its report on the "East Asian miracle," the World Bank (1993) noted that since 1960, the eight high-performing Asian economies (HPAE) (Japan, Hong Kong, Korea, Taiwan, Singapore, Malaysia, Indonesia, and Thailand) have grown at about 5.5% in per capita terms, more than twice as fast as the rest of East Asia (2.4%), roughly three times as fast as Latin America (1.8%) and South Asia (1.9%), and five times faster than sub-Saharan Africa. The report noted that the HPAEs maintained important fundamental policies like macroeconomic stability, the principle of shared growth, high savings rate and heavy investment in human capital, stable and secure financial system, and limited price distortion as well as openness to foreign technology. In addition, they also actively promoted selective interventions like mild financial repression, keeping real interest rates positive but low, directed credit, selective industrial promotion, and export-promoting trade policies. These interventionist policies were deemed necessary largely because they helped to address the critical problem of a class of market failures, that is, coordination failures, particularly in the early stage of development. The complementary key ingredient to ensure success, however, was that the government distributed rewards, often in the form of privileged access to credit or foreign exchange, on the basis of competitive performance rather than encouraged rent-seeking activities. Thus, selective interventions were disciplined by competition via either markets or contests. In addition, the existence of a high-quality civil service that was insulated from political interference and had the capacity to impartially monitor performance has been crucial to such selective intervention and to ensure contest-based competition.

On the other hand, various economists, including Paul Krugman (1994) and Alwyn Young (1993, 1995), as well as Kim and Lau (1994, 1996), have used growth theory and accounting to show that growth in East Asia could be largely attributed to sheer increase in the inputs of labor and capital and very little to total factor productivity or more productive use of these inputs. Recent evaluation of the empirical evidence, however, has indicated that Young's numbers were subject to large measurement errors. Studies by the Union Bank of Switzerland (1996) and Aziz (1996), have shown stronger total factor productivity gains, amounting to around 2–2.5% between 1978 and 1996, compared with a weaker 0.3% for the United States. However, despite the controversy over measurement errors, it is clear that total factor productivity for East Asian countries has not been strong in their early stage of industrial takeoff,[2] indicating certain fundamental weaknesses in the structure of firms, lack of technology and brand names, and weak R&D, as well as product and process development capability, noncompetitive product and factor markets, weak and poorly regulated banking and financial sector, as well as the high cost burden of an economy based on patronage and cronyism.[3]

PUBLIC POLICIES IN SINGAPORE

The economic success of Singapore in the past three decades demonstrated both the power of the neoclassical view and the importance of the revisionist perspective to complement the explanation of high growth. As the neoclassical view correctly pointed out, Singapore's growth was characterized by a high savings rate (34–45% of GDP since the early 1980s), heavy investment in human capital, fiscal and monetary prudence leading to macroeconomic stability, minimal price distortion, a stable and secure financial system, and extreme openness to international trade, investment, and technology transfer. In addition, as the revisionists stressed, the story of Singapore also demonstrated the necessity and capacity of a country with no natural resources to create national competitive advantage through selective industrial promotion and infrastructure development and continuously renew it by upgrading of industrial structure.

The traditional justification for public sector involvement is that of externalities and other forms of market failures. To the extent that much basic research, manpower training, infrastructure support for national competitive advantage and technology diffusion have public goods characteristics, they create significant positive externalities that cannot be easily appropriated by the investing parties. Consequently, the private sector would tend to underinvest compared to what is deemed socially desirable. Another justification for public sector intervention is the failure of the capital market in allocating finance and pooling risks for R&D projects involving high fixed costs, a long time horizon, and great uncertainty. On the other hand, public sector involvement may also be socially inefficient due to agency problems, rent-seeking by special interest groups, and other sources of government failures.

The Singapore government has involved itself as a key player in the economy largely on the justification of weak institutional structure in the early stage of development, coordination failures, positive externalities, and perceived pervasive market failures in a small open economy. It assumes the function of facilitator for human resource development, investment in research and development, and internationally competitive infrastructure in national hardware and software. The approach adopted by the government is often strategic and proactive, not *ad hoc* and reactive. The lead time needed in factor creation is frequently taken into account, so institution building often occurs with a view to the future.

This creation of national competitive advantage is crucial for Singapore, as it has very little natural factor endowment besides its human resources and geographic location. Foreign and domestic investments will stay in Singapore only if it is able to offset its natural resource disadvantage with a man-made advantage: superior national infrastructures. In the early stage of development, Singapore's geographic location gave it a natural base to build sea and air transport facilities that served to establish its competitive position as a regional hub for physical production and transport (manufacturing, *entrepôt* trade, and distribution). The recent development of information and telecommunications infrastructure is a logical next step to further strengthen Singapore's role as a regional hub for information production and communication (financial and business services, regional headquarters operations, R&D, design, regional marketing, training and technical support services, etc.).

To illustrate the government's role in economic development, it is instructive to look at the creation of national competitive advantage through heavy investment in information-telecommunications infrastructure for the promotion of information technology since the second half of the 1980s. It has proved to be fairly successful so far. To update our account of Singaporean experience, we consider an ambitious National Technology Plan unveiled in 1991 to usher the nation into the innovative phase of development. It entailed a $2 billion research and development fund. This was followed by the Second National Science and Technology Plan in 1996. While there are indicators for success, the verdict is still out on this ambitious project.

Creating National Competitive Advantage in Information-Telecommunications Infrastructure

The rapid diffusion of the application of information technology (IT) means that a new order of international division of labor is evolving. National competitive advantage in information-telecommunications infrastructure, both at the hardware and software level, particularly the rapid accessibility of information and the ability to process and use the results speedily to sharpen the competitive edge of enterprises and nations, will increasingly determine the new international hierarchy of nations. IT provides the rapid capability to integrate design, manufacturing, procurement, sales, and administrative and technical support services in any enterprise. With the geographic dispersion of production base, procurement, design, sales, and marketing from the headquarters location, the urgent need to have centralized coordination in a regionally central physical location has become imperative for major multinational companies (MNCs). An efficient and cost-effective national information-telecommunications infrastructure thus becomes critical for a regional business services center like Singapore. In particular, an efficient information-telecommunications infrastructure helps to reduce transaction costs, leading to improved efficiency in existing intraorganizational operations as well as on external market exchanges. In addition, it enhances value creation, that is. enabling new products and services to be delivered and new value-creating processes to be performed that were previously not possible.

The IT sector in Singapore, encompassing activities associated with the production and dissemination of information goods and services, has been identified as a key industry since the 1980s. There is a multiagency exercise for developing and promoting information-telecommunications infrastructure and development. Apart from the direct telecommunications facilities offered by Singapore Telecom, the other statutory body that has been actively promoting IT and related computerization activities is the National Computer Board (NCB), which was established in 1980. The comprehensive National Information Technology Plan (NITP) was developed by the NCB and other public agencies as a blueprint for all aspects of IT development in Singapore in 1986. The plan included specific objectives and deadlines for training people; creating an IT culture; enhancing the communications infrastructure; generating and supporting IT applications; fostering a world-class indigenous IT industry that includes software, hardware and computer services; and pioneering new information technology applications through R&D.

Since 1986, the implementation of the NITP has achieved significant success. The Civil Service Computerization Program has been successfully implemented and extended to the private sector to develop a nationwide information system. National electronic data interchange (EDI) networks, including Tradenet, Medinet, Buildnet, and Lawnet, have been established. A wide array of IT training institutions is developing specialists in communications, integrated manufacturing, artificial intelligence, and software engineering.

A notable success story of creating national competitive advantage through an efficient information-telecommunications infrastructure has been the implementation of Tradenet. Initiated by the government and run by Singapore Network Services (SNS) since January 1, 1989, Tradenet has been an unqualified success in helping to manage Singapore's huge external trade of $257 billion a year—2.9 times the GNP. It has helped to save Singaporean traders an estimated $1 billion a year. International trade has traditionally involved an enormous amount of paperwork. With Tradenet, however, traders simply fill out one electronic form, which can be submitted by modem to the Trade Development Board's main computer 24 hours a day. Information is then routed, again electronically, to the appropriate government agencies from among the 18 involved in issuing trade documents. Approvals, often generated with the help of expert systems, are deposited in the electronic mailbox of the trader, typically within 15 minutes. To further reduce paperwork, application fees and custom duties are automatically debited from the trader's bank through electronic funds transfer. Tradenet also automatically routes approved permits to the Port and Civil Aviation Authorities to facilitate the physical clearance of goods. As part of the information-telecommunications competitive infrastructure, an expert system for container planning, a system called Portnet was developed to work with Tradenet. This system allows for the electronic declaration of vessel calls, electronic data interchange links with other ports for processing arriving ships, and artificial intelligence (AI) based pattern recognition systems that automatically encode container numbers (Sisodia, 1992).

The National Computer Board has also been instrumental in spearheading the establishment of IT research institutes and the collaboration with the private sector. The Information Technology Institute (ITI) was established in 1986 to conduct applied R&D. In 1989, in collaboration with AT&T Bell Labs, the Information Communication Institute of Singapore (ICIS) was formed to provide telecommunications software training at the postgraduate level. With the assistance of the Japanese government, the Japan-Singapore Artificial Intelligence Centre (JSAIC) was established in 1990 to promote AI technologies.

The diffusion of IT usage expanded significantly throughout the 1980s and 1990s. NCB IT surveys indicated that organizations in Singapore employing 10 persons or more that had computerized their operations has risen from 13% in 1982 to 59% in 1987 and reached 90% by 1994. The percentage of establishments with local area networks has also risen steadily to reach 58% by 1994. In addition, the production and export of IT hardware and software emerged rapidly into a major industry, with foreign IT companies playing a dominant role. Direct exports of IT sales rose by an annual average rate of 37% between 1982–1994 to reach S$2.2 billion by 1994. Domestic IT sales increased at a somewhat slower rate of 24% during the same period to reach S$2.8 billion by 1994.[4]

The next phase of Singapore's strategy is aimed at transforming commerce, financial, business services, and society to create an "intelligent island." The government has dubbed this new plan "IT 2000" (National Computer Board, 1992). Singapore proposes to build a National Information Infrastructure, which will enable the national information, communication, and transaction system to work. In this case, Singapore's small size has been turned into an advantage. The physical infrastructure needed to support the information age can be more easily put in place in a country of Singapore's dimensions. Singapore is thus poised to become the world's first fully networked society, one in which all homes, schools, businesses, and government agencies will be interconnected in an electronic grid.

The IT 2000 Report set forth the vision that, within 15 years, Singapore will:

be among the first countries in the world with an advanced nation-wide information infrastructure. It will interconnect computers in virtually every home, office, school and factory. The computer will (by then) evolve into an information appliance, combining the functions of the telephone, computer, TV and more. It will provide a wide range of communication modes and access to services. Text, sound, pictures, videos, documents, designs and other forms of media can be transferred and shared through this broadband information infrastructure made up of optical fibres reaching to all homes and offices, and a pervasive wireless network working in tandem.

At the core of the IT 2000 vision is a "3C" view of IT—compute, conduit, and content. The driving force of IT in the 1990s and beyond will hence be the development of an advanced, ubiquitous information network, the digitization of contents, and the expansion of the multimedia content industries. In line with this strategy, a policy decision was made to accelerate the islandwide deployment of optical fiber by 2005.

The National Information Infrastructure Plan represents what can happen when a government assumes an instrumental position in actively shaping and investing in creating national competitive advantage. It underscores the importance of identifying and investing in certain key capabilities. There are very few inherent competitive advantages that nations and corporations can continuously count on. Advantages thus have to be created and continuously renewed. Singapore has leveraged its single natural advantage of strategic location by establishing world-class transportation system and materials-handling facilities and extended such "hubbing" into the financial and other business services activities by establishing a sophisticated communications and information technology infrastructure. Singapore now positions itself as a "value-added switching node" and a gateway in the dynamic Asia-Pacific region.

The importance of information-telecommunications infrastructure in supporting Singapore's competitive advantage as a regional financial and business center has been confirmed by successive rounds of international surveys of business leaders as reported in the annual *World Competitiveness Report*. In the 1995 report, for example, Singapore's telecommunications infrastructure was given a rating of 97.5 out of 100, which not only topped the league of newly industrializing nations but was also ahead of some of the OECD countries as well. The Singapore government clearly recognized that its competitive advantage lies not in creating new technologies but in rapid exploitation and application of technologies already developed elsewhere. This "fast follower" strategy emphasized building up the nation's technology absorption capacity—the effectiveness of scanning, learning, assimilating, and possibly improving upon available technology created by others to gain competitive advantage, while leaving the task of risky exploration of new technologies to more advanced nations with far greater resources (Wong, 1992).

Singapore's drive to create an information, networked society has a built-in dilemma: there is an inherent conflict between the democratization of information creation and access and the government's long-standing concern to control the information its citizens receive for fear of undermining national values. It would not be too presumptuous to surmise that, eventually, the democratization of information creation and access will gradually undermine the government's control of information in a fully networked society.

National Technology Plan

For the past 30 years, Singapore has gradually moved from a low-wage production base to a high value-added manufacturing and services hub in the Asia-Pacific region. Increasingly, its labor has become too expensive relative to that of the regional economies, which are fast catching up in skill, technology, and managerial expertise. To sustain competitiveness, Singapore needs to move to an innovation phase of development and promote activities with more innovative and design content. Consequently, Singapore must increase its capacity to undertake research and development at an international standard.

This process has already begun but has been somewhat slow. For example, national expenditure on R&D increased from $38 million or 0.2% of GDP in 1978 to $460 million or 1.0 of GDP in 1990. Private sector spending on R&D expanded from $26 million in 1978 to $380 million in 1990. The private sector therefore accounted for more than half of the total national expenditure on R&D by 1990. In 1978, Singapore had only 1,672 people working in R&D; by 1990, this number had risen to 7,004. The number of research scientists and engineers (RSEs) as a proportion of the labor force also rose from 8 per 10,000 in 1978 to 28 per 10,000 by 1990 (National Science and Technology Board, 1991).

However, Singapore is still a long way behind the world leaders or the other NIEs. Other economies like the United States, Europe, Japan, Taiwan, and Korea all have plans to boost science and technology. Korea, which spent about 2.6% of its GDP on R&D in 1994, has developed a detailed plan to raise its level of R&D spending to 5% of GDP by the year 2000. Taiwan, which spent 1.8% of its GDP on R&D in 1994, planned to increase it to 2% in the 1990s. Similarly, while the number of research scientists and engineers (RSEs) per 10,000 labor force in Singapore rose from 29 in 1990, to 37 in 1992, it is still substantially lower than that of the other NIEs like Taiwan (54) and Korea (40), let alone the more developed countries like Japan (91), the United States (69), Germany (58), France (51), and the U.K. (46).[5] Realizing the severe competition from the other NIEs that are ahead in promoting science and technology and to uplift the state of Singapore's science and technology base, the government formed the National Science and Technology Board (NSTB) in early 1991 with the mission to develop Singapore into a center of excellence in selected fields of science and technology so as to enhance national competitiveness in the industrial and services sectors. The NSTB published a National Technology Plan called the "Window of Opportunities" in September 1991.

Realizing the limited capacity for a small economy to undertake basic research, the National Technology Plan concentrated on that part of research directed toward economic upgrading. Thus, Singapore's science and technology research would have to be result-driven; that is, it must produce results eventually relevant to economic upgrading and competitiveness. In order to be successful in "industry-driven" R&D, the government realized that the private sector must undertake the bulk of these R&D activities because the best measure of the value of such R&D activities would be the willingness of profit-seeking organizations to commit funds and resources toward it.

Realizing the effect of high fixed cost, long time horizon, and great uncertainty in hindering private sector investment in R&D, the government felt that by sharing part of this extra cost and risk, it would encourage more private sector R&D and foster national competitiveness and economic vigor. Thus, the government decided that it should play a more proactive coordinating and facilitating role to promote these efforts. Its role was to gauge what resources companies needed in order to undertake more R&D and then to find the means of providing the support.

The specific targets set out in the National Technology Plan were for total national expenditure on R&D to reach 2% of GDP by 1995, a minimum 50% private sector share of this total, and a ratio of the number of scientists and engineers engaged in R&D activities of 40 per 10,000 labor force by 1995.

To achieve these specific targets, the National Technology Plan set out the main thrusts that government would take in the next five years to achieve these targets and how it intended to provide the environment that would support active and widespread R&D by companies in Singapore. The key recommendations were:

—A $2 billion Research & Development Fund to support industry-driven R&D over the next five years;

—Provision of grants and fiscal incentives to encourage more R&D by the private sector;

—Assistance in developing and recruiting R&D manpower, domestically and overseas;

—Support and funding for research centers and institutes that can train manpower or provide technological support to enable companies to undertake their R&D; and

—Assistance for commercialization and infrastructure support.

More specifically, research and development expenditures and priorities would be focused on the following means of technology: information technology, microelectronics, electronics system, manufacturing technology, materials technology, energy, water, environment and resources, biotechnology, and food and agrotechnology as well as medical services. The NSTB has proposed several ways to use tax incentives to promote R&D, for example, extension of pioneer status up to an additional two years for companies that are prepared to undertake specified R&D activities in Singapore, similar extension of postpioneer concessions, double-deduction for R&D expenses, accelerated depreciation for capital expenditure incurred in acquiring approved know-how or patent rights, and tax exemptions for incremental income earned and for R&D reserves. In addition to fiscal incentives, the plan proposed to attract more Singaporeans into R&D and to supplement this with research talent from overseas. The government helped to defray part of the training cost through the provision of scholarships, financial aid, as well as specific grants.

More importantly, successful commercial exploitation of R&D required the ability to bring together other assets such as finance or capital, marketing skills, distribution network, and competitive manufacturing capabilities. Start-ups typically have difficulties commercializing their research findings because they do not possess, or cannot find, all the requisite elements. NSTB was also tasked to assist start-ups by helping to bring the elements together. For example, administrative policies could be changed and institutional barriers removed to encourage greater tie-ups between the research institutes and industry. If finance or managerial expertise were lacking, NSTB could also assist in matchmaking through strategic partnerships, joint ventures, or direct equity investments in the start-ups. In short, the aim was for the NSTB to develop into a "one-stop Technology Assistance Center" covering the entire life cycle of R&D.

It is still too early to assess the relative success of the Singapore government's role in fostering R&D in sustaining competitiveness. There were, however, some indications that things were moving in the correct direction. The R&D survey in

1995 indicated that Singapore spent a total of $1,175 million on research and development in 1994, up from $756 million in 1991. This meant that R&D spending was 1.2% of the GDP, indicating that Singapore was somewhat behind schedule to reach its goal of 2% R&D expenditure by 1995. On the other hand, the number of research scientists and engineers also rose from 34 per 10,000 in the labor force in 1991 to 42 per 10,000 in 1994, exceeding the National Technology Plan's (NTP) target of 40 per 10,000 by 1995. There were some indications that some private companies were beginning to build up core industrial capabilities in key technologies. The private companies were also accounting for an increasing share of total R&D expenditure, amounting to 63% in 1994. This has also exceeded the NTP's target of 50% by 1995. Examples of core industrial capabilities in key technologies included the many public sector bodies, that have developed such capabilities, such as the Institute of Systems Science, which was recently selected as one of four foreign partners in the Japan Real World Computing Sixth Generation Initiative. In the private sector, Hewlett Packard's R&D team in Singapore developed its first color ink-jet and portable printer. Motorola's local team was responsible for a credit card-sized pager and other telecommunication products. In addition, more strategic alliances between private companies and public sector organizations and between Singapore and other countries were being formed. The Glaxo-Institute of Molecular & Cell Biology Centre set up in early 1993 and the Apple-Institute of Systems Science Centre set up in 1992 were examples.[6] However, one source of weakness is that about three-quarters of R&D expenditure were still undertaken by foreign companies, especially in key industries like electronics, chemicals, and pharmaceuticals, as well as in the services industries.

In addition, the NSTB has spearheaded R&D growth through the strategic development and funding of 13 research institutes and centers in various technological areas to form a technology infrastructure to support industries, coinvested in 62 corporate R&D centers through industry R&D grants, invested substantially in development and funding of manpower-related grants, fostered economically relevant R&D and strategic research in the universities, promoted a culture of innovation and entrepreneurship, as well as established a network of international linkages for collaborative R&D.

The second phase of the National Technology Plan, entitled "National Science and Technology Plan—Towards 2000 and Beyond," was launched in 1996 to further develop Singapore's science and technology capability over the next 5–15 years. The vision was for Singapore to build a world-class science and technology base, especially in selected fields, that matched Singapore's competitive strengths and that would spur the growth of new high value-added industries. The target is to reach an R&D expenditure share of GDP of 1.6% by 2000 and 2% by 2005 as well as RSEs per 10,000 labor force of 65 by 2000 and 90 by 2005.

The focus of technology development would be on the first tier, that is, comprising the development, innovation, adaptation, and acquisition of short-term technologies. Over the next 5–10 years, some 70% of the government's resources will be directed to this tier. The next two tiers, consisting of indigenous R&D and technology development for medium-term leadership, as well as strategic research for long-term leadership, will constitute the remaining 30%.

The focus, as in the first NTP, would continue to be the key emerging technologies, including:

—Information technology/telecommunications

—Microelectronics/semiconductors

—Electronic systems

—Manufacturing technology

—Materials and chemicals technology

—Environmental technology, energy, water and resources

—Biotechnology

—Food and agrotechnology

—Medical sciences

In developing capabilities, the strategic thrust would continue to be on meeting the demand of manpower through the expansion of postgraduate education; raising the profile of an R&D career; upgrading career development programs for researchers; attracting foreign R&D manpower from developed countries; government support and incentives through cofunding of private sector R&D; fiscal and financial support for technology acquisition; strengthening technology infrastructure through enforcing a certain degree of market discipline upon research institutes and centers so as to achieve greater industry relevance and orientation as well as better operational efficiency and effectiveness; and fostering technology innovation and commercialization through nurturing technological start-ups.

CONCLUSION

In justifying government intervention in fostering economic development, a key rationale is the pervasive existence of imperfect markets and incomplete information, leading to pervasive market failure. As noted by Stiglitz (1989), while traditional literature characterizes market failures as the exception to the general rule that decentralized markets lead to efficient allocation, in the new view, the presumption is reversed. Only under exceptional circumstances are markets efficient. This makes the analysis of the appropriate role of government far more difficult, as the issue becomes not identifying market failures but identifying large market failures where there is scope for significant, welfare-enhancing government intervention.

In the case of Singapore, the unique feature of smallness and compact size could have made government intervention more effective and manageable, leading to less government failure. In addition, being small, the law of large number does not apply as readily; hence, it can be argued that pervasive market failure for competitive factor and product markets calls for an interventionist approach.

It is, however, significant to note that the emphasis on government intervention in Singapore is largely geared toward production rather than consumption or redistribution. Instead of intervening or deploying resources to create a welfare state, the emphasis of intervention was in actively creating national competitive advantage through physical infrastructural investments, national information infrastructure, R&D subsidy, and manpower development to strengthen long-term productive capability. In addition, an open, liberal, and often proactive immigration policy to attract skilled foreign workers to settle in Singapore has acted as a major policy to enhance the pool of human skill.

Government interventions in the factor market have been more controversial and have not produced expected success. For example, intervention in the labor market has proved to be counterproductive. In addition, some of the intervention in the capital market like the central provident fund forced savings scheme that led to a savings and investment rate of above 40% of GDP has resulted in weak capital productivity and poor total factor productivity performance (Young, 1993; Toh and Low, 1992). On the other hand, the central provident fund played a very important role in mobilizing capital for infrastructural and public housing development in the early stage of development. This contributed substantially to social and political stability in a young immigrant society as well as laying a strong foundation for rapid industrialization and eventually the evolution as a hub city in the ASEAN region.

It is noteworthy that the public sector in Singapore is strong, noncorrupt, and run in a much more commercial manner compared to that of most other countries. Civil servants have a market-oriented evaluation and reward system, with bonus and performance system built in. In addition, the public sector as a whole has its annual bonus tied to the overall performance of the economy. With the public sector's bottom line tied directly to fostering economic growth, the incentive system has been able to galvanize the public sector in servicing private sector interest in growth and development. In addition, the market-based system has also significantly injected market rationality into public sector intervention, helping to avoid large and wasteful public sector projects, as well as vast rent-seeking activities. Hence, interventions tend to be more market-facilitating, -correcting, and -enhancing rather than distorting. In addition, Singapore has the advantage of a small, open economy constantly under the check of international competitive forces so that policies or interventions that are too market-distorting would be fairly rapidly overwhelmed by international competitive forces.

The cultural element that facilitates government intervention and leadership in East Asia is the greater emphasis on the interest of the group, community, or state over that of the individual. Under this cultural milieu, it is considerably easier for the government to harness resources and mobilize the private sector to pursue major development goals, more so when the process of recruitment of the public sector allows it to capture a large share of the best and most dedicated minds in the country.

It is not clear, however, whether some of the success in government intervention in Singapore and the other NIEs is merely a function of their stage of development. As a follower in the process of economic catching up, it is not as difficult to identify the priorities in industry, infrastructure investment, R&D expenditure, manpower development, and so on. However, as the case of Japan shows, when these countries gradually reach the technological frontier and are also in the process of pushing forward the frontier, the same policy success of government intervention could no longer be replicated. The recent increasing emphasis by the Singapore government on creating an innovative culture is an indication of such concern.

NOTES

1. The author was a participant in this two-year exercise in drawing up the SEP. The SEP exercise is similar to the close consultation and deliberation between the elite economic bureaucracy and the private sector in the process of policy formulation as emphasized by the revisionist school of thought (see Johnson, 1982).

2. Incidentally, this is not too different from the early stage of industrial development of the United States and Japan. For example, Abramovitz and David (1973) have shown that total factor productivity (TFP) growth for the United States between 1853 and 1907 has been around 0.5%. Similarly, others have shown that real growth for Japan between the Meiji Restoration and World War I could be largely attributed to physical capital accumulation.

3. The recent currency crisis showed up some of these weaknesses.

4. See NCB IT Usage Survey, various years.

5. *The World Competitiveness Report*, 1993.

6. See speech by the Minister of Trade and Ministry in *The Straits Times*, September 3, 1993.

REFERENCES

Abramovitz, M., and P. A. David. (1973). "Reinterpreting Economic Growth: Parables and Realities." *American Economic Review* 63: 428–439.

Amsden, A. (1989). *Asia's Next Giant: South Korea and Late Industrialization*. New York: Oxford University Press.

Aziz, J. (1996). "Growth Accounting and Growth Processes." Working paper 06/116. Washington, DC: International Monetary Fund.

Chen, E.K.Y. (1979). *Hyper-Growth in Asian Economies: A Comparative Study of Hong Kong, Japan, Korea, Singapore and Taiwan*. New York: Macmillan.

Fei, J.C.H. (1983). *Evolution of Growth Policies of NICs in Historical and Typological Perspective*. Honolulu: East West Center.

Friedman, M., and R. Friedman. (1980). *Free to Choose: A Personal Statement*. New York: Harcourt Brace Jovanovich.

Johnson, C . (1982). *MITI and the Japanese Miracle: The Growth of Industrial Policy 1925–1975*. Palo Alto, CA: Stanford University Press.

————. (1981). "Introduction: the Taiwan Model." In J. Hsiung et al., eds., *Contemporary Republic of China: The Taiwan Experience*. Westport, CT: Praeger.

Kim, J. I., and L. J. Lau. (1996). "The Sources of Asian Pacific Economic Growth." *Canadian Journal of Economics* 29 (Special Issue): S448–454

Kim, J. L., and L. J. Lau. (1994). "The Sources of Economic Growth in the East Asian Newly Industrialized Countries." *Journal of Japanese and International Economics* 8(2): 235–271.

Krugman, P. (1994). "The Myth of the Asian Miracle." *Foreign Affairs* 73(6): 62–78.

Lim, C. Y. (1988). *Policy Options for the Singapore Economy.* New York: McGraw-Hill.

Low, L., and M. H. Toh. (1992). *Public Policies in Singapore: Changes in the 1980s and Future Signposts.* Singapore: Times Academic Press.

Mason, E. et al. (1980). *The Economic and Social Modernization of the Republic of Korea.* Cambridge, MA: Harvard University Press.

Ministry of Trade and Industry. (1979). *Economic Survey of Singapore.* Singapore: Ministry of Trade and Industry.

National Computer Board. (1995). *Singapore IT Industry Survey.* Singapore: National Computer Board.

———. (1992). *A Vision of an Intelligent Island—the IT2000 Report.* Singapore: National Computer Board.

National Science and Technology Board. (1991). *National Technology Plan: Window of Opportunities.* Singapore: National Science and Technology Board.

Patrick, H. (1977). "The Future of the Japanese Economy: Output and Labor Productivity." *Journal of Japanese Studies.*

Sisodia, R. S. (1992). "Singapore Investment in the Nation-Corporation." *Harvard Business Review* (May–June).

Stiglitz, J., et al. (1989). *The Economic Role of the State.* Oxford: Basil Blackwell.

Toh, M. H., and L. Low (1992). "Total Factor Productivity in Singapore: Some Myths and Issues." Mimeo.

Union Bank of Switzerland. (1996). "The Asian Economic Miracle." *UBS International Finance* 29 (Autumn).

Wade, R. (1990). *Governing the Market—Economic Theory and the Role of Government in East Asian Industrialization.* Princeton: Princeton University Press.

White, G. (1988). *Developmental States in East Asia.* New York: Macmillan.

Wong, P. K. (1992). "Economic Growth and Information-Telecommunications Infrastructures in Singapore." Working paper, Centre for Management of Technology, Singapore.

World Bank. (1993). *The East Asian Miracle: Economic Growth and Public Policy.* New York: Oxford University Press.

Young A. A. (1995). "The Tyranny of Numbers, Confronting the Statistical Realities of the East Asian Growth Experience." *Quarterly Journal of Economics* 110: 641–680.

———. (1993). "A Tale of Two Cities: Factor Accumulation and Technical Change in Hong Kong and Singapore." *NBER Macroeconomics Annual.* Cambridge: MIT Press.

10

Public Policies in the Hong Kong Economy: Emphasis on Manufacturing

Y. C. Richard Wong

Hong Kong is generally regarded as the freest economy in the world, and the Hong Kong government is known for its laissez-faire economic policy. This is, by and large, a correct portrayal of what has been taking place in Hong Kong in the postwar years. In this chapter, I consider several issues relating to the manufacturing sector. First, what are the essential features of Hong Kong's laissez-faire economic policy? Second, why did the Hong Kong government choose to implement such a policy, when, for most of that period, Britain adopted a socialist-oriented policy? Third, what implications did a laissez-faire policy, have for the development of the economy and society? Fourth, what is the future of the laissez-faire policy, especially in light of restoration of sovereignty over Hong Kong from Britain to China? My discussion is partly analytical and partly historical. I develop some of my key points through an analysis of a few important events that had a major impact on Hong Kong's development and policy environment.

It is important to appreciate that although in the area of economic affairs, Hong Kong had adopted a largely laissez-faire approach to policy matters, in the area of social policy Hong Kong has been quite statist. This has important implications for Hong Kong development and its policy environment. However, I do not look at issues outside the economic area, even though they may have an effect on economic policies.

THE POLITICAL ECONOMY OF ECONOMIC POLICY

In 1945, Hong Kong's population was about 600,000. Today it is 6.5 million. At the end of the war, Hong Kong's per capita income was about one-fourth of that in Britain. Today, it exceeds that of the United States by a small amount. This rapid rate of economic growth is not uncommon in this part of Asia.

Hong Kong's economic miracle is largely attributed to the adoption of a laissez-faire economy policy. The key features of this policy are minimal government intervention in the market, the rule of law, free and unfettered trade, open and competitive markets, a simple and predictable tax regime, low tax rates, balanced budgets, limited public expenditures, a stable currency, and price stability.

Hong Kong in the postwar years has been characterized by an unusual degree of economic and civic freedoms. On the other hand, Hong Kong's largely administered relationship among economic, civil, and political freedoms, is complex and perhaps still inadequately understood.

To some extent the absence of political freedoms has made it possible for the colonial administration to implement its laissez-faire policy. Two factors are important. First, an administration that is legally and politically not accountable to the public makes it possible for the personal convictions of senior administrators to prevail in a colonial administration. It is, to some extent, a historical accident that the chief architect of Hong Kong's economic policy was a financial secretary who held office throughout the 1960s. Sir John Cowperthwaite was a believer in laissez-faire and put his convictions into action. The tax regime and fiscal system have survived to the present and are, to a large extent, enshrined in the basic law. His successors have, by and large, continued that policy to this day. The fact that budgets proposed by the administration were never challenged by an appointed legislature made it possible for a laissez-faire policy to be sustained. Eventually, the benefit of the policy was able to command sufficient intellectual and popular following to become entrenched and to survive legislative challenge from an increasingly elected legislature that began to emerge in the 1980s.

Second, a foreign colonial administration governing an alien population in the post–colonial era naturally felt sufficiently constrained in its political behavior to wish to minimize its obtrusiveness. The British government at the end of war was more concerned with its own economic recovery than with the affairs in a far-off city. Its main concern, which it took great pains to communicate to the colonial administration, was that Hong Kong must not become a fiscal burden to the British government. Diplomatically, the rise of China probably contributed to the short-term approach of the colonial administration. Civil servants, on the whole, were keen to minimize mistakes, doing as little as possible so that they could retire comfortably back to Britain after a stable and colorless career.

Third, in order not to alienate itself from the community, the administration would selectively incorporate public opinion in its policymaking process through a consultation process through some 400 advisory committees whose members were appointed. To some extent, the administration saw itself as balancing the various vested interest groups and holding them in abeyance, at the same time taking into account some of their legitimate concerns.

It is no doubt true that as a small economy without natural resources beyond its geographic location and an excellent harbor, Hong Kong had little choice but to pursue a free trade policy in order to improve its standard of living. This was a lesson that the more interventionist Singaporean government soon learned after its own independence. Nevertheless, the colonial setting in a post–colonial era and accidents of history had an important effect.

THE RISE OF LABOR-INTENSIVE MANUFACTURING

Before the war Hong Kong was primarily an *entrepôt*. Manufacturing was largely absent. The population in Hong Kong was predominantly made up of sojourners who did not consider the territory to be their home. Export-oriented, labor-intensive manufacturing emerged only after the war. Three factors contributed to its rise. First was the arrival of numerous Shanghai industrialists. Second was the arrival of workers and peasants with their families from Guangdong. These immigrants chose to stay in Hong Kong permanently. The population of Hong Kong rose from 600,000 to 2.1 million between 1945 and 1951. Third, the United Nations embargo against China during the Korean War effectively killed Hong Kong's *entrepôt* trade.

Viewed in its historical context, the rise of manufacturing in Hong Kong occurred because of a dramatic shift in Hong Kong's comparative advantage in the postwar years. These changes were largely the result of external events that had little to do with Hong Kong's own development. Export-driven industrialization was the result neither of a trade promotion policy nor of an industrial policy. In this sense the industrialization of Hong Kong had little to do with government policy. It simply emerged. The government did not promote it or stand in its way. If the government wished to take any credit for its policy, it was to provide a legal, economic, and business environment that allowed entrepreneurs and workers to flourish. Hong Kong's manufacturing sector was well supported by entrepreneurs and professionals who had arrived from Shanghai in the areas of shipping, banking, retail business, movies, and professional services. The British and Chinese bankers and traders indigenous to Hong Kong also provided valuable financial support and overseas networks.

One of the most significant events in the development of manufacturing in Hong Kong was the imposition of voluntary export restraints on textiles and garments by the U.S. government through the Multi-Fiber Agreement (MFA). The Hong Kong government's response was unique in that it decided to allocate the quotas to manufacturers according to their previous performance. It also allowed the manufacturers to trade these quotas on the market freely. As a result it created a uniquely efficient system for the utilization of these scarce and valuable quotas. The quota allocation system also avoided the problem of public corruption associated with government administration of quotas. This episode is particularly revealing of the government's economic philosophy and approach to economic policy.

The industry was able to capture scarce economic rents and to expand into high value-added products. It became by far the most important industry in Hong Kong during the 1960s and the 1970s. Nevertheless, the annual exercise of trade negotiations with the U.S. government brought Hong Kong trade officials into close collaboration with the textile and garment manufacturers. The Textile Advisory

Board became one of the most powerful advisory committees. Influential manufacturers took turns in sitting on the board, and many were appointed to the Legislative
and Executive Councils. It has often been jokingly said that the Jockey Club, Hong
Kong Bank, and Jardines were the three most influential power groups in Hong
Kong. If there is, indeed, some truth in these jokes, then one certainly should not
omit the textile and garment lobby. The success of this group in persuading
government to fund the development of the technical institutes and colleges, the
polytechnics, the Vocational Training Council, the Productivity Council; to exempt
trucks from expensive licensing requirements; and to provide industrial land at a
cheaper price is evidence of the group's enormous influence. In the past, people
joked that the Trade Department's most important job was to administer the textile
and garment quotas. Indeed, the influence of this powerful lobby continues into the
second generation with the appointment of some of their children as Legislative
and Executive Council members.

Although there were other manufacturing industries, none of them had the
political influence and sophistication of the Shanghai textile and garment lobby.
However, these other industrialists also benefited from the successful lobbying of
the textile and garment manufacturers. The policies that they obtained and that the
government was willing to concede did not favor one set of industries over another,
although they were clearly pro-industry.

THE CHANGING FORTUNES OF MANUFACTURING

The first golden era of the textile and garment manufacturers was the 1960s,
when the enormous growth of the young female labor force provided these
labor-intensive industries with its most important support. These workers were the
baby boom generation of the immigrants who had arrived in the immediate postwar
years. By the 1970s, these young women workers had reached their marriage and
maternity years and were withdrawing from the labor force. The problem of labor
shortage was compounded by the first oil shock of 1973. A huge, industrial lobbying
effort emerged. The government finally succumbed to the political pressure and
established a Committee on Industrial Diversification to look into the matter. The
report was issued in 1977 and included recommendations on enhancing productivity and the development of new products and markets. However, it was soon
overtaken by events.

China began to open its economy in 1979. In the span of 18 months between
1980 and 1981 some 400,000 people crossed the border from China into Hong
Kong. The tide was stemmed after the Hong Kong government started to repatriate
immigrants from China. The sudden influx solved Hong Kong's labor shortage
problem literally overnight. As real wages fell, industrial output rebounded. Labor-
intensive manufacturing acquired a new lease on life.

In the 1980s manufacturing both expanded and migrated across the border into
South China. The abundance of low-wage labor there provided the labor-intensive
manufacturing sector with its second golden era. Many firms were able to expand

their production almost 10 times. Huge fortunes were made within a very short span of time. Unfortunately, to the dismay of many women workers who were beginning to return to the labor force in the 1980s after they had completed their childbearing and child rearing years, they were finding that many manufacturing job opportunities were gone, and they were competing against younger workers in China. China's opening occurred at a very opportune time for Hong Kong. It took place at a time when Hong Kong's comparative advantage in labor-intensive manufacturing was ending, but the existing knowledge and skills in operating labor-intensive manufacturing had not yet disappeared or become obsolete.

The predicament of the quota-driven textile and garment industry is particularly interesting. Although Hong Kong was no longer competitive in manufacturing low value-added textile and garment products, the quotas themselves were valuable. To utilize them profitably, it was necessary to import workers. A new lobbying effort to bring in workers from China was supported by business but bitterly opposed by workers. Finding itself caught between two camps, the government tried to strike a middle ground by allowing a limited number of imported workers and required that employers pay imported workers the same wages as those provided to local workers. It is interesting to note that business sector support for imported workers was not limited to the manufacturing sector alone and certainly not to the quota-driven textile and garment industry. A proposal to allow businesses to bid for the quotas was not accepted by government because of the successful lobbying of the textile and garment industries. The proposal, which would result in an efficient allocation of the labor import quotas, did not favor the low value-added textile and garment industries.

THE REEMERGENCE OF INDUSTRY AND TECHNOLOGY POLICY

Although the expansion of labor-intensive industries into China provided a golden opportunity for the growth of Hong Kong manufacturers, the future of manufacturing was not assured. First, the prospects of Hong Kong's old manufacturers in low value-added production operating across the border were not certain. Increasingly, Hong Kong was adding value through servicing manufacturing production in China rather than engaging in production per se. Second, the attempt to upgrade productivity into high value-added production in China was having some major difficulties. The lack of protection for intellectual property rights and the arbitrariness of government behavior in China were deterring investments in R&D and the adoption of high value-added production processes. The problems encountered in managing and retaining key management, technical, and skilled staff and the uncertainties inherent in controlling the production process made it risky to develop knowledge-intensive production in China.

Some new manufacturers were retracing their steps and hoping to return to Hong Kong. Unfortunately, the cost structure in Hong Kong was becoming prohibitive. The opening of China had fundamentally transformed Hong Kong's economic structure. Today, less than 10% of GDP and employment is still classified as manufacturing. Some of it is not really manufacturing but simply a statistical artifact of the classification system. Labor costs are expensive, and although a large proportion of students continue to study science and engineering subjects in the schools and universities, few of them aspire to work in manufacturing. Furthermore, housing costs are so expensive that hardly any foreign companies have an interest in investing in manufacturing in Hong Kong.

Nevertheless, manufacturers with an interest in high value-added processes have continued to press the government to develop industrial estates, science parks, and funding to support applied research. Their efforts are also supported by the universities, which probably would benefit from additional research grants. The Industry and Technology Development Council is now distributing more funding for such purposes, although the amounts are still quite modest by the standards of most industrialized countries and those in the East Asia region. It is interesting to note that the funding actually is provided to very specific projects with a well-defined problem or application. As a consequence some "picking of winners" is inevitable, but the effect will be limited by the funding that is available. The government has also announced the establishment of a new Informational Technology Bureau for the purpose of promoting and coordinating the use and development of information technology in the territory.

The Industry Department is now believed to be willing to accommodate the proposal to establish a government credit guarantee fund to support small and medium-size enterprises to be administered by the banks. This idea would not have been entertained in the past but is finding favor with the current administration, perhaps as a concession to business to demonstrate that the government is supporting industry. The funds to be made available will be limited.

THE FUTURE OF INDUSTRIAL POLICY

Our discussion of Hong Kong's past reveals that government has on the whole been reluctant to take an active role in formulating an industrial and technology policy. In particular there is no policy that is explicitly discriminatory in developing selective or strategic industries. This is not to say that the government has not adopted policies that have favored industries as a whole over other nonindustrial sectors. But these policies are primarily focused on providing human capital formation, land resources, information dissemination, and, to a lesser extent, selective funding for research and development. At no time were credit policies and fiscal measures used to support industries either generally or selectively.

These industry support policies were put in place largely as a result of intense and effective lobbying from industry interests rather than the product of government proactive initiatives. They are best described as the reluctant but politically necessary concessions that the administration had to undertake to accommodate the clamor of vocal and powerful vested interests.

The future of industry and technology policy depends on a number of factors. The new Special Administrative Region government that came into office on July 1, 1997, is likely to be, by inclination, more explicitly pro-business than previous administrations. The legislature is likely to be more representative of organized business interests, but the difference today is that instead of being appointed members, the organized business interests will be elected through functional constituencies and by an electoral college. They are, therefore, likely to be more entrenched than under the British administration. The government may, therefore, be more sympathetic to business lobbying interests, including both old and new manufacturing interests.

The restoration of sovereignty over Hong Kong from Britain to China is unlikely to have a major impact on industrial policy. It may, however, speed up the coordination of cross-border movement of goods and people and the development of large infrastructure projects that were neglected in the previous years due to political quarrels between the British and Chinese governments. These issues are not directly industrial policy, as traditionally understood. But resolution of these questions could have a significant effect on further integration of the Chinese hinterland as a manufacturing base of Hong Kong. If this occurs, it would be another significant boost for Hong Kong's manufacturing sector.

Fears that China will interfere in Hong Kong's economic affairs have not materialized. The fact that many old industrialists from Hong Kong have cultivated the Chinese leadership probably reflects the political savvy of these people in hedging their bets rather than a sign of the Chinese leadership's inclination to interfere in Hong Kong's industrial policy.

Despite Hong Kong's growing penchant to flirt with industrial and technology policy, the main thrust of that policy is likely to be sector-neutral. Measures that are likely to be nonneutral and selective are unlikely to be widely adopted with any major commitment of resources. The Hong Kong government is poorly equipped to intervene with the market process on a large scale simply because it does not command the resources necessary to do so. A low tax rate makes it difficult to finance large recurrent spending for industrial policy in an era where there are powerful competing social demands for scarce budgetary resources. The huge reserves accumulated by the government are largely derived from land-related revenue, which had increased enormously as a result of asset price inflation in the past decade. It is unlikely that future recurrent spending will be financed by such one-time revenue increases. Furthermore, the currency crises in a number of countries in Asia this year and the recent speculative attacks against the Hong Kong dollar will give government a compelling reason to keep its reserves out of reach.

As Hong Kong's economy is already dominated by the service sector, the competing demands for government attention will inevitably neutralize the lobbying efforts of the industrialists. The Industry Support Fund is now no longer the only fund the government has financed. A separate and new Services Support Fund had already been established and is functioning. The importance of technology is not perceived primarily as an industrial concern but affects all sectors. For this reason, it is quite likely that although the commitment to a laissez-faire economic policy will be weakened, it is unlikely to be abandoned entirely by government. It will still be the last line of defense of a government that must hold the interest groups in abeyance, is limited in its ability to intervene because of fiscal restraints, and has to demonstrate its ability to maintain prosperity and stability to a highly mobile population and investors that could leave at will if government becomes too interventionist.

11

Economic Policy in Thailand: Some Successes and Some Failures

Mingsarn Kaosa-ard

In the early 1990s, Thailand, along with seven other countries, was hailed as an Asian miracle. By 1996, Thailand started to encounter a balance of payments deficit, followed by successive revelations of financial plight, leading to massive foreign exchange outflows. Finally, the Thai government decided to convert the fixed exchange rate to a managed float system and announced that real growth, which used to be 7–10%, would not exceed 1% in 1997. In less than six months, Asia's fifth Tiger had turned into a sick cat. Since then conditions have worsened, so that the decline in 1998 was almost 7 percent.

This chapter traces the weaknesses underlying the real sectors of the Thai economy and examines public policies for industry, natural resources, tourism, and the environment. The chapter begins with an overview of Thailand's development, followed by an analysis of the fundamental conditions of the country's progress. The final section explores elements underlying the systematic breakdown of institutional maintenance in Thailand.

THE THAI ECONOMY

Thailand's transformation from an agriculturally dominant structure to an industrially dominant one became statistically apparent in 1981, when for the first time the value-added from manufacturing surpassed that of agriculture. In 1985, the value of manufactured exports started to exceed that of agriculture, and since that point, manufacturing exports have been accelerating. From 1988 to 1993, the average growth rate of the manufacturing sector was as high as 14% annually, and from 1988 to 1990, Thailand registered double-digit growth. In 1994, the value-added of the manufacturing sector accounted for 28.5% of gross domestic product

(GDP), and the value of manufacturing exports accounted for 80% of the total export value. The expansion of industrial exports was an important feature of Thailand's economic change, and the industrial sector took on a leading role in generating substantial exchange earnings for the Thai economy.

The first period of industrialization in Thailand (1970–1979) can be characterized as import substitution. The 1980s witnessed Thai industrialization becoming more export-oriented. There have also been structural changes within subsectors of manufacturing. During the early stage of industrialization, consumer goods had a high market share. Later, the market share of food industries declined noticeably and gave way to textiles and garments. Industries that expanded rapidly between 1987 and 1993 included automobile parts, machinery, electrical components, hide products, basic metal products, preserved and canned food, textiles and clothing, and, finally, gems and jewelry. Rapid expansion was not limited to export-oriented industries; mining-related industries, especially in areas related to construction, also grew at a high rate to meet expanding domestic demand. Industries that grew at lower rates were basic industries such as timber and timber products, tobacco, food, and beverages.

Toward the end of the 1990s, the growth and the competitiveness of the export sectors, in particular, food-based sectors, started to slow down. Manufactured exports, which accounted for 25% of real GDP growth in the early 1980s, was reduced to 11% by 1989–1990. Between 1991 and 1993, the overall industrial growth performance subsided for most industries. The few industries whose growth rates continued to increase were automobile parts, electrical components, basic metal products, and petroleum products.

A factor that effected a change in the structure of Thailand's industrialization was foreign investment. Although the country has a long history of foreign investment, foreign investment in Thailand and South Korea was considered among the lowest in Asia-Pacific countries until 1985. Following the yen's appreciation in 1985, foreign investment in Thailand rose rapidly due to the relocation of Japanese production plants (later, Taiwan and Hong Kong plants would also move). In 1987, Japanese investment in promoted sectors exceeded cumulative investment from the previous 20 years. In particular, Japanese investment has provided the technical foundation for Thai industries with respect to the automobile parts industry and the electronics industry, among others. It is worth noting, however, that the shift to highly capital-intensive industries (such as the iron, steel, and petrochemical industries in the 1990s) was mainly driven by local investment. Domestic investment was made possible by the liberalization of local capital markets and by heavy borrowing from overseas banks by Thai private firms.

Thailand's economic structure remains highly unbalanced. This is for a number of reasons. First, Thailand's economic growth initially centered around the primary city of Bangkok. In 1990, the population of Bangkok still accounted for as much as 57% of the country's urban population, compared to 31% in other developing countries with a similar economic performance. The rapid expansion of the city has created several problems, such as overcrowding, traffic congestion, and a deteriorating urban environment. These problems have consumed much of the government's budget, which otherwise could have been allocated to poverty-stricken areas or other more productive uses.

Second, although the industrial sector generated high income for the economy, this did not translate into employment opportunities for the Thai labor force. Although the agricultural sector generates substantially less income, it employs a much larger proportion of the labor force. In 1996, agriculture contributed only 12.8% to GDP, yet this sector absorbed as much as 53% of the country's total labor force. Thailand's attempts to decentralize industries have had limited success. Until only recently, many industrial activities remained in close proximity to the Bangkok Metropolitan Area (BMA) and the eastern region and extended only 200 kilometers toward the western region.

Third, expectations of sustained growth and increasing land scarcity in the late 1980s and early 1990s created an explosive boom in the land and securities markets, sharply boosting land prices and salaries of white-collar workers in real estate and the financial sectors. Wages for blue-collar workers also increased but not to the same extent as those of white-collar workers.

Finally, until the 1980s, the growth of the economy was largely nature-based and relied heavily on land and marine resources. These resources were depleted rapidly.

An important implication of these changes is that the agricultural sector experienced "Dutch disease" effects, that is, resource outflows to the more lucrative nontraded sectors such as real estate and securities. As a result, both agriculture and agricultural-based sectors (the main pillars of the Thai economy) were substantially weakened. Compounding this problem is inadequate human resource development, which has proven to be a major obstacle hindering Thailand's move into high-technology industries.

International Trade

Exports have been the engine of economic growth in Thailand. The five main manufacturing exports that were the driving force of the Thai economy between 1984 to 1987 were canned food, textiles, leather products, machinery, and electrical products. These sectors contributed to three-quarters of total economic growth during the period, although toward the end they began to display signs that they were losing steam.

From 1987 to 1993, Thailand, Indonesia, and Malaysia had the highest industrial growth rates in the Asia-Pacific Rim. During this period, these countries experienced similar growth in manufactured exports: 28% for Thailand, 29% for Indonesia, and 30% for Malaysia. Thai exporters have increasingly faced international competition, especially following China and Vietnam's vigorous entries into the world market. In early 1996, the Thai export sector began to display troubling signs; for instance, in the first and second quarters export growth was negative. This downturn triggered concern among investors and eventually led to capital flight.

Competitiveness

A study on Thailand's revealed comparative advantage (RCA), using data collected for the period 1990–1995, provided early warnings that Thailand was becoming less competitive in a number of export industries. These industries included processed canned seafood (of which Thailand is the world's biggest supplier), preserved fruits and vegetables, garments, leather products, rubber products, electrical machinery, and domestic appliances. The study indicated that the competitiveness of 13 out of 20 textile and garment products declined between 1990 and 1993.

Trade Agreements

In 1994, Thailand's tariff rates averaged approximately 17.7%, a level lower than the World Trade Organization (WTO) requirements. For this reason, the WTO agreement on tariff reductions will not have any significant effects on Thailand's tariff structure (which in turn affects the country's industrialization process). On the other hand, the ASEAN (Association of South East Asian Nations) Free Trade Area (AFTA) agreement is expected to impact the structure of Thailand's industries to a greater extent than the WTO agreement, since the average tariff rate of Thailand is higher than the rates of other ASEAN countries. For instance, Indonesian tariff rates average around 11.6%, and the Philippines rates average at 6.7%, as compared to Thailand's average of 14.2% in 1997. Under the AFTA agreement, by the year 2000, Thailand's overall tariff rates must be reduced by 50%, leaving the tariff rate for the manufacturing sector at an average of 9.0%. In this regard, it is imperative that the Thai industrial sector regains its comparative advantage by increasing skilled labor and by improving efficiency in important industries such as automobile parts and electronics. Basic industries, such as the petrochemical and steel industries, must also be strengthened. In addition, there should be a reallocation of resources away from industries that are losing their comparative advantage toward new and competitive opportunities.

TOURISM BOOM

The period 1987–1996 can be termed the golden decade of Thai tourism. The number of foreign tourists increased from 2.6 million in 1987 to 7 million arrivals in 1995. This number is projected to increase to 9.6 million arrivals in 2000 and will continue rising to 11.2 million arrivals by 2003, representing approximately 1% of the world's total arrivals. This indicates that Thailand has ample opportunities to attract additional new arrivals and expand its market. Thailand's foreign exchange earnings from international tourism in 1995 were approximately 14% of total export earnings and 49% of the total income from the service sector. The foreign exchange income from international tourism has been greater than the country's top-ranking manufactured exports, including garments, computer components and equipment, rice, jewelry, and plastic products.

Tourism products are composite products, comprising a bundle of goods and services from three major areas: tourist attractions, general services used by tourists (or the "industry component"), and services provided by the government. Attractions include nature-based and historical tourism resources, culture, local cuisine, and the availability and quality of shopping. Government management consists of the provision and management of infrastructure, sanitation, safety and other travel-related services such as visa issuance, immigration, customs, and so on. The industry component includes transportation, accommodation, catering, guide services, and so on.

All components must be taken into account when evaluating the competitiveness of tourism. In September 1996, a Thailand Development Research Institute (TDRI) survey was conducted that included 389 international tourists and 45 international travel agencies. The purpose of the survey was to rank Thailand in comparison with its competitors in the Asia-Pacific region in terms of the three components explained earlier. The survey illustrated that, in terms of overall appeal and efficiency, foreign tourists ranked Thailand third (preceded by Australia and Japan and followed by Singapore and Indonesia). Tourist agencies, however, ranked Thailand as second only to Australia. Among the 12 items listed under attractions, Thailand was ranked the highest in five categories: historical sites, culture, people, food, and nightlife.

An evaluation of government management revealed it as a major obstacle to a sustained tourism boom. Apart from visa applications, Thailand ranked low in several aspects of government management, including entry services (such as immigration and customs service) to the broader management of infrastructure (inter- and intracountry communications, urban traffic, health, and sanitation). Among the areas that need the greatest improvements are Bangkok's traffic congestion, pollution control, and tourist safety. It can be concluded from these results that government management is the major constraint to further expansion of tourism. Sector projects, such as the Eastern and Southern Seaboard, which support manufacturing industries, have slowly penetrated those areas considered to be prime locations for tourism. In addition to environmental stress, rapidly increasing demand for tourism also competes for infrastructure improvement funding.

Natural resources and the environment are strained not only because they are used as production inputs for the tourism industry but also because they must absorb the outputs from industry. Despite the impressive evaluation of Thailand's tourism competitiveness, there are clear warning signs that Thailand's tourism resources are overstressed. A study by the Tourism Authority of Thailand (TAT) revealed that 172 tourist sites in 49 provinces are in critical condition and in urgent need of restoration. This is additional evidence in support of the argument that tourism problems in Thailand are the result of supply stress, not demand shortage.

NATURAL RESOURCES AND THE ENVIRONMENT

The change in the structure of industrialization from agricultural processing (or simple production) to large-scale production (involving sophisticated technology) has led to an increase in industrial pollution and hazardous wastes. For example, a joint study by the Department of Industry and the Department of Pollution Control indicated that, at present, Thailand has more than 1 million tons of industrial hazardous waste, and it is expected that this will increase to nearly 3 million tons in the next five years. Currently, the hazardous waste treatment facility (originally, a pioneer project) can process only 10–15% of the total amount of hazardous waste produced. The remaining untreated waste is stored in factories or released into waterways or the atmosphere or dumped in forest reserves.

Thailand's economic development has relied heavily on the accelerated depletion of its valuable natural resources and on treating the environment as a waste sink. Water and air pollution increasingly requires attention, as well as a sizable budget. A study by the Asian Development Bank reported that by the year 2000, the amount of pollution in Thailand will be 2.5 times 1990 levels, resulting in a situation where Thailand's pollution problems exceed those of every other Asian country, with the exception of South Korea.

PLANNING AND POLICY MAKING IN THAILAND

To understand policymaking in Thailand, one has to first understand political development in Thailand. Up until 1992, the Thai political regime evolved from authoritarianism and military control, through various periods of "semidemocratic" regimes (for example, Prem's 1980–1988 term as a nonelected prime minister leading an elected Parliament). Since 1992, Thailand could be described as a fully democratic system, with a rural-based, elected government, that is, elected and installed by the rural population. Ministers are largely parliamentarians from various provinces who think locally, rather than nationally (let alone internationally). The influence of primarily Western-trained economic technocrats varied under different political regimes. Their glory days were those under the Prem and Anand (1991–1992) governments.

Public policies in Thailand are manifested in national and sectoral plans. The major function of the national plan by the National Economic and Social Development Board (NESDB) is to provide a reference for budgetary purposes; subsequently, each ministry develops its own plan in accordance with this national plan. Government projects will be approved by the Bureau of the Budget if they are consistent with the national plan. Generally, national and sectoral plans do not set priorities according to cost-benefit estimates, nor do they take into account budget constraints. After the plans have been translated into investment programs and projects, the Bureau of the Budget will consider them in the context of resource constraints. As a result, all ministries tend to include as many ideas as possible in the plans. Moreover, the national plan is ineffective with regard to policies and projects involving government spending. National plans are generally ineffective at providing guidelines for institutional reform, such as the implementation of the polluter-pays principle and the innovative uses of economic instruments, for example, taxes or charges.

In the early 1990s, national planning evolved into a more people-centered, rather than project-oriented approach. The eighth national plan is indicative of this viewpoint. Line ministries resorted to more and more sectoral planning, which, if approved by the Cabinet, can also be used as a budget reference. In addition, sectoral master plans are also used to divide responsibilities (and also the cake) of involved agencies, both in the public and the private sector. The telecommunication master plan is a case in point.

Another important feature of Thai policymaking is that legislation supporting each line minister is usually brief and vague and bestows substantial discretionary powers to the ministers via ministerial regulations and, in particular, notifications (notifications being the actual means for policy implementation). The parliamentarians' incentive is therefore to hold executive posts in these ministries rather than to legislate.

INSTITUTIONAL FAILURES: CASE STUDIES

Macroeconomic Policies

Until 1996, Thailand's success in stimulating growth while maintaining stability was attributed to its prudent macroeconomic management. The country had nine years of fiscal surplus, and public debt was only 15% of GDP (1977), making Thailand one of the least publicly indebted countries in the world (TDRI, 1997).

The macroeconomic management of Thailand was generally conservative. Yet in 1993, the Finance Ministry made a bold move and opened the Bangkok International Banking Facility (BIBF) in the hopes of promoting Thailand as another financial center of Southeast Asia. Foreign, low-interest loans poured into Thai financial intermediaries, who busily dished out loans to local investors without proper project feasibility and risk assessments. Many of these loans went to the bubbly real estate sector and the securities sector. Finally, when export stagnation triggered a warning sign to international creditors, the real estate sector was the first to collapse, followed by their financial backers. The economic meltdown followed.

The economic turmoil that ensued was not simply the result of policy failures. It was the result of a breakdown in the institution that governs macroeconomic management. The existing macropolicy institution is a legacy from a major reform in 1958. Macroeconomic policies are managed by four agencies: the NESDB and the Bureau of the Budget, both under the Prime Minister's Office; the Ministry of Finance; and lastly, the Bank of Thailand. Until recently, these four agencies were armed by a corps of highly competent, Western-trained economists known as "the technocrats."

Until the mid-1990s, macroeconomic policies were left in the hands of the technocrats in the four agencies. The sectoral policies (i.e., the line ministers' policies) were the playing field of ministers who wished to distribute rent among their own factions, constituents, and, in all likelihood, their own pockets. Following 1994, political ministers started to make their presence felt in both the Ministry of Finance and the Bank of Thailand. The most outstanding indication of their influence is the Bank of Thailand's reluctance to devalue the baht in 1997, out of fear of political repercussion (TDRI, 1997).

The decline of the quality of the technocrats owing to brain drain into the private sector during the boom years was thought to be key to the penetration of the patronage system into these core agencies. Although this explanation may describe what happened in three of the agencies, it is not applicable for the Bank of Thailand. The bank's remuneration system was far above that of the civil service, and it has been able to retain high-quality staff. In the bank's case, an outdated management structure—it was designed in the early 1960s—grants a very high level of power and autonomy to the governor. This may have been appropriate during the period of human resource scarcity, but it has become untenable in the 1990s, when a cadre of equally competent officers is now available (TDRI, 1997). Intense competition for top jobs eventually invited factionalism and patronage from the politicians who had finally reached the Bank of Thailand through the Ministry of Finance.

Industrial Policies

Thailand does not have industrial targeting or pick-the-winner policies. The industrial sector of Thailand has been primarily shaped by the nation's trade tax regimes (tariffs and export taxes mainly on agricultural products) and various sectoral policies, for example, capacity controls, local content requirements, and so on.

Industrial policy in Thailand can be described as moving toward a lesser degree of market distortion for a number of reasons. First, tariff policy is the responsibility of the Ministry of Finance, which until recently had not been manipulated by executive decisions. Second, important sectoral policies, especially capacity control, were abolished under the Anand governments. Third, a freer trade regime is required by WTO and AFTA. Finally, after decades of academic attacks, the case against arguments supporting infant industry has perhaps received some respect from ruling technocrats.

Natural Resources and Environmental Policies

Natural resource and environmental policies are areas where interventions from executive decisions are severely intensive. This renders law enforcement weak. On a positive note, Thailand's electoral boundary was small enough to allow local patrons to enter national politics. These influential people tend to have a substantial stake in their local natural resources, and gaining political power at the national level allows them to change the rules of the game, as well as the rule keepers. One example of negative national influence outside local areas occurred with a land scandal whereby land that had previously been a forest reserve was transferred to an urban millionaire, although under the law only farmers were legally eligible. Legal cases on converting public land are often related to politically influential people. Another incident occurred in 1997, when an environmental tax on granite production was quickly dropped because it would have affected the constituents of one of the government's coalition parties. Thus, environmental protection policies that conflict with interest groups are often not implemented and remain only on paper.

Tourism Policy

For almost a century, tourism policy in Thailand has emphasized expanding the number of foreign tourists visiting the country through aggressive international advertising campaigns. This policy exists despite the fact that tourism problems in recent years have been the result of excess demand on resources. Tourism policy is an area that, to date, has not been greatly affected by executive decisions. One major reason for this is the small government budget involved. Much of the tourism budget is utilized for promotional purposes overseas. This occurred because higher-level government officials incorrectly perceived tourism in Thailand as suffering from demand problems. The new tourism master plan approved by the Cabinet in 1997 includes budget requests for the rehabilitation of tourism sites in the provinces. However, owing to budget constraints, the budget package has been postponed until the present fiscal situation improves.

FINAL REMARKS

In the late 1980s, the Thai economy evolved to the stage where growth could not be sustained without a substantial injection into the accumulation of new productive capital for the purpose of overcoming natural capital depletion. Instead, massive capital, both domestic and borrowed, was poured into speculative sectors. During the same period, brain drain from the public sector rapidly weakened administrative capacities. Political developments, which fostered links between the administrative and business sectors, brought about changes in the rules of the game, which resulted in management's favoring more opportunistic groups. The public sector brain drain shook not only management's ability but also its integrity. Moreover, frequent changes in the ministerial portfolios forced the relatively uninformed government to concentrate on addressing emergencies and short-term problems, rather than formulating a long-term vision and undertaking structural and preventive changes. Policy decisions are often made without sufficient and solid studies supporting them. The breakdown of governing institutions observed in the natural resource and environment sector finally reached the financial sector, and, as a result, financial crises are occurring one after another, and the economy dives deeper and deeper.

Until the current political system is reformed, Thailand has little hope of remedying its economic ills and implementing sensible public policies. Meanwhile, the only mechanism at work is the reduction of real wages, which, if occurring rapidly and to a large enough degree, will eventually stimulate the export sector.

REFERENCES

Mingsarn Kaosa-ard, et al. (1997a). *Thailand's Industrial Master Plan.* Bangkok: TDRI.
————. (1997b). *Thailand's Tourism Master Plan.* Bangkok: TDRI.
TDRI (Thailand Development Research Institute). (1997). *Thailand's Boom and Bust.* Bangkok: TDRI.

12

Economic Development and Malaysian Public Policies

Azmi Setapa and Shigeyuki Abe

Until the recent currency crisis, Malaysia represented one of the success stories of East Asia. Initially dependent on primary commodities, Malaysia has transformed itself into a modern industrial economy with high value-added output. Since independence in 1957, Malaysian public policy has endeavored to promote industrialization along with overarching ethnic equity objectives. Flexible policy has enabled Malaysia for many years to achieve its objectives of growth and equity, but these gains are now called into question. The contagion of the Asian currency crisis hit Malaysia in 1997 and has caused economic and political difficulties. To deal with the crisis, the government, which had relaxed foreign capital controls in 1986, recently announced a policy of restricting foreign capital and fixing the exchange rate. This policy approach contrasts sharply with the recommendations of the IMF and with policies instituted elsewhere in East Asia.

This chapter discusses Malaysian public policy in relation to its philosophy, background, issues, and objectives. We consider the basis for Malaysia's long period of expansion and the issues and policy responses during the current crisis. We hope that this analysis will shed some light on the future direction of the Malaysian public policy by reviewing development policies from a consistent perspective.

BASIC PHILOSOPHY OF MALAYSIAN PUBLIC POLICY

Malaysian public policy is based on economic, social, and political issues that are particularly important and sensitive in a multiracial society. The broad objective of Malaysian public policy is to strengthen ethnic unity and to maintain social stability so that national development policies can be effective to reach high and equitable economic growth.

The basic premise for formulating public policy in Malaysia is the issue of ethnicity. Ethnic inequality exists in Malaysian society due to income disparity between *bumiputras* (Malays and other indigenous people) and *non-bumiputras* (Chinese and Indian). Although other factors such as religion and cultural differences exist, the economic factor is the most significant in the Malaysian context. *Bumiputras*, particularly the Malays, constitute 55% of the total population. They are mostly farmers in the agriculture sector and live in the rural areas. Many Malays fear that their economic backwardness will eventually lead to *non-bumiputras'* taking political control of the country. Thus, the governing party, the National Front, which has representation from the three major races in Malaysia—Malays, Chinese, and Indians—believes that the ethnic inequality issue must be overcome to ensure long-term social stability. Other issues such as education also fall within the ethnic inequality issue since the majority of *bumiputras* possess a very low level of education. Similarly, regional development is another factor since most of the *bumiputras* live in rural areas, whereas most of the *non-bumiputras* live in towns. The formulation of public policy must address the development issue in a multi-ethnic context.

The philosophy behind Malaysian public policy begins with the relationship between social stability and economic prosperity. It is well accepted that social stability is a prerequisite for economic prosperity. Many believe that, in turn, economic prosperity and stable economic growth strongly influence social stability. There are clearly also other forces involved—many cultural and social issues do not have a clear connection with economic development. These could be tackled by other policies such as an education policy. But, in economic policy, the Malaysian government has emphasized the linkage between social stability and economic prosperity as a central tenet of policy formulation.

THE ROLE OF THE GOVERNMENT

The public sector has played an important role in Malaysia's economic development. The percentage of the public sector expenditure (PSE) to GNP increased steadily until the mid-1980s and declined sharply afterward (Table 12.1). The high percentage of the PSE to GNP indicated strong government involvement in the economy until the mid-1980s. This involvement was important particularly at the early stage of development, where the private sector was not fully developed. For instance, in the 1960s and 1970s considerable government expenditure was required for basic infrastructure facilities. At the early stage of development, the economy was constrained by a very weak private sector. The government provided infrastructure facilities and also other services such as financing, business, and so on that otherwise could have been carried out by the private sector. Thus, it was the task of the government at the early stage of development to provide facilities for

Table 12.1
The Growth of Government

Year	PSE (RM million)	PSE/GNP (%)
1970	3,568	29.3
1975	8,652	40.0
1980	24,340	47.4
1985	31,482	43.8
1990	47,933	43.2
1995	50,624	24.3
1996	58,493	24.5

Note: PSE refers to public-sector expernditure.

the development of the private sector. For this purpose, government had to carry out many education, training, and business programs.

Government involvement was also necessary at that time because of social market failures. With sharp income inequality in a multiethnic society like Malaysia, ethnic integration was at risk. The government was placed under tremendous pressure to enhance ethnic integration after the 1969 riot. This event forced the government to implement the New Economic Policy (NEP) in 1971. The government's involvement in the economy declined sharply from 1985 onward. This was due to large budget deficits from 1981 to 1984 because of falling commodity prices that brought the Malaysian economy into a recession. This budget pressure influenced the government to introduce the privatization policy in 1983.

The privatization policy implicitly indicated the government's desire to reduce its role in the economy. It marked a change in the role of the government, the engine of growth in the 1960s and 1970s, to a minimum level. From 1983 onward, the private sector became the engine of growth.

Besides reducing the government's budgetary burden, privatization was intended to improve economic efficiency and productivity. Many analysts doubted the positive influence of privatization on productivity and efficiency, though the government claimed many improvements had been made. One clear obstacle to improving efficiency and productivity is the lack of competition in privatized markets. Unless the government introduces more competitors, privatization may not be consistent with the central free market premise that competition brings about efficiency.

THE DEVELOPMENT PLANS

Malaysia has drawn up and implemented many development plans. Like other developing countries, Malaysia adopted import-substitution of consumer goods in the initial industrialization effort of the First Malaysian Plan, 1966 to 1970. Malaysia then established a number of free trade zones (FTZs) while keeping traditional import-substitution. Export promotion along with a traditional import-substitution policy can be called a "dual industrialization" approach. In the 1980s, Malaysia extended import-substitution to include some heavy industries. Government-led projects included automobile, steel, aluminum refining, and so on. The national car, Proton SAGA, is the most famous project of this period.

The most famous plan is the New Economic Policy, which was launched in 1970. This plan is unique in its emphasis on distribution issues. The attempt to redress economic differences between ethnic groups will be discussed at greater length later.

In the mid-1980s, Malaysia first experienced a brief period of negative growth due to the collapse of primary product prices: oil, rubber, and tin. At this time, Malaysia changed its policy stance to put greater emphasis on growth than on distribution. The first Industrial Master Plan (IMP) was issued around this time. The Fifth and Sixth Malaysian Plans implemented the IMP. As a result of this policy change the Malaysian economy grew at an average annual rate of more than 8% for nine years from 1988. The ratio of manufacturing to GDP jumped sharply. The most recent plan, the Seventh Plan, introduced *cluster-based industrial development*. This plan aims at productivity growth and quality improvement. A number of *megaprojects* were also initiated.

New Economic Policy

The philosophy behind the NEP was economic efficiency leading to high economic growth and a distribution of resources that could lead to equity among the different ethnic groups. Thus, the broad and long-term objective of the NEP was "growth and equity." More specifically, the objectives of NEP were as follows:

—to eradicate poverty

—to accelerate the process of restructuring the society so as to eliminate the identification of races based on economic functions

The second objective had two aspects. First, employment was to be restructured by sector and occupation, eliminating the "ethnic division of labor" that had been created during colonial times. Second, the ownership and control of wealth were to be restructured. Specifically, Malays were to hold 30% of corporate sector assets in 1990.

While the NEP concentrated on the racial economic imbalance, it alluded to more general goals. The process involved the modernization of rural life, rapid and balanced growth of urban activities, and the creation of a *bumiputra* commercial and industrial community in all categories and at all levels of operations, so that Malays and other indigenous people would become full partners in all aspects of the economic life of the nation.

All NEP goals were to be reached in the context of economic growth. No one was to suffer any loss of a job, income, or business, although, obviously, some loss of opportunities to improve one's job or increase one's income or business was implicit in the redistribution plan.

National Development Policy (NDP) and the IMP-2

The NEP expired in 1990. Even before this expiration date, a liberalization policy on investment and business had already started in 1986, though, to a certain extent, this policy threatened the full achievement of the NEP targets. The National Development Policy (NDP) was introduced in 1991 based on the 1986 liberalization policy. The emphasis on the *bumiputra* economic development was retained, but the NDP included none of the specific redistribution and restructuring targets that characterized the NEP. The general goal of the NDP was to turn Malaysia into a fully developed nation by the year 2020. This plan is also known as Wawasan (Vision) 2020. Relative to the NEP, the NDP was much more in line with the free market, where things move based on the efficiency principle, and less dependent on subsidies. In other words, the government was gradually reducing protection for *bumiptras* and leading them into a freer competition.

The NDP establishes some fundamental targets. Malaysia's objective is to grow over 7% for the entire 30 years of the plan, which assures an eight-times larger GDP. The objective is to extend Japan's doubling income plan for 30 years. As part of its development initiatives, in 1996 Malaysia announced a Multimedia Super Corridor (MSC) plan. This plan is to connect Cyberjaya, which is the core of MSC and to be completed by 2005; Putrajaya, which is a new administrative capital city to be completed by 2000; Kuala Lumpur; and a new international airport by optic fibers. By providing this modern infrastructure, Malaysia plans "Seven Flagship Applications." They are electronic government, telemedicine, R&D clusters, worldwide manufacturing web, borderless marketing centers, national multipurpose card, and smart schools.

The Seventh Malaysian Plan and the Industrial Master Plan 2 (IMP-2) started in 1996. Malaysia planned to upgrade its industrial structure and to join the group of industrial countries by 2020. IMP-2 emphasizes the MSC and the development of information technology as key to this end. The construction of MSC hinges upon how to finance its enormous budget and how to secure the assistance and siting in Malaysia of information technology-oriented multinational corporations (MNCs).

RECENT DEVELOPMENTS

Recent developments have raised serious questions about Malaysian prospects and policies. The success of Malaysian policies of rapid growth with equity was already threatened before the advent of the 1997 crisis. Malaysia grew at a very high rate in a compressed period of time. This brought labor shortages and wage increases. Managerial people and technicians, in particular, were in short supply. At the present time, we can observe that multinational corporations are shifting their production sites from Malaysia to other countries. Some of the world's leading MNCs, including Philllips (Netherlands), Matsushita Panasonic (Japan), and Inventic (Taiwan) have shifted their production lines to China and Indonesia in face of rising wages and for other reasons.[1] Moreover, Malaysia has depended on foreign labor. Dirty work, including construction and plantation labor, has been carried out by foreign workers.[2] With acutely increasing wages and shortages of labor, new industries such as electronics might draw on foreign labor in the future. This might cause another racial problem and might give most of the technology transfers to foreign workers, contrary to the initial objective of enhancing Malaysia's indigenous human capital.

In 1997, the currency crises brought contagion effects and some political unrest in 1998. Let us briefly discuss the chronology of the Malaysian policy after the crisis. Thailand's devaluation of the baht triggered a financial crisis. In September, Malaysia called for speculative currency trading to be outlawed. In December 1997 an austerity package was announced. This was an 18% cut in government spending, higher interest rates, and a cutback in lending. This caused a liquidity squeeze that flared into recession. In May 1998 it was revealed that Malaysia's economy shrank by 2.8% in the first quarter, and, further, in August the economy contracted by 6.8% in the second quarter. A number of mega pipeline and new airport projects were halted due to the bad economic climate, though others seem to be still under way. On September 1, 1998, Malaysia imposed a wide array of capital controls to insulate the country's economy from foreign attacks and fixed the currency at 3.8 ringgit to the U.S. dollar. Subsequently, responding to political pressures, the Central Bank reduced interest rates and provided much needed liquidity.

It is not clear at this point in which direction Malaysia is going. In the past there have been big swings in policy stance, but the current one is one of the biggest, and it is a swing back from liberalization and globalization to isolation and restriction.

EVALUATION AND TENTATIVE CONCLUSION

What judgments can one reach with regard to the success of Malaysian development policies?

In 1970, 49.3% of the Malaysian population was categorized as poor. Official estimates for 1990 recorded that the poverty rate had declined to 15%. Unpublished research carried out by Ishak Shauri from the National University of Malaysia found that urban poverty had been virtually eliminated, and rural poverty is shrinking rapidly in Peninsular Malaysia, mainly because of growing opportunities for nonagricultural work. However, the latest report by the Economic Planning Unit revealed that although poverty has declined sharply, the income distribution as shown by the Gini coefficient had worsened. The NEP was successful in restructuring the employment sector. The number of *bumiputras* (Malays and other indigenous people) in the industrial sector had increased sharply from 173,000 in 1970 to 918,000 in 1990. In the services industry, the involvement of *bumiputras* had also increased from only 213,000 in 1970 to 1.2 million in 1990. However, if the employment structure is divided according to position held, the *bumiputras'* involvement at high-level positions is still not adequate. The NEP was also quite close to its target of restructuring corporate ownership. *Bumiputra* ownership had increased sharply from 2.4% in 1970 to 20.3% in 1990. Although this achievement was below the targeted level of 30%, no doubt this is still a significant achievement and successfully laid a strong foundation for *bumiputras* to enter a freer business world. It is worth noting that the ownership of *non-bumiputras* also increased, from 32.3% in 1970 to 46.2% in 1990. Thus, there was a sharp decline of foreign ownership from 63.3% in 1970 to only 25.1% in 1990.

Regional economic integration can be clearly seen where economic dualism declined sharply because of better infrastructure development. The rural areas became integrated into modern Malaysian society. The dual economy also diminished due to intensive education, training, and industrial programs carried out in the rural areas.

Malaysia also was successful in transforming the quality of life of its population. The Human Development Index (HDI), developed by the United Nations Development Program, ranked Malaysia at fourth place in terms of its improvement in the HDI, which is calculated based on several factors such as level of education, life expectancy, and health services.

Racial dissatisfaction is diminishing sharply with the adoption of more open and liberal public policies. The modern *bumiputra* community is quite capable, and most of them no longer require subsidies and protection to excel in business.

The Malaysian economy is undergoing a rapid structural shift. From an agricultural economy, which exposed to fluctuations in commodity prices, Malaysia has changed its economy into a modern one depending largely on manufacturing exports. The contribution of agriculture to GDP fell from 31% in 1970 to only 19% in 1990. Presently, the agriculture sector contributes only 11.3% to total GDP. The contribution of manufacturing to GDP rose from 13.4% in 1970 to 26.9% in 1990. Presently, the manufacturing sector contributes 37% to total GDP. The number of farmers declined sharply from 50% of the population in 1970 to only 25% in 1990.

Over the years, as the emphasis shifted back and forth from distribution to growth and from control to liberalization to reflect economic conditions, Malaysian economic management has been quite successful. A strong interventionist public policy pursuing a redistribution target normally leads to inefficiency and slower growth due to the trade-off relationship between growth and redistribution. Heavy emphasis on poverty eradication and restructuring employment, ownership, and control of business would lower the growth rate below what it would otherwise have been. However, this theoretical perception has not corresponded to Malaysian experience. Not only has Malaysia enjoyed rapid economic growth in the aggregate, but it has also achieved qualitative changes. Malaysia has upgraded its trade and industrial structure. This achievement is quite astonishing for a country where public policies strongly emphasize distribution and social integration. Occasionally, the empahsis on distribution was lifted temporarily for the sake of more currently critical economic objectives, that is, growth, but the Malaysian government generally puts an equal emphasis on distribution and has succeeded in attaining conflicting goals.

In view of the long-term success of public policies, a shift toward controls and inward orientation represents a serious change of direction. Controls may be costly to long-term economic performance. Krugman (1998b), who alleges that Asian countries need temporary currency controls, warned that preliminary indications for Malaysia are not encouraging. Krugman (1998a) went on to argue, "A country that proposes to use currency controls to gain some economic breathing room must be especially careful to limit such abuses, bending over backwards in its efforts to do the right thing on other fronts." In the 1980s, Jeffrey Sachs used to urge troubled Latin American economies to combine "external heterodoxy" with "internal orthodoxy"; that is excellent advice here. The ultimate goal of the external heterodoxy should be to be able to return to world capital markets after a fairly brief interval."[3]

The gigantic projects that are the national target toward 2020 are dependent on foreign participation. Foreign MNCs and inflows of capital are the key to Malaysia's future.[4] Foreign businesses are wary of government intervention. Currency controls and other restrictions are a second-best option, hopefully temporary in nature. Malaysia will enjoy more fruits of economic growth if confidence can be restored, and the world economy behaves well so that Malaysia can lift its restrictive policies in the near future.

NOTES

1. See Aoki (1998).

2. According to the Malaysia International Trade and Industry (MITI), the total number of foreign workers was 1.05 million in 1993. Agriculture received 432,000 (27% of total labor in agriculture); construction, 266,000 (48.2%); manufacturing, 177,000 (10%); and services, 179,000 (9.3%).

3. See Krugman (1998a).

4. In fact, during the boom phase after 1986, the ratio of foreign capital in domestic investment had been over 50% for the period 1987–1992 and peaked in at 71% in 1989 (Aoki, 1998).

REFERENCES

Aoki, Takeshi. (1998). *Introduction to Malaysian Economy.* (In Japanese) Tokyo: Nihon Hyoron.

Cho, George. (1990). *The Malaysian Economy: Spacial Perspective*. London: Routledge.
Krugman, Paul. (1998a). "Malaysia's Opportunity?" *Far Eastern Economic Review* September 17.
——— . (1998b). "Saving Asia: It's Time to Get Radical." *Fortune* September 7.
Malaysian Ministry of Finance. *Economic Report*, various issues.
MITI (Malaysia). (1996). *Second Industrial Master Plan 1996–2005*. Kuala Lumpur: MITI.

13

The Philippines and the Asian Crisis: Has it Turned the Corner?

Florian A. Alburo

OVERVIEW OF POLICY REGIMES

This chapter traces the evolution of policy in the Philippines in order to evaluate whether public policy has enabled the country to take off into a self-sustained growth path. We examine this issue in the context of the Asian crisis, which is seen here as a short- and medium-run event. The basic question is whether the country has transformed its policy landscape to assure a long-run, sustainable growth path—has it turned the corner in spite of the crisis?

The next section thus ventures into examining some "missed opportunities" that the country had in terms of policies. Many important reforms were taken by different policy regimes but could not be sustained in the next ones. We want to flag these and evaluate their significance. The third section establishes the situation of the Philippines in the light of the Asian financial and currency crisis. In the concluding section we propose to answer the question, have these policies made the economic environment "turn the corner," so to speak?

The Philippine economy is often described as in a "boom-and-bust" cycle or "stop-and-go growth." Even more serious is a characterization that these gyrations do not move the country into a higher-growth performance plane but remain on the same cyclical path. Golay (1961) had early on ascribed the cycle of political elections as driving this path. Baldwin (1975) also later on documented the correspondence between economic performance and the four-year election cycle. What is peculiar about the Philippines is the seeming inability of the economy to significantly move up into higher-growth cycles. If we look at the more recent, long-term aggregate picture of the economy between 1980 and 1996, we also see a cycle that tracks the annual growth rate of the components of the GNP. Notice the cycle apparent in the periods 1986 and 1991 and then the appearance of another cycle in the periods 1992 and 1996, assuming that the peak of the current cycle's growth happened in 1996. There is a similar cyclical path of the economy in the early period of the 1960s until the period of 1969, the last election held before martial law was declared in 1972.

What is troublesome about these cycles is that previous peaks are seldom exceeded in the next cycle's peak. The point is that the country's economic growth has not been moving in upward cycles over the long haul.

Many factors lie behind this lackluster economic progress in the last few decades. At the macrolevel, the trade policy regime has been an important determining factor. Like a mirror of the aggregate, the country's trade is also described as a hybrid of protection and liberalization philosophies. Although the Philippines, as other Asian countries, followed a path of import-substitution, the Philippines did not break off this path as early as did the others. Consequently, there was never a full departure from a protectionist era.

Indeed, the heavy protection that went with import-substitution in the 1950s and the 1960s was subsequently supplemented by promotional efforts for industrial exports in the 1970s through the creation of export-processing zones and bonded warehouses. The trade regime was tied closely to the industrial policy regime.

Various estimates of the degree of protection in postwar Philippines indicate that the country was sheltered from the rest of the world trading system through a complex system of controls. The country remained "open," like the other Asian countries, though the manner of its openness was through this complex system. The works of Baldwin (1975), Valdepenas (1970), and Power and Sicat (1971), among others, document this protection system. The price comparisons of Baldwin show that implicit protection exceeded 200% in some products, depending on their essentiality. Yet, in the same breath, certain industries were encouraged through liberal imports for their inputs and control of imports of final products.

Cast along a timeline, the country's short experience with a liberal trade regime did not result in a structural change that could sustain growth. Restrictions were cumulatively reinstituted beginning 1970 amid promotion incentives to stimulate exports (Alburo, 1986).

The dual thrust of protection and selected liberalization failed to develop a thriving trade and exports sector and to deepen industrial growth in the 1970s. Thus, while the Philippines fared well or even better than other Asian countries in 1970, the 1980 export figures show the country had lagged behind. Table 13.1 shows a comparison of merchandise exports between the Philippines and several Asian countries. Note the comparability of exports in 1970 and the dramatic divergence of trade performance in 1980 and the succeeding years.

There are four identifiable policy episodes in the country's trade regime: (1) 1962–1965, (2) 1970–1975, (3) 1980–1983, and (4) 1986 onward. These are described elsewhere (Shepherd and Alburo, 1991). All of these were meant to correct trade distortions, including tariff rates above 100%, the cascading nature of tariff rates along industrial processes, quantitative and nontariff trade restrictions, and other controls. Invariably, the analyses of the country's trade regime point out

Table 13.1
Merchandise Exports (in billions of U.S. dollars)

COUNTRY	1970	1980	1985	1990	1995
The Philippines	1.1	5.7	4.6	8.2	17.5
South Korea	0.8	17.5	26.4	64.0	125.0
Taiwan	1.4	19.8	30.5	66.2	111.6
Singapore	0.8	18.2	21.5	49.3	118.3
Thailand	0.7	6.5	7.1	23.4	56.4
Malaysia	1.6	12.9	15.1	28.7	74.0
Indonesia	1.1	21.9	18.5	25.7	45.4

Source: IMF, *International Financial Statistics* (various issues). Washington, DC: IMF.

several broad and interrelated implications. First are the persistent distortions to the trade environment since the immediate postwar period. These were manifested in the variety of restrictions to trade transactions. Though there were periods of liberalization, these were short-lived and did not trigger significant structural changes. These spurts of freer trade interspersed with protection created more uncertainty and policy instability than if the trade policy framework had been more consistent.

Second, it is quite obvious that these distortions altered relative factor prices that industries had to face in making production and trade decisions. In particular, the deliberate policies of providing liberal trade rules for certain inputs for essential industries together with restrictions to imports of their outputs made factor prices diverge from their international marginal rates of transformation. In fact, restrictions themselves make the exchange rate overvalued, which adds to already distortionary relative factor prices. This means that for a long time the Philippines had a lower capital–rent ratio than elsewhere. This meant firm behavior was biased toward using more capital-intensive means of production than if factor prices were more neutral. In a country with relative abundance of labor, employment was further jeopardized.[1]

Finally, the overall pattern of resource allocation, especially among industries, is clearly driven by the underlying protection system. The growth of industries in value-added terms has not seen a change in relative distribution during the course of several decades. Aside from the industrial composition, the protection system also drives the allocation of aggregate output according to end use. In the process, growth is also affected as the importance of consumption relative to investment goods impacts on the trade-off between present and future outputs.

Related to the trade regime is the country's exchange rate policy. The early and meticulous computations by Baldwin (1975) of effective exchange rates for different classes of imports and exports provide evidence that for a given nominal rate, effective rates vary depending on the bank penalties imposed through Central Bank policies. Overall, however, both the effective exchange rates, based on various surcharges imposed on the kind of imports and based on traditional calculations of real effective exchange rates, tend to show that the peso has historically been overvalued by at least 20%. The overvalued peso made the cost of (imported) capital cheaper than otherwise. This has spawned the adoption of more capital-intensive methods in production, given the bias in relative factor prices. It might be argued that even if these "cheap" imports induce import and capital intensity, they are industry-neutral. The point, however, is that this factor intensity bias is systematic. Put differently, factor endowment use is systematically more diminished than under alternative conditions.

Also related to the trade regime is foreign investment policy. Philippine investment laws have historically been nationalistic, defining large areas of the economy as off-limits to foreign capital and equity, with the exception of remnants from the American occupation of the country that had allowed parity rights and was preserved under the Laurel-Langley Agreement. As the economy faced up to greater trade and its linkages with foreign investments, liberalization meant carving up special locations and zones for these, limiting equity participation by setting ceilings and areas and creating the Board of Investments (BOI) to oversee the policy. The country recently passed a new Foreign Investments Act (FIA) of 1991, consolidating previous investment laws. The main feature of the FIA is a specification of a Foreign Investment Negative List (FINL), which identifies specific areas of investments for which there are restrictions to foreign equity participation. In all other areas not listed in FINL, foreign investors are allowed up to 100% equity. The FINL itself has three categories (List A, B, and C). Lists A and B specify industries, products, or services for which foreign equity is limited by the constitution or existing laws. In the FIA, List C is supposed to contain "investment areas in which existing enterprises already serve the needs of the economy and the consumers and in which foreign investments need not be encouraged further." So far, List C remains empty. Although the FIA still needs to be strengthened, it serves to project an environment of greater liberalization. There are not yet standard provisions that have to be integrated such as the carry over of net operating losses. The Retail Trade Nationalization legislation allowing foreign equity participation in retail trade is yet to be completed and passed into law.

From this description of the trade and related regime, it seems to be the largest domain of public policy in the Philippines both in its historical past and in the present. Its effects on the overall resource allocation, relative prices, and other sectoral and social concerns are widespread. Its definition and management have therefore occupied central government attention and action and are a setting for various interest groups of the economy to influence.

In summary, the more important public policies in the Philippines are captured in the realm of trade and related regimes. Over the course of the country's economic history, policy regimes changed with political leadership. These were confronted with issues of policy reforms and how to adjust in order to secure continued economic growth. Each political regime has therefore had the latitude to understand the economic problems it faced and to put in place public policies to address them. In many cases each government administration drew an agenda laying out what public policies it wanted to pursue, creating the necessary legislation (where needed) and building the constituency for them.

MISSED OPPORTUNITIES

The previous section indicated that the Philippines has carried out many public policies and other economic reforms throughout its history. Some were implemented vigorously, others halfheartedly, and many more reversed at midstream. Whatever the actions taken, it would be useful to examine a number of these. Indeed, we want to be able to trace policy opportunities that the country had and took at critical junctures of its economic performance, even more so those that it failed to take.

Unlike other economies, the Philippines, with neither strategic resource nor income cushion, can ill afford policy mistakes without suffering significant welfare reduction. Public policies, especially those that improve the overall economic environment, are therefore critical. Among the policy areas, most that generated action as well as opportunities revolved around trade and related reforms.

The decontrol of 1962 was the first major economic policy change in the country. The new political leadership adopted a swift abolition of the control apparatus, and the economy's indicators immediately showed its effects. Indicators of import premiums fell drastically. Yet in the aftermath of this public policy the new administration altered the tariff and customs code raising rates among many products to over 100% and lowering the rates for others. This became the forerunner of the cascading nature of the tariff system (Valdepenas, 1970). An accompanying policy change was the devaluation and realignment of the currency by almost 100% overnight (though in the previous two years there had been an effective multiple exchange rate system in operation).

Although the decontrol measures freed international trade, the widespread revision of the tariff rates effectively blunted their impact. The import premiums approximate the average tariff rate. But when cast in terms of the effective protection rates these were more distortionary.[2] The liberalization of commercial trade and the devaluation may have corrected the policy flaws of the past, but the opportunity for retaining the policy's neutrality was clearly missed.

The devaluation by more than 50% in 1970 was the single major public policy of the administration. But rather than freeing commercial trade (since restrictions had cumulatively been reinstituted), the government adopted selective liberalization, created processing zones, and expanded quantitative restrictions. The government failed to appreciate the importance of combining the devaluation with liberalization or to understand the implications of a further distortion to the commercial policy.

The program for liberalization in 1980 under the Tariff Reform Program (TRP), calibrated to run for four years, did not touch upon the need for a foreign exchange rate adjustment. Perhaps the gradual phasing of the TRP did not necessitate its immediate change, but it seems clear that it was an important part of the reform. The economic crisis of 1983 forced the abrupt termination of TRP, though the codal changes were continued since restrictions were enforced anyway.

As a public policy instrument, the TRP had a systematic process of narrowing the tariff rates to reduce their cascading nature, removing quantitative restrictions, and reinstituting freer trade. Unfortunately, it did not take into consideration many issues related to the sequencing of products for liberalization.[3] Thus, aside from the major neglect of exchange rate adjustments, there were internal policy questions. While the 1983 crisis opened an opportunity for further and broader public policy changes, it was obvious that its root causes were principally political, even if it has been argued that the economic fundamentals were already troublesome (De Dios, 1984).

The new government in 1986 crafted a new economic agenda altogether without completely abandoning previous programs such as the TRP. But it emphasized the need for comprehensiveness in public policies, appropriate sequencing, and a packaged approach to implementation (Alburo et al., 1986; Bautista and Lamberte, 1996). The new government restarted the aborted liberalization program following a similar phasing. But it was confronted by a larger set of public policy debates—land reform, government reorganization, privatization, deregulation, debt problem, population policy, tax reforms, and so on—beyond the macroeconomic essentials. Indeed, the economic agenda became more open since the new government fundamentally abolished the existing constitution (and opted for a Freedom Constitution), allowing for many potential changes. In the end the route taken for public policy was conservative—many reforms had to wait for a Congress to convene and hold public debates, and reorganization had to be completed.

In the aggregate policy framework, the new government effectively carried through where the previous government had left off before the 1983 crisis. It chose to ignore the needs for accompanying public policies as part of a complete package of reforms. The opportunities for undertaking bolder measures were there—reservoir of global goodwill after the 1986 revolution, sharp declines in the world price of oil, low inflation rate in the country, generous support from international institutions, among others—yet national policies were caught in conflicts within the government.

Although the economy experienced an unprecedented growth rate in 1988 (mainly arising from a low base), there was not enough cushion to withstand the effects of the coup attempts that followed. The economy suffered a fall beginning in 1989 until 1991. Whatever reforms that were initiated by the government also suffered by way of further postponement, cancellation, or review. The economic slowdown was not conducive to aggressive public policies. Major crises took place among some of the major services (e.g., power), which took their toll on economic performance.

The new government in 1992 first instituted damage control, paying attention to the restoration of services. Its own economic agenda did not initially differ from its predecessor, though it subsequently crafted a direction for national government. This included a radical tariff reform moving toward a 5% uniform tariff by 2004 and a comprehensive tax reform program. The national government also succeeded in shepherding the country's accession to the World Trade Organization and the Uruguay Round of Multilateral Trade Agreement. The government also pushed for greater deregulation, especially of previously closed sectors such as telecommunications and accelerated privatization. Yet despite the lowering of trade barriers, the government failed to recognize the importance of the accompanying exchange rate adjustment.

What patterns of "missed opportunities" can be drawn from this brief description of the aggregate policies taken over the course of the country's economic history? A major criterion to use is the replication of the economic problems that require policy actions in various periods. It is, of course, debatable whether the root causes of similar manifestations of economic problems are always the same. Yet whatever is the root cause, self-replicating problems indicate missed opportunities.

Two of these are in the area of aggregate trade and exchange rate policies. The start of the Macapagal administration (1962–1965) saw a bold and swift exchange rate adjustment—large devaluation and the elimination of multiple exchange rates. At the same time this administration completely decontrolled the economy. But it missed the opportunity of rationalizing the tariff structure when it revamped the system with ceilings exceeding 100%, latent cascading rates, and the retention of a classification by essentiality.[4] Perhaps the lack of widespread knowledge and use of effective protection rates limited the government's appreciation of its policy actions.

In the succeeding devaluation in 1970 by the Marcos administration (1966–1986), there was no accompanying liberalization of trade transactions. Instead the government opted to adopt an open trade policy for defined geographic zones and continue a protection network elsewhere. It missed the opportunity of realigning the domestic economy with the rest of the world despite empirical evidence of the problem.

The 1980 reforms, on the other hand, paid particular attention to trade distortions without an accompanying exchange rate adjustment. Moreover, the elaborate and complex system of licensing, quantitative restrictions, and other nontariff barriers made the sequencing of the reforms difficult to formulate and follow. Thus the comprehensiveness of the reforms could not be achieved either. Though there was a significant advantage in pursuing comprehensiveness since policy control was centralized, many varying vested interests prevented this from taking place.[5]

In the aftermath of the 1986 revolution, the policy agenda was wide open. The Aquino administration (1986–1992) had a coterie of directions but could not agree on a set of priorities. Thus public policies were a restart of previous reforms minus items that were clearly remnants of a dictatorial economy (e.g., abolition of the human settlements ministry). Import liberalization and tariff reforms were major refinements of what could not be carried out at the end of the Marcos regime. There were, however, many more missed policy opportunities—from land reform to an aggressive exchange rate policy. The setting for an exchange rate adjustment combined with trade liberalization was there, but eventually only the latter was implemented.

A radical and accelerated trade reform was on the agenda in 1990 (tariff simplification to four rates) but failed to be carried out. Instead a different and softer executive order (E.O. 470) phased tariff changes over five years. But the economic crisis of 1991 forced an across-the-board 9% import levy. Not only was the eventual reform watered down, but the rates were raised as well.

The liberalization of foreign exchange rules was part of the Ramos administration (1992–1998) agenda to respond to the global changes in the form of the Uruguay Round Trade Agreements, the ASEAN Free Trade Area, and Asia-Pacific Economic Cooperation (APEC). In addition, this administration successfully incorporated a uniform tariff rate of 5% by 2004 into revisions of the underlying executive order on tariff rates. But surprisingly absent again was the accompanying exchange rate adjustment, even if the numbers already indicated a potential balance of payments problem.

In all, the compelling support for these "missed opportunities" is that the replicated problems are not new. Indeed the concerns about the adverse effects of public policies have been invariant over time. The debate in 1986 is a replication of the debate in 1962 (Alburo, 1986). The country need not relate to the aggregate policies of other developing countries but relate to its own history.

The missed opportunities were not so much the absence of policies but rather the combination of policies to address concrete problems. The experience shows that either commercial policy changes take place, or exchange rate policy changes, but seldom both. This is a question neither of timing nor of sequencing since these are not considered at all in the discussions. In short, the need for a package of public policies, not modular components, was clearly missed.

Each policy pronouncement taken had a time horizon of the administration's term and not toward a long-term vision of the economy. If there was one, it was couched in anticipation of a second term. Thus five-year plans for a four-year term implied the desirability of continuing office to assure the plans are completed. The Marcos administration had the opportunity to cast a long-term horizon for the economy and undertake the necessary policies to achieve them. In fact, in this administration the 25-year plans were started. Yet the actual policies taken were far short of maximizing the future benefits of the economy.

IN THE CONTEXT OF THE ASIAN CRISIS

One observes in the Philippines that the crisis that began in July 1997 with the baht devaluation is viewed from at least two standpoints. On one hand, there is the view that the country is simply an innocent bystander to an economic problem that is in other countries. Even if the Philippines is indirectly affected, it has already taken the necessary policies to withstand a potential injury. The country's "fundamentals" are correct. On the other hand, there is the view that these fundamentals were weak to begin with, and the crisis only served to highlight them despite the respectable performance of the economy in the last few years.

Without having to impute causality to the indicators, there are several symptoms of the crisis. Among them are (1) the surge of short-term capital, mostly in the form of portfolio investments relative to the flows of foreign direct investments, (2) a bubble in the economy shown by exuberance in the stock markets and price inflation of real estate and nontradables, (3) the rapid expansion of domestic credit extended by the commercial banking system, (4) a widening current account deficit, and (5) an overvaluation of the local currency.

The Philippines experience with short-term capital inflows has been relatively recent. In fact the portfolio capital component of them was negligible before the 1990s. Yet this surged, beginning in 1993. From U.S.$156 million in 1990 this rose to U.S.$6.9 billion in 1996. The inflow of foreign investments in the Philippines showed a sharp increase after 1992 with a consequent scaling down of foreign direct investments.

Apart from the inward flows of short-term portfolio investments, the country's financial institutions also tapped the global markets for both short-term and long-term foreign exchange resources. In the former, borrowings were utilized to take advantage of interest rate differentials and the stable exchange rate for onward lending to local borrowers in local currency. For the latter, the institutions floated long-term bonds in international markets. Again the data show that borrowings, especially by banks, surged, but beginning only in 1995. Total foreign exchange liabilities (short and long) stood at U.S.$4.7 billion in 1993 and surged to U.S.$17.8 billion by 1997 (June). Though there may be issues here with regard to the use of foreign currency deposit unit (FCDU) of offshore banks in the Philippines, the fact is that borrowings by the private sector escalated in two years between 1995 and 1997.

Portfolio investment inflows in the Philippines have found their way into the property sectors, in the stock markets, or in financial institutions, among others. Driven by continued privatization of public enterprises, initial public offerings by corporations, and overall "irrational exuberance," these investments drove up asset prices and created large paper gains in the stock market. Evidence of the decline in the property bubble can be readily observed in the rapid decline in property prices around the prime areas of the country, the shelving of planned property construction, the sharp drop in prices of club and golf course shares, and the drop in stock prices since 1996.

Domestic credit had annual growth rates in excess of 50% beginning in 1996, with an increasing proportion going into financial institutions, real estate, and business services. Commercial bank loans to the manufacturing sector tapered off during the same period of rapid domestic credit growth. Indeed there is consistency in the timing of these changes in the behavior of financial institutions, especially during the mid-1990s.

Although these surges appear to be significant especially if viewed in potential trends, the stock magnitudes are far from alarming. Of the U.S.$44.8 billion external debt of the country (June 1997), only U.S.$8.5 billion, or 18.9% are short-term in maturity, with the rest medium- and long-term. More than half of the debt is owed by the private sector, with the central bank accounting for 24% of the total. Finally, 25% of the debt is owed to Japan, with another 24% owed to bondholders and noteholders and 18.5% owed to multilateral agencies. The rest are spread evenly across the United States, the U.K., France, and Germany. Banks, financial institutions, and suppliers account for 26.8% of the external debt in terms of institutional creditor, with another 30.3% owed to bilateral agencies (e.g., export agencies).

In terms of the trade and current account deficit characteristic, the Philippines has had a trade problem for some time, and it has been persistent. On the other hand, its current account deficit has fluctuated over the years, narrowing the trade deficit with surpluses in the services trade and net transfers. As a major source of overseas contract workers, these Filipino workers send remittances, which partly pay for the country's trade deficits. In fact without these the Philippines current account would have been in a worse position. The current account deficit as a percent of GNP never hit above 6%, with the exception of the second quarter of 1996. But in the second quarter of 1997, before the actual crisis took place, the current account deficit stood at 6.7% of GNP, which somehow was a threshold during the Mexican crisis. The narrowing of the gap between the two deficits has been covered by the surge in the net services trade. For example, this item had an inflow of U.S.$4 billion in 1994 from U.S.$1.5 billion in 1990.

The overall balance of payments (BOP) of the Philippines has been positive for most of the years between 1990 and 1996, principally because of a positive capital accounts position. In turn, this has been carried by more significant inflows of medium- and long-term loans. Only in 1995 did the net portfolio account begin to be significant in the capital accounts.

A widening goods trade deficit is a reflection of the competitiveness of the Philippines export goods. The extent to which a nominal exchange rate is unable to adjust relative to competing countries partly determines the extent of the deficit. To portray this more accurately, the real effective exchange rate (REER) is often calculated. The calculation of a real effective exchange rate is quite sensitive to the base year chosen, the countries included (and excluded) in the calculation, and the price indices. Thus there are many such indices. A broad REER includes the competing countries of Singapore, South Korea, Taiwan, Malaysia, Thailand, Indonesia, and Hong Kong. A narrow REER includes only Indonesia, Malaysia, and Thailand. There was overvaluation only in late 1995 for broad REER and a worsening for the narrow REER. By any measure the peso has been overvalued for a long time. Another calculation of a real exchange rate is simply the nominal exchange rate deflated by the country price index and adjusted to a common year. By showing these individual country indices, one is able to compare the movement of the index over time without having to arrive at a single index weighted by the partner country's share in trade. On this basis, again, the Philippines currency has been overvalued relative to Thailand, Indonesia, Malaysia, and China. Even after the early part of 1997 the Philippines still was not able to recover its lost competitiveness from a base year of 1988.

In summary, it is evident that the Philippines had all the symptoms of a financial crisis, even if it is actually not suffering from the crisis that exploded in the region. What has kept it from acquiring the severity that others have experienced is the late exposure to the symptoms. This does not mean that the measures being taken to address the root causes of the "Asian flu" should not be applicable to the country as well.

CONCLUDING REMARKS

The evolution of policies in the Philippines shows that they suffered from frequent reversals, occasional paralysis, and deliberate delays. They often were not carried through changing government regimes. Both historical data and more recent indicators tend to support such characterization of the policy environment. While there does appear to be a semblance of cumulative reforms (e.g., the continued improvement of investment laws since the 1950s), their effects have yet to be seen.

Thus the country, unwittingly, has not been caught at the center of the Asian crisis that has engulfed a number of other countries. But this is not because the Philippines has done well in its policy arena. That it has been sheltered from the onslaught of the financial crisis is not necessarily due to healthy fundamentals. Looking at the anatomy of the crisis, it is rather because the Philippines has not achieved the openness of the others.

It is beyond the scope of this chapter to assess the immediate damage or long-term impacts of this crisis. There is no doubt that recovery will come, sooner or later. Though the debate on the merits of open economies will continue, what is more important is the response to the recovery toward long-term growth. As market corrections take place, as relative prices reflect less distortions, and as institutional support is created, the task obviously shifts to the country's ability to sustain a new momentum for growth. In this sense there is some question whether the Philippines can manage a more open economy, given its history as described in this chapter.

If the country is yet to "turn the corner" in its policy environment, it becomes doubtful if it can sustain a growth path beyond an earlier recovery. After all, quick recovery may not be more important than a self-sustaining trajectory after the crisis shall have passed.

NOTES

1. The share of employment in the manufacturing sector has practically remained at 10–12% during the past three decades despite the fact that the labor force has more than doubled during the same period.

2. It is unfortunate that when this first policy move toward decontrol and tariff adjustments took place, there were no studies of effective protection. The later calculations are effectively irrelevant.

3. Many products that were inputs into downstream industries were scheduled for liberalization later than the liberalization of the downstream products.

4. The Central Bank classification of imports (by degree of essentiality and whether consumer or producer goods) was not abolished and continued to be the basis for subsequent tariff code specification. Institutional apparatus for intervention by product category remained.

5. Examples of these are described in Shepherd and Alburo (1991, pp. 228–229).

REFERENCES

Alburo, Florian. (1986). "Import Liberalization Revisited." University of the Philippines School of Economics Discussion Paper 8611 (September).

Alburo, Florian, et al. (1986). *Economic Recovery and Long-Run Growth: Agenda for Reforms*. Manila: Philippine Institute for Development Studies.

Baldwin, Robert E. (1975). *Foreign Trade Regimes and Economic Development: The Philippines*. New York: National Bureau of Economic Research.

Bautista, Romeo M., and Mario M. Lamberte. (1996). "The Philippines: Economic Developments and Prospects." *Asian-Pacific Economic Literature* 10(2) (November), pp. 16–31.

De Dios, Emmanuel S., ed. (1984). *An Analysis of the Philippine Economic Crisis*. Quezon City: University of the Philippines.

Golay, Frank H. (1961). *The Philippines: Public Policy and National Economic Development*. Ithaca, NY: Cornell University Press.

Power, John H., and Gerardo P. Sicat. (1971). *The Philippines; Industrialization and Trade Policies*. London: Oxford University Press.

Shepherd, Geoffrey, and Florian A. Alburo. (1991). "Liberalizing Foreign Trade in the Philippines." In Demetrius Papageorgiou et al., *Liberalizing Foreign Trade*, vol. 2. Oxford: Basil Blackwell.

Tecson, Gwendolyn, et al. (1995). *Philippine Trade and Industrial Policies: Catching Up with Asia's Tigers*. Manila: Philippine Iinstitute for Development Studies.

Valdepenas, Vicente B., Jr. (1970). *The Protection and Development of Philippine Manufacturing*. Manila: Ateneo de Manila University Press.

14

Macroeconomic Policy: A Foundation for Indonesia's Sustainable Economic Development

Boediono and Hartadi A. Sarwono

Over the past three decades of the implementation of six five-year development plans, Indonesia's economic performance has been remarkable. The objectives in each five-year development plan are basically aimed at improving the living standards and welfare of the people, along with creating a strong foundation for the succeeding stage of development. Throughout those years, the government has maintained its focus on preserving stability, equity, and growth, the three pillars of Indonesia's development trilogy. By retaining this focus, Indonesia has been able to continue to attain high levels of economic performance.

During the past three decades the country has been growing in real terms at an average of almost 7% a year—a growth performance that ranks among the 10 fastest in the world and that is on a par with that of other dynamic East Asian countries. Another remarkable feature of this performance has been the structural transformation of what was an agricultural economy toward a more industrialized economy. The economy has become more diversified and less dependent on oil, with the private sector playing a greater role in the economy. More importantly, the basis of exports, which was dominated by primary products, including oil and agricultural products, has increasingly shifted toward manufacturing and services products. The financial sector also grew in size and sophistication, though the growth now is probably not sufficiently balanced by prudent regulations designed to anticipate and reduce risk.

The favorable economic performance achieved was attributed mainly to structural adjustment policies undertaken by the government since the 1980s. Those measures, which are comprehensive in nature and cover various sectors, were intended, among others, to cope with a number of severe challenges encountered by Indonesia's economy at the beginning of the 1980s. In addition, the continued structural adjustment process of the economy depends first and foremost on maintenance of macroeconomic stability. In this regard, prudent macroeconomic policies have been adopted to ensure that economic reforms proceed in a stable macroeconomic condition.

Now, we are living in the new era of globalization. The strategy of structural adjustment policies and prudent macroeconomic management embraced by Indonesia contributes to globalization and expanding opportunities for Indonesia's economy to share in its benefits. However, the integration of the developing countries, including Indonesia, into global markets brings serious challenges and makes them more vulnerable to external disturbances. Despite Indonesia's strong macroeconomic performance, a number of underlying weaknesses have made this country susceptible to adverse external shocks. Structural rigidities arising from regulations in domestic trade and import monopolies have impeded economic efficiency and competitiveness. At the same time, the relative stability of the rupiah during most of the 1990s, together with high rate of return on domestic investment, both encouraged and facilitated a high level of private foreign borrowing. Also, the rapid expansion of the financial system since the 1980s has left a number of banks with significant amounts of nonperforming loans due to over expansion of credit to sensitive sectors such as property and construction.

In the wake of the recent currency turmoil in the region, the exchange rate has depreciated to alarming levels. The plummeting of the rupiah has led to very large increases in the rupiah debt service costs of banks and corporations that had borrowed from abroad. In this sense, the Indonesian crisis can be understood as a "crisis of success," caused by a boom of international lending followed by a sudden withdrawal of funds. However, this is more than the bursting of an unwanted bubble. Much of the economic activity supported by the capital inflows was highly productive, and the loss of economic activity resulting from the sudden reversal in capital flows has been enormous. Moreover, since the currency depreciation has engendered a substantial rise in interest rates, the burden of paying for, and collecting, domestic currency loans has also increased, further straining the position of corporations and financial institutions, particularly those that were already weak.

From the outset of the recent currency crisis, the government has taken strong corrective actions with support from the International Monetary Fund. The package is based on three main elements: (1) a stabilization program through monetary and fiscal policies, (2) a fundamental restructuring of the financial sector, and (3) further deregulation of the domestic economy. Indeed, this package is consistent with the macroeconomic policy and strategy of Indonesia as elaborated upon in this chapter.

THE STRATEGY: STRUCTURAL ADJUSTMENT AND PRUDENT MACROECONOMIC POLICIES

Indonesia's progress over the last three decades has been the result of consistent structural adjustment policies and prudent macroeconomic management. Achieving sustainable economic development requires not only a continuous process of structural reform to increase the supply response of the economy but also the maintenance of macroeconomic stability. To achieve significant economic growth and to ensure continuous progress in the equity of income distribution, economic activities should be performed under stable macroeconomic conditions. This long-standing development trilogy has guided policymakers and government officials for the last three decades.

Structural Adjustment Policies

In the late 1960s, restoration of economic stability following widespread social unrest, disruption of production, hyperinflation, huge budget deficits, and default on international debts was the first priority of the New Order government under President Suharto. The support of the international donor community was crucial to efforts to stabilize the economy, and the ascendancy of the economic technocrats played a key role in restoring confidence of both donors and private investors. The credibility of the government's stabilization program following a substantial devaluation was established through the eradication of the budget deficits, thereby bringing money supply growth down and taming inflation.[1] The government also unified multiple exchange rates, abolished exchange controls, and opened the inward capital account both to attract flight capital back into the economy and to bring in foreign direct investment (FDI). These steps were highly successful, and between 1970 and 1972 the government took the unusual route of opening up the outward capital account, removing the restrictions on outward capital transactions.

Trade policies, which were partly liberalized in the late 1960s, became steadily more inward-looking and protectionist in the period of 1973–1985. The oil boom reduced pressures to earn foreign exchange and provided additional funds for development programs. Import-substitution industrialization was followed during these years. Inward FDI flows were increasingly regulated and made subject to the government's priorities. A plethora of export controls and taxes were imposed as well. The financial sector came under increased regulation, and all sorts of credit controls were imposed between 1973 and 1982.

Financial Sector Restructuring

Indonesia's strategy for stimulating economic growth changed fundamentally in 1983, when the era of the oil boom ended. The economy had to be restructured completely to reduce the dependency on government development activities. The sharp drop in oil prices caused adverse impacts, as reflected in the drastic decline in foreign exchange earnings and government revenues, lower imports, and lower investment. The unfavorable oil price reduced the role of government and the capacity of the public sector to act as the engine of growth. Therefore, the private sector was expected to assume a greater role in economic development, and the financial sector was expected to increase its ability to mobilize the necessary funds. The private sector, thus, became the primary engine of growth and job creation. To this end, the financial sector plays an important role as an intermediary between depositors who have a surplus of funds and investors who need those funds for their activities. Indonesia, like other developing countries, faces a gap between limited savings and increasing investment needs. Therefore, efforts to adjust the financial system aim to enhance the strategic role of banks and other financial institutions to support economic development and constitute an integral part of the overall structural adjustment policies.

Structural adjustment in the financial system is fundamentally a two-pronged process.[2] First, it involves removal of direct controls over prices and quantities, combined with an easing of the process that governs the entry and exit of financial institutions. The result should be that economic choices would be determined mainly through the interaction of market forces. Second, it requires the imposition of prudential regulations that ensure clear and sufficient information is available to all, reduce excessive risk, and minimize opportunities for fraud and manipulation at the expense of the general public.

The financial reforms in Indonesia have been carefully phased and only gradually implemented. Initially, in 1983 the reforms were focused on removal of credit and interest rate controls on the banking system, while developing indirect, market-oriented instruments of monetary policy to replace direct credit ceilings. Policies with respect to international trade and inward FDI remained highly restrictive, even though outward capital transactions were unrestricted, and domestic financial reform had been initiated. This is precisely a reverse sequencing of liberalization reforms compared with that suggested by the conventional wisdom based on the experience of the "Southern Cone" countries of Latin America. Indonesia succeeded in opening up the capital account prior to beginning domestic financial reforms as well as in instituting both types of financial reforms prior to real economy reforms in its reverse sequencing of policy reforms.

In October 1988, another package was launched, aimed at deepening the financial system, increasing fund mobilization, and improving the effectiveness of monetary policy.[3] This package permitted the establishment of new private banks, the opening of branch offices of banks and nonbank financial institutions, and rural credit banks. The banking system still had priority, simply because it was dominated by very large, but highly inefficient, state-owned banks. Meanwhile, in line with the development of the banking sector and efforts to create a sound banking system, we were also concerned about prudential measures. For this reason the Central Bank introduced capital adequacy requirements (CAR) based on BIS (Banks for International Settlements) standards, regulations on legal lending limits, net open positions, loan-to-deposit ratios, allowances for earning assets losses, and limitations on foreign commercial borrowings. More importantly, reforms were also carried out in the legal framework in March 1992, when a new Banking Act was set, superseding the former Banking Act issued in 1967.

The measures just mentioned have undoubtedly encouraged more advanced banking activities. However, in line with this development, the Central Bank remains very aware of the importance of maintaining financial stability. Our long period of experience has shown that financial stability is a necessary condition to support economic development. We therefore saw that steps to increase prudential measures were vital, and in recent years the Central Bank introduced some measures aimed at promoting "self-regulatory banking" within the banking industry, while further restructuring the industry.

The government also took a number of steps to reinvigorate the moribund stock exchange and to encourage the development of the insurance and pension systems. It has taken steps to liberalize the capital market with the aim of creating a conducive environment for investors. In December 1987 and December 1988, the government took further steps to energize the capital market that had slumbered through a decade of existence. The regulation limiting daily price swings to 4% of the price of a stock was abolished, and foreigners were allowed to buy shares. Foreign securities houses were also given the green light to form joint ventures with local partners. It is true, of course, that the sudden emergence of competition in 1989 from equity markets had a profound effect on how banks marketed themselves to customers. Furthermore, a new capital market law was also enacted in 1995 to strengthen the legal foundation of the market.

Structural Reforms to Improve the Supply Response of the Economy

One of the key factors in sustaining Indonesia's economic development has been the ability of the government to recognize promptly and respond appropriately to rapid changes in the economic environment, both domestically and internationally. Against this background, Indonesian policymakers foresaw that adjustment measures had to be taken in order to put in place all the essential elements that, in the long run, would constitute the basis for sustainable economic development. The structural adjustment measures affect many facets of the economy. To give some focus to the Indonesian experience, there are three basic components to structural adjustment: getting prices right, letting markets work, and reforming public institutions, especially financial institutions.[4] The objectives of structural adjustment policies have been to enhance the economy's resilience and efficiency as well as to improve the economic structure, to diversify and promote exports, especially non-oil/gas exports, to encourage the mobilization of savings, and to step up the participation and role of the business community and the people at large in development so as to lay a broader and stronger foundation for further development in the years ahead.[5]

The first step of the reform process was started in the late 80s after the complete collapse of petroleum prices in 1985–1986. The trade reforms were urgently needed to boost nonoil exports to support of the balance of payments. The economy had to be opened to international markets through a series of deregulation measures that dramatically eased foreign investment rules, reduced tariffs for most commodities, rationalized the tariff structure, and greatly reduced the number of commodities protected by nontariff barriers. Those measures were a crucial factor in building and maintaining foreign investors' confidence and creating a conducive environment for investment.

Nontariff barriers (NTBs) were substantially reduced after 1986, and tariffs replaced the NTBs in many industries. Tariff cuts were also initiated, and restrictions on inward FDI were also loosened. Between 1990 and 1993, very little was accomplished in terms of further import tariff reform as the Uruguay Round negotiations stalled. Between 1990 and 1993, the simple average (unweighted) tariff remained at about 20%. The success of the Uruguay Round negotiations in 1994 helped to break the logjam in trade policy reform, and tariff cuts became deeper. Between 1994 and 1997, the simple average tariff was steadily reduced to only 11%, leaving Singapore as the only country in Southeast Asia with lower tariffs. As a member of the Association of Southeast Asian Nations (ASEAN), Indonesia also began to implement tariff cuts on a preferential basis under the Common Effective Preferential Tariff (CEPT) scheme. By the end of 1997, most restrictions on inward FDI, including divestiture requirements on new investments, were all but eliminated. The pace of deregulation has increased both domestic and foreign direct investment and drove Indonesian industry and, indeed, the entire economy to new levels of openness and competitiveness.

PRUDENT MACROECONOMIC MANAGEMENT

Sound macroeconomic policies, in which fiscal, monetary, and banking policies constitute integral elements, have been the hallmarks of Indonesia's impressive economic performance. Stable macroeconomic conditions are essential for overall economic development. Therefore, achieving stability has been our consistent endeavor for years. In this regard, the focus on macroeconomic stability is aimed at managing domestic demand by controlling inflation and keeping the current account deficit in check. Prudent and consistent fiscal and monetary policies are central to this effort.[6] First, fiscal policy, including all elements of government revenue and expenditure, has been modified through steps to simplify the tax system, reduce subsidies, and ensure efficient expenditures in order to sustain a dynamic balanced budget. Second, monetary policy comprised aspects to safeguard the stability of the rupiah in terms of both domestic prices (inflation) as well as foreign currencies (exchange rates). In general, monetary policy is directed to keep liquidity growth at levels adequate to support the targeted rate of economic growth without giving rise to internal and external imbalances. In addition, a managed floating exchange rate system is adopted to ensure the competitiveness of export commodities as well as to allow the market mechanism to work in foreign exchange markets.

Fiscal and monetary policies were carried out with respect to their responsibilities to provide a proper framework for a market-oriented economy, resulting in broader economic efficiency. The government has aimed over these years for stable and sustainable noninflationary growth. With these policies in place, the macroeconomic environment has remained stable and predictable. Inflation has exceeded

10% only once in the past dozen years. The current account deficit has been maintained at a manageable level, and foreign exchange reserves have remained close to the equivalent of five months of imports. Interest rates have been maintained at positive real values in order to stimulate savings and, subsequently, investment. Real effective exchange rates that were kept realistic have enhanced the competitiveness of export commodities in world markets.

The persistence in pursuing macroeconomic stability has also inspired a high level of confidence in Indonesia's economic fundamentals and the government's credibility. This has been fostered and strengthened further by a strong conviction that the government will not take drastic measures in adjusting the economy, in particular, in the financial sector. Accordingly, this macroeconomic stability is also reflected in our financial stability. Stability in the financial system is very important, as the economy is increasingly integrated with the global economy. While we continuously promote market mechanisms through a series of financial reforms, we have been able to maintain stability in financial markets with less intervention whenever there is a shock to the economy.

RECENT DEVELOPMENT IN ECONOMIC AND FINANCIAL STRUCTURE

Following structural adjustment measures adopted by the government, Indonesia's economic structure developed favorably toward a more balanced structure. In the early years, the economy was noted for its heavy dependence on the primary sector, especially on oil and gas. In recent years, the sources of economic growth have become more diversified. The manufacturing sector share in GDP increased sharply. Nonoil/gas exports, especially the manufacturing products, increased significantly, outpacing oil and gas exports. The same thing occurred in the government's domestic revenues. Nonoil/gas revenues became more important, exceeding revenues from oil and gas. With a more diversified economy, it is expected that the economy will be more resilient against external shocks.

Furthermore, Indonesia's economic fundamentals have been much stronger as a result of prudent macroeconomic policies, which have been executed in conjunction with a series of market-oriented reforms. A stable macroeconomic condition has provided a better environment for business activities. In the last decade, economic growth has increased substantially, averaging 7.5% annually in real terms. Income per capita increased to more than $1,200 in 1996 from a little more than $500 in 1985. The high economic growth rate was also helped by a relatively low average inflation rate. The relatively low inflation rate was an essential factor, which enabled Indonesia to sustain high growth rates for a long period. As a result of this satisfactory economic performance, Indonesia is now categorized as one of the most dynamic emerging markets.

Fundamental Changes in Indonesia's Economic Structure

Indonesia's favorable economic performance has been accompanied by a fundamental change in economic structure. First, the role of the private sector in the national economy has grown, partly reflected by the increase in the ratio of private sector investment to GDP from 25% in 1985 to more than 35% in 1996. The second fundamental change is the shift of economic structure from the agriculture sector to the manufacturing sector. The contribution of manufacturing to GDP increased from 17% in 1985 to 25% in 1996, while the contribution of the agricultural sector decreased from 25% to around 16%. The third fundamental change is that the Indonesian economy is increasingly integrated with the world economy. Indonesia's exports to GDP ratio rose from 20% in 1985 to more than 25% in 1996, while ratios of foreign direct investment to GDP and to exports rose from 0.6% and 3%, respectively, to 3% and 13%. Fourth, the level of integration may also be seen in the ratio of banks' foreign liabilities to GDP, which rose from 0.6% in 1985 to more than 6% in 1996. Last but not least, we have also recorded a shift of oil exports to nonoil exports, with nonoil exports rising from approximately 30% of total merchandise exports in 1985 to more than 75% in 1996. Within the government's budget, the proportion of nonoil revenue has surged as a proportion of domestic revenue, from less than 30% to around 76% over the same period.

These changes have brought with them some consequences. In conjunction with the greater role of the private sector, macroeconomic management is increasingly dependent on the market mechanism, and the government's role is increasingly directed toward efforts to create and maintain a level playing field to ensure that the market mechanism works smoothly and fairly. Moreover, the integration of Indonesia's economy with the world economy has necessitated the use of more sophisticated macroeconomic management and reduced the government's direct role in the implementation of national development. In the past, private sector business activities did not have any significant impact on national efforts to maintain economic stability. Now, as the private sector's contribution to GDP has become greater, the private sector—particularly the large-scale businesses—can no longer disregard the implications of their business activities on macroeconomic stability. To achieve sustained growth—which has always been the government's aim in managing the economy—policies must also be directed at the micro level.

In the financial sector, our banking industry has recorded dynamic growth, both in terms of the number of banks or offices and in terms of the mobilization of financial resources. As of 1997 we have 239 banks with more than 6,000 bank offices, compared with 124 banks with about 1,900 bank offices in 1988. Meanwhile, propelled by more advanced information and communication technologies, the banking industry has become more modern and able to cope with increasingly complex financial activities. Financial products have become more varied. Once limited to demand deposits, savings, and time deposits, they have now broadened to include the sale of securities in financial markets, such as certificates of deposit, shares, and bonds. We have also seen the introduction of modern technology like automatic-teller machines (ATMs) and electronic funds transfers (EFTs). The type of financing provided has also widened from traditional credit disbursements to purchases of securities, such as commercial paper issued by the business sector. Moreover, there are increasing signs of asset securitization, so that the relationship between assets and liabilities in bank balance sheets has begun to diminish, and off-balance sheet activities have increased. As a result, banking income has also begun to shift from credit interest to fee-based income.

Rapid technological advances have encouraged innovations in financial activities. The development of information and communication technologies has increased the number of new financial products, including derivatives. In the future, we are likely to see many financial breakthroughs, including the use of computer networks and electronic money. Technological progress has also encouraged the rise of transactions across national borders and increased the number of banks operating outside their national borders, a process described as financial globalization.

More importantly, financial reforms have fostered a more effective market mechanism within the banking system, thus enhancing its function as a financial intermediary. Efforts toward deregulating our banking industry, for example, have led to increased competition among banks, prompting greater efficiency. Banks are now more independent in terms of being able to set their own business strategies. They have become more market-oriented, as reflected in the price banks have established for deposits and loans as well as in the variety of new financial products they have introduced for their consumers.

The capital market has also grown rapidly. The number of companies listed on the Jakarta Stock Exchange increased tremendously, from 24 companies at the end of 1985 to 267 companies in 1996. Over the same period, funds mobilized from the issuance of shares rose sharply from Rp89 billion to Rp215 trillion. Trading of shares on the Jakarta Stock Exchange has risen sharply, from Rp3 billion in 1985 to Rp76 trillion in 1996. These trends indicate the increasing tendency of businesses to move away from relying solely on bank credit toward more diversified sources of finance.

Apart from the issuance of shares or bonds on the stock exchange, businesses may also obtain alternative financing for their business activities by issuing commercial paper or obtain financing from other financial institutions such as from leasing companies, venture capital, and factoring companies. As in the case of shares and bonds issued on the stock exchange, the business activities of these other financial institutions have also accelerated recently. This shows that financing needs, which used to be obtained only from banks, have begun to shift to alternative sources of funds.

ENTERING INTO THE THIRD MILLENNIUM: CHALLENGES AND OPPORTUNITIES

Today, we are living in a completely new era. Now, as the twentieth century comes to a close, the world economy is undergoing another profound change:

globalization. A change that transforms the world economy is reflected in widening and intensifying international linkages in trade and finance. It is driven by a nearly universal push toward trade and financial market liberalization, increasing internationalization of corporate production and distribution strategies and technological change that is fast eroding barriers to the international tradability of goods and services and the mobility of capital. Markets for merchandise trade are expanding, more and more services are becoming tradable, and capital is flowing in increasingly diverse ways across countries and regions in search of profitable investments.

In the financial sector, globalization has led to a fundamental transformation in the financial industry. This transformation takes place in at least three forms.[7] First, there is a process of "financial transnationalization." In recent years, the operations of financial institutions have been broadened and therefore are not limited to any particular country or region. Financial markets in the world have become unified, and national or regional borders have become obscure. The second form is the new innovations in financial activities. The development of information and communications technology has also increased the number of product and process innovations, including new financial products in the form of new financial assets derived from other financial assets, that is, financial derivatives. The third form of financial globalization is the tendency toward securitization with a merging process in the operation of commercial banks and securities institutions. Recently, banks have become increasingly aggressive in the financial market through the utilization of derivative financial instruments and the securitization of assets.

A prominent feature of the ongoing global economic change is that the developing countries, including Indonesia, are active participants as both agents and beneficiaries of the change. Formerly dependent on natural resources, Indonesia has developed a thriving manufacturing sector, increasingly sophisticated financial markets, and a broad range of export-oriented industries. Private and government enterprises have become market-oriented and global in their outlook.

The government has committed itself to continue to assist in this market-oriented process, bearing in mind the growing linkages between world markets, especially financial markets, and the importance of competitiveness. It will continue to manage the economy in a prudent and realistic way in the belief that sound economic fundamentals are the basic building blocks for healthy and sustainable growth. While seeking to maintain robust growth, close attention will be paid to the balance of payments position, while maintaining the long-run commitment to an open economy. Export industries are expected to be an engine of growth of the economy. The government will continue to encourage changes in the production sector through structural reform aimed at trimming the high-cost economy. In this case, structural reform in the real sector of the economy will focus on the reduction of monopolies and restrictions to trade. Sustainable economic growth will depend on increasing productivity and efficiency in the real sector, providing infrastructure, and strengthening human resources. Changes in the government's role, in particular, improvements in markets and regulatory frameworks, greater reliance on the private sector, and more efficient public investment and services, will be critical in this effort.

Macroeconomic Policy in a Rapidly Changing Environment

Alongside the new opportunities in trade and external finance offered by globalization have come new challenges of macroeconomic management in an increasingly open, integrated, and competitive global economy. The integration of the developing countries into the global financial market, however, makes them more vulnerable to external financial disturbances. A more integrated capital market has exposed the smaller and less developed capital markets to the spillovers of turbulence from capital markets in the industrial countries. As capital tends to seek higher returns, capital flows will move easily from one country to another. The result of this is a vastly higher volume and greater rapidity of cross-border capital mobility, a development that has markedly complicated the tasks of managing domestic liquidity.

Policymakers are confronted more and more with a new discipline, the need to maintain the confidence of the market participants, both domestic and international. In view of the rapid growth of the financial and banking system, coordination of macropolicy (monetary policy) and micropolicy (financial sector policy) has taken on far greater significance.[8] Therefore, in the current era of globalization it is important that the effort to build a sound, stable financial system be integrated into the overall task of macroeconomic management.[9]

As mentioned earlier, rapid mobility of capital has given rise to a number of difficulties in managing domestic monetary policy. The difficulties will be heightened under a relatively fixed exchange rate system. Under less flexible exchange rate policy, capital inflows will immediately boost the growth of the money supply, thereby undermining the effectiveness of measures designed to control monetary expansion. When this situation exists, closing an existing, open economic system is no longer a realistic option. Neither is it possible to fend off capital inflows through a frontal counterattack. Hardly any country in the world is bolstered with adequate foreign reserves to counter international capital movements, leaving a monetary authority with little option but to make continuous adjustments to domestic monetary policy in line with international trends.

RECENT CURRENCY TURMOIL AND GOVERNMENT POLICY RESPONSES

As Indonesia's economy becomes more integrated into the global economy, it will also become more sensitive to disruption on an international scale. Any event, economic or otherwise, in Indonesia or in other countries will quickly spread into global financial markets. Recently, the abrupt shift in the foreign exchange market since the middle of July 1997 reflects, in part, much stronger contagion effects from the regional currency crisis than expected. The currency crisis that has plagued

Indonesia's economy is apparently more serious, more widespread, and more lasting than first thought. From mid-July 1997 to early January 1998, the cumulative depreciation of the rupiah reached 70%, with over half of this decline occurring since the end of November 1997, while the fall in the Jakarta stock exchange index reached 50%, both the largest declines in the region. The enormous depreciation of the rupiah did not seem to stem from macroeconomic imbalances, which remained quite modest (Table 14.1). Instead, the large depreciation reflected a severe loss of confidence in the currency, the financial sector, and the overall economy.

The Strategy

From the outset of the currency crisis, the government, supported by the International Monetary Fund, has taken strong corrective action based on three key components: tight monetary and fiscal policies, a fundamental restructuring of the financial sector, and further deregulation of the economy.

First, the authorities will maintain a tight fiscal and monetary policy stance, designed to stabilize fluctuations of the currency, improve monetary conditions, and narrow the current account deficit. Substantial fiscal measures have been put in place to keep the budget from a large deficit, while monetary policy will be kept tight, as necessary, to stabilize the exchange rate. Second, prompt and decisive action will be taken to restore the health of the financial system, including closing unviable banks. Third, a broad range of structural reforms, many of which are linked to issues of governance, will be implemented, including the liberalization of foreign trade and investment, dismantling domestic monopolies, allowing greater private sector participation in the provision of infrastructure, and expanding the privatization program.

These three components are actually bolstering the two aspects of the strategy of fundamental macroeconomic policy elaborated in this chapter: *prudent macroeconomic management* and *structural adjustment policies*, which include economic and financial reforms. We realized that our efforts to fundamentally reform the economy have to be strengthened and accelerated.

Macroeconomic Policies

To strengthen the effectiveness of monetary management, Bank Indonesia has turned to greater exchange rate flexibility through a gradual widening of the intervention band in the rupiah exchange rate against the U.S. dollar. This policy aims to stem heavy flows of speculative, short-term capital while also promoting interbank foreign exchange transactions. Moreover, on August 14, 1997, the government decided to abandon the rupiah-managed floating exchange rate system by eliminating the intervention band for the rupiah exchange rate. Market forces will determine the rupiah exchange rate, with the authorities influencing the market indirectly through fiscal and monetary policy. The Central Bank can, of course, still intervene in the market at its own discretion. A significant tightening of liquidity

Table 14.1
Indonesia Macroeconomic Indicators

	1992	1993	1994	1995	1996	1997
GDP AND MAJOR COMPONENTS						
Nominal GDP (trillion Rp)	282.4	329.8	382.2	454.5	532.6	624.3
Nominal GDP (billion US$)	139.1	158.0	175.5	197.7	227.3	126.0
Real GDP (change %)	7.2	7.3	7.5	8.1	8.0	5.0
Private Consumption (change %)	3.5	6.5	5.8	6.3	9.1	4.5
Private Investment (change %)	5.2	6.9	16.1	14.1	14.8	4.5
Government Consumption (change %)	5.8	0.1	2.3	3.4	3.8	1.5
Government Investment (change %)	5.4	2.9	4.7	7.4	14.8	14.1
Exports (change %)	14.7	6.6	9.0	4.3	5.5	11.2
Imports (change %)	6.6	4.4	13.3	16.8	7.8	8.2
PRICE AND LABOR						
GDP Deflator (%)	5.4	8.9	7.0	8.7	8.5	10.7
Consumer Price Index (change %)	4.9	9.8	9.2	8.6	6.5	11.1
Unemployment Rate (%)	2.7	3.1	4.4	7.0	4.9	N.a.
FINANCIAL MARKET						
M2 (change %)	20.2	22.0	20.2	27.6	29.6	23.2
Short Term Interest Rate (%)	16.7	11.8	14.3	17.2	17.3	20.7
Exchange Rate (Rp/US$)	2,030	2,087	2,164	2,253	2,343	4,911
BALANCE OF PAYMENTS						
Trade Balance (FOB % of GDP)	4.8	5.4	4.6	2.8	2.6	4.4
Current Account Balance (% of GDP)	-2.2	-1.5	-1.7	-3.4	-3.4	-2.7
EXTERNAL DEBTS						
Government Debts (billion US$)	48.8	52.5	58.6	59.6	55.3	54.9
Private Debts (billion US$)	24.6	28.1	37.9	48.2	54.9	65.9
Total Debts (billion US$)	73.4	80.6	96.5	107.8	110.2	120.8
POPULATION (millions)	186.04	189.14	192.22	195.28	200.00	205.00

Source: Bank Indonesia data bank.

conditions backed this policy. Since the crisis began, Bank Indonesia's monetary strategy has been to support the rupiah exchange rate and limit any increase in inflation by maintaining a firm monetary stance.

The government is fully committed to maintain a sound fiscal policy, based on a balanced budget principle, which precludes domestic borrowing. Consistent adherence to this principle has permitted the government to accumulate a surplus of 1% of GDP in 1996/1997 and 1997/1998. However, with the sharp depreciation of the rupiah and the deterioration in the economy, it is no longer feasible to aim at a surplus of 1% of GDP in 1998/1999. The budget has, therefore, been framed to strike an appropriate balance between preventing undue deterioration of the fiscal position and avoiding an excessive fiscal contraction. On the expenditure side, the government plans to postpone or reschedule major state enterprise and infrastructure projects. To reduce economic distortions and strengthen the fiscal position, the government intends to adjust administered prices with the aim of gradually eliminating subsidies on fuel and electricity. On the revenue side, the government has already announced increases in excises on alcohol and tobacco, which will effectively raise revenue from these items by 80% and 10%, respectively. In addition, the government will remove all value-added tax (VAT) exemptions, introduce a 5% local sales tax on gasoline, and raise the luxury sales tax.

Maintaining Indonesia's impressive record of poverty reduction over the past 30 years, through the provision of basic education, health, and other social services, is an integral part of the government policy framework. Yet large numbers of poor still remain, and it is imperative that the fiscal and monetary policies do not result in a worsening of their economic and social conditions. In these circumstances, special government initiatives will be necessary. In particular, the government plans to introduce community-based work programs to sustain the purchasing power of the poor in both urban and rural areas. In addition, budgetary allocations for social spending will be increased, so as to ensure that all Indonesians receive at least nine years of education and better basic medical services.

Financial Sector Restructuring

The weaknesses in the financial sector had their origin in the rapid expansion of the banking system and nonbank financial institutions since the early 1990s and problems of inadequate risk management and supervision, which ultimately led to a situation where a number of banks had significant amounts of nonperforming loans. Lending beyond legal limits and other shady dealings had become common at some of the private banks. Banks and nonbank financial institutions were also exposed to a potential downturn in the property sector, as this lending had grown rapidly over the past three years. Given this pre-crisis situation, Indonesia's financial sector was not prepared to withstand the financial turmoil that swept Southeast Asia starting in July 1997. The Central Bank was working to steadily overcome banking problems, but these efforts were overtaken by the spreading financial chaos in Southeast Asia.

The reverse sequencing of structural adjustment policies creates problems when adverse investment selection by financial institutions becomes serious. Problems are compounded when domestic projects are financed by overseas loans denominated in dollars, and exchange rate risk is not taken into account by the borrowers. The plunge in asset values, including stocks, real estates, and domestic currency instruments, worsens the financial sector plight and illustrates the dangers McKinnon and others have pointed out in the literature.[10] The extent of adverse investment selection and bad loans as well as clearer estimates of outstanding debt need to be clarified and dealt with. Failure to address the issues of transparency and to provide better information on the financial situation of the banking sector can threaten financial stability.

Therefore, a comprehensive restructuring of troubled financial institutions aimed at restoring the soundness of the financial system will also be key to the success of the government program. On November 1, 1997, 16 insolvent banks were closed, and weak, but viable, institutions have been required to quickly formulate and implement rehabilitation plans. At the same time, steps are being taken to minimize future systemic risks. In particular, the legal and regulatory frameworks will be strengthened by establishing strong enforcement mechanisms and introducing a stringent and clear exit policy.

However, the continued depreciation of the rupiah, high interest rates, and the slowdown in economic activities since then have led to a marked deterioration of the financial condition of the remaining banks. With public confidence in domestic private banks yet to recover, the process of "flight to quality" (to state and foreign banks) and "flight to safety" (to foreign currencies, especially the U.S. dollar) has increased the fragility of the financial system. This deterioration has been exacerbated by deposit runs and capital flight, forcing banks to increasingly resort to Central Bank liquidity support. Restoration of investor confidence is once again a high priority. The adoption of strong measures to correct the problems in the financial sector, including the writing off of nonperforming loans, should be accompanied by strengthening of institutional reforms. In order to restore the confidence of depositors and creditors, both domestic and foreign, in the Indonesian banking system and to reestablish the soundness of the system, the government is undertaking a comprehensive program to rehabilitate the system. The program comprises two main elements: first, the provision of a full guarantee by the government to all depositors and creditors of locally incorporated commercial banks and second, the establishment of the Indonesian Bank Restructuring Agency (IBRA), which will be responsible for rehabilitating those banks that are at present not sound and do not have good prospects of restoring themselves to soundness.

Structural Reforms

Structural impediments to economic activities are also at the center of market concerns about Indonesia's future prospects. As mentioned before, Indonesia has made substantial progress in opening up to international competition and deregulating the domestic economy. Notwithstanding these efforts, numerous barriers still stand in the way of both imports and exports, while some sectors are not open to foreign investment, and extensive regulations restrain domestic competition. Governance issues intersect with a number of restrictions, adding to perceptions of inequity and creating uncertainty for domestic and foreign investors. Unless structural reforms are accelerated, and governance issues dealt with, both foreign and domestic investment and, therefore, growth will be adversely affected.

To address these issues, the government has launched a bold strategy of structural reforms, aimed at bringing the economy back to a path of rapid growth, by transforming the "high-cost economy" into one that would be more open, competitive, and efficient. To achieve this transformation, the strategy called for foreign trade and investment to be further liberalized, domestic activities to be further deregulated, and the privatization program to be accelerated.

CONCLUDING REMARKS

Looking ahead to the twenty-first century, we can expect that increased uncertainty and competition will characterize the world economy. The recent economic crisis has provided a bitter experience to the Indonesian economy. Widening and intensifying international linkages in trade and finance can be a boomerang to the economy. Indonesia has been in the forefront of countries anticipating the new era of global trade and financial markets. Experiences have shown that in facing challenges, Indonesia has always responded by continuing the adoption of the two macroeconomic strategies: (1) structural adjustment policies, which include financial sector restructuring and real sector reforms, and (2) prudent macroeconomic management, in which the role of monetary and fiscal policies becomes increasingly important in pursuing stable macroeconomic conditions.

The need for efficient and competitive financial and real sectors is critical to building a solid foundation for sustainable economic growth. Therefore, efforts to further reform the financial system and improve efficiency in the real sector constitute an integral part of the overall structural adjustment policies. Indonesia is confident that the policies of growth on the supply side of the economy, combined with good management in the demand side of the economy that it has adopted in the past, will continue to serve it well in the years to come.

NOTES

The views expressed in this chapter are those of the authors and do not represent those of the Bank Indonesia. We thank all participants of the ICSEAD Workshop 97 for valuable comments. The discussions we had in Kitakyushu were also indispensable for revising this chapter. However, the authors are solely responsible for possible errors.

1. Comprehensive discussions concerning Indonesia's economy around that period can be seen in Hal Hill, *The Indonesian Economy since 1966: Southeast Asia's Emerging Giant* (Cambridge: Cambridge University Press, 1996).

2. This argument it elaborated on at length by Ali Wardhana in "Financial Reform: Achievements, Problems, and Prospects," Keynote Address, Australian National University Indonesia Update Conference, August 1994.

3. Theoretically, the 1988 package was in line with the argument of "financial deepening" suggested by Edward Shaw, *Financial Deepening in Economic Development* (New York: Oxford University Press, 1973).

4. See Ali Wardhana, "Structural Adjustment in Indonesia: Export and the High Cost Economy," Keynote Address, the 24th SEACEN Governors Meeting, Bangkok, January 1989.

5. For elaboration, see Adrianus Mooy, Inaugural Speech at the University of Indonesia, 1991.

6. For further elaboration see J. Soedradjad Djiwandono, "Financial Sector Liberalization and Reform: The Experience of Indonesia," paper presented at the 29th Asian Development Bank Annual Meeting Seminar on Financial Sector in Transition, Manila, the Philippines, April 1996.

7. For further elaboration, see J. Soedradjad Djiwandono, "Indonesia amidst the Dynamic Economies in the Asia-Pacific Region," paper presented at the Asia-Pacific Roundtable organized by Stanford University, January 1996.

8. See also Michel Camdessus's speech in the IMF-World Bank Annual Meeting, 1996.

9. See John Lindgren et al., *Bank Soundness and Macroeconomic Policy* (Washington, DC: International Monetary Fund, 1996).

10. Ronald McKinnon, "The Order of Economic Liberalization: Lessons from Chile and Argentina," *Carnegie-Rochester Series on Public* 17 (Autumn 1982), pp. 59–86.

15

Development in China, 1978–1998*

Tongsan Wang

China has experienced a high rate of economic growth for 20 years and has made remarkable achievements since reform and opening up to the rest of the world started in 1978. According to the official statistics, from 1978 to 1997, the average annual growth rate of GDP was 9.8% (Figure 15.1). Economists take great interest in the "Chinese miracle." This chapter considers China's development policy over the past two decades.

In the report of the 14th Communist Party Congress in 1992, Chinese leader Jiang Zemin noted China's "historical course from rural reform to urban reform, from reform of the economic system to that in other fields, and from enlivening the domestic economy to opening to the outside world." The development achievements of the past two decades can be attributed to successful policy reforms and the opening of the domestic economy to international influence. In the course of reforming the old system, the vitality of the economy improved. By opening to the outside world, China joined other countries in learning advanced technology, obtaining necessary investment capital, and making use of its comparative advantage. The macroeconomic management system set up and perfected in reforms has played an increasingly important role in economic development. The central government controls the speed and quality of economic development and maintains rapid, long-term growth by formulating industrial policy and by using financial and monetary instruments. Three aspects of Chinese development policy are:

—Economic system reform;

—Opening to the outside world;

—Strategy and policy of macroeconomic development.

*This chapter was written with the assistance of Tao Li, Yanqun Zhang, and Li Wang.

Figure 15.1
Economic Growth of China, 1978–1997

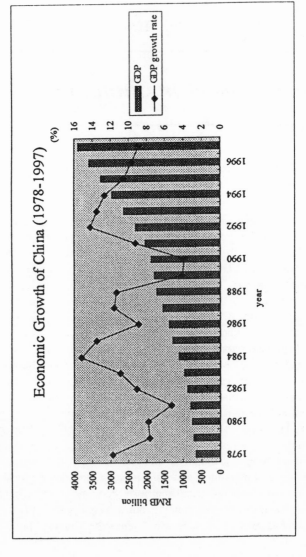

Economic Growth of China (1978-1997)

Source: China Statistical Yearbook, 1997 and previous years.

REFORMS: INSTITUTIONAL INNOVATION AND ECONOMIC DEVELOPMENT

China's reform is generally regarded as "gradual reform," different from "radical reform" carried out in the former Soviet Union and the Eastern European countries. The gradual reform approach is key to rapid growth in China. The critical difference between the two approaches is that radical reforms were designed in advance, so to speak, artificially. In contrast, Chinese leaders and economists had no clear advance designs of their final aims, directions, and steps. In fact, most of the policies of reforms were developed and implemented (Lin, 1995), just as, in the words proposed by Deng Xiaoping, the chief architect of China's reform, "groping stones to cross the river." Institutional innovations have ranged across every field from macromanagement to micro-operations.

Chinese reforms have undergone three stages:

—The takeoff stage (1978–1984),

—The full-swing stage (1984–1992),

—The deepening stage (1992–   ) .

THE STAGES OF REFORMS

First Stage (1978–1984)

The 10 years of "Cultural Revolution" that ended in 1976 drove the economy to the edge of collapse. Many Chinese politicians and intellectuals realized that the political route based on class struggle had to be terminated and that China should concentrate on economic reconstruction. At that time, the great majority of common people believed that as long as China focused on the economy instead of political movements, its economy would develop rapidly, and living standards would improve. The political route based on class struggle was ended at the Chinese Communist Party's 11th National Congress in December 1978. At that meeting, leaders adopted the idea that "the focus of work [should be] shifted to economic development" and made a decision to move toward "reform and opening."

The reforms began in rural China, mainly at the micro- or household level. The system of contracted responsibilities for the household with remuneration linked to output broke through the enforced egalitarianism that had existed in the rural economy and had reduced peasants' incentives. Under the new scheme, once peasants had met their output quotas to the collective or village, they were permitted to sell the rest on the free market. As a result, the output of food increased by a big margin, and rural production developed rapidly. In this period, the central government also experimented with reforms for management of some state-owned enterprises and partially loosened state plan controls for enterprises in order to increase incentives. These changes were limited in scope and depth. Collectives, individually owned enterprises, and especially township enterprises developed gradually with the encouragement and help of the central government. The main success was the development of the rural economy. In general, the reforms did not deal with the fundamental contradictions of the Chinese economic system.

Second Stage (1984–1992)

In this stage, the focus of reforms was shifted from rural areas to cities. In 1987, at its 13th National Congress, the party stated that the socialist planned economy was inherently a consensus system between market and plan. Planned adjustment and market adjustment were both means to control economic development. Privately owned firms and "foreign-funded enterprises" would be a necessary and profitable supplement to the socialist economy for a long time to come.

At this stage of the reforms, the main focus was to break through the constraints imposed by some traditional concepts. The policies of this stage were to increase the vitality of state-owned enterprises by setting up contracted responsibilities for them. Under a "dual-track" system, market prices coexisted with centrally planned prices. At the same time, the central government reformed macroeconomic policies and began to carry out reforms in taxation and in financial institutions.

Third Stage (1992–Present)

After three years' effort, inflation was restrained, and economic order took a favorable turn. However, when concerns about igniting inflation flared once more, the central and local governments were overcautious for a time. As a result, economic growth during 1989–1990 was reduced to 5%. In 1992, with a return to high growth, economic reforms entered a new stage.

In October 1992, at its 14th National Congress, the Chinese Communist Party set the goal of establishing a new system, a "socialist market economy." After more than 10 years of experimentation, China confirmed the direction of reforms. The party advanced the thesis that it was basic to China's economic system to retain a dominant position for public ownership in addition to developing other forms of ownership; the two models of ownership would operate side by side. In December 1993, the Chinese government set up the basic framework to establish a market economy:

—Establishing a modern enterprise system with "clearly established ownership, well-defined power and responsibility, separation of enterprise from administration, and scientific management";

—Fostering and developing the market system to serve as the basic means of regulating the allocation of resources and building a unified and open market with orderly competition;

—Transforming the government's functions and establishing and perfecting the macroeconomic control system.

In 1994, China took great steps in reforming finance, taxation, banking, foreign trade, foreign exchange, and pricing. Next, we look more closely at rural reforms and state-owned enterprise reforms.

Rural Reforms

China is an agricultural country with a huge population. Agriculture occupies a core position in the national economy. The central government has always emphasized that agriculture is, in fact, the foundation of the economy. As noted earlier, before 1978, under the People's Commune system, the peasants had no incentives to produce, and, as a consequence, labor productivity was low.

At first, rural reform was carried out spontaneously by the peasants themselves. For example, in the initial stage, in a poor village in An Hui Province, the peasants divided the land among the households. Some neighboring villages followed An Hui's example. Within a year, it was clear that this policy was efficient, and the output of agricultural products in these villages had increased by a big margin. Some local leaders acquiesced in, and approved of, the reforms, and then the central government affirmed the system formally and spread it to the whole country. This new system was usually called the *household responsibility system*. As noted earlier in this chapter, it established contracted responsibilities on a household basis but allowed households to sell the surplus on the market so that remuneration was linked to output. At first, the contract deadline for landholdings was limited to three years, but this was too short a time to stimulate peasants' investment in improving the soil. In 1984, the contract period was extended to 15 years and then to 30 years in 1995. At present, the National People's Congress is formulating laws on contracted lands in order to protect peasants' profits and safeguard stable development of agriculture.

There were great gains from rural reform. From 1978 to 1982, the gross value of national agricultural output increased 7.8% per year. The annual growth rate was 9.5% in 1983, then up to 14.5% in 1984, exceeding the average annual growth of 3.2% during 26 years from 1953 to 1978 (Table 15.1). In 1984, per capita income reached renminbi (RMB)355, an increase of 21.2% over the previous year. The output of the main agricultural products increased substantially. The output of grain and cotton, for example, totaled 40.7 and 60.7 billion tons, respectively. China's production of cotton leaped to first place in the world. Some economists estimated that half the increase of agricultural output came from the improvement of labor productivity reflecting innovations in the rural operating system.

However, there were still problems in the new rural system. The major problem was that small agricultural plots slowed agricultural mechanization because peasants operating small plots of land could not realize the benefits of mechanized production. As the contribution of institutional innovation to economic growth slowed, the growth rate of agricultural output decreased. From 1985 to 1988, the growth rate of value-added in agriculture was only 3.1%. Therefore, new institutional innovations were called for in agriculture and rural areas. Since 1990, the

Table 15.1
Agricultural Output, 1978–1997

Year	Gross output value of agriculture (RMB billions)	growth rate of gross agricultural output (%)	Gross crop output (million tons)	Growth rate of gross crop output (%)	Per capita net income of rural residents (RMB)
1978	139.7	8.1	304.77	-	133.57
1979	169.76	7.5	332.12	9.0	-
1980	192.26	1.4	320.56	-3.5	191.33
1981	218.06	5.8	325.02	1.4	223.44
1982	248.33	11.3	354.50	9.1	270.11
1983	275.0	7.8	387.28	9.2	309.77
1984	321.41	12.3	407.31	5.2	355.33
1985	361.95	3.4	379.11	-6.9	397.6
1986	401.30	3.4	391.51	3.3	423.76
1987	467.57	5.8	402.98	2.9	462.55
1988	586.53	3.9	394.08	-2.2	544.94
1989	653.47	3.1	407.55	3.4	601.51
1990	766.21	7.6	446.24	9.5	686.31
1991	815.70	3.7	435.29	-2.5	708.55
1992	908.47	6.4	442.66	1.7	783.99
1993	1099.55	7.8	456.49	3.1	921.62
1994	1575.05	8.6	445.10	-2.5	1220.98
1995	2034.09	10.9	466.57	4.8	1577.74
1996	2342.87	9.4	504.54	8.1	1926.07
1997	2470.92	5.3	494.17	-2.1	2090.13

Sources: *China Statistical Yearbook*, 1997 and previous years; *A Statistical Survey of China*, 1998.

central government has tried to enlarge the scientific and technical input to agriculture. It has adopted a series of measures to encourage "big farming households" to lease land so that they can mechanize and operate on a large scale. The central government is trying to find a way to further stimulate peasants' incentives and to improve agricultural output in ways other than increasing the price of food.

Town and Village Enterprises

The gains in productivity and income coming from rural reform made available financial and labor resources at the local level. These were turned into a success story with the rapid development of town and village enterprises (TVEs) As is shown in Table 15.2, the gross value of industrial output of the TVEs increased at extraordinary rates, particularly during the booms of 1984–1988 and 1991–1994. The TVEs, which are largely light and processing industries operating on a small scale, have far outdistanced the state-owned industries (SOEs). Beginning with a share of only 11.6% in 1978, the TVEs accounted for more than 50% of industrial output by the mid-1990s. These firms operate with a "hard" budget constraint; they must cover their costs. Despite the fact that they remain under collective ownership, they are guided by market forces. It should be noted, however, that their advantage in terms of growth is offset by the fact that they frequently operate on a small scale, with low capital intensity and primitive technology.

OPENING TO THE WORLD ECONOMY

When the People's Republic of China was founded in 1949, China's international trade was limited to the socialist bloc. After the relationship with the USSR was broken in the late 1950s, China had to develop its economy by self-reliance and implemented a "closed door" policy. In the 11th Party Central Committee Congress, responding to the changes in international circumstances, the party put forward the "opening up" policy. In the 20 years since, the economy has been greatly opened to foreign trade and influence. This has not only contributed directly to Chinese economic development but also supported China's reform.

China's opening up was a gradual process. It began by setting up the special economic zones (SEZs) to open the coastal and riverine cities, then to opening the frontier cities, and finally to opening in all areas. The setting up of SEZs and economic experimentation areas (EEAs) improved local economic growth and encouraged economic reform and additional plans for opening more broadly. The SEZs that served as the testing grounds for reform and opening were not only the window to the outside world but also the forerunners of economic system reform and of the construction of the market economy. They provided much valuable experience for the development of the whole Chinese economy. They played demonstrative, diffusive, and leading roles in making institutional changes, upgrading industries, and opening China more widely to the outside world. According to the official statistics, the GDP of the five special economic zones (Hainan, Shen-

Table 15.2
Development of Township and Village Enterprises (TVEs)

Year	Gross value of industrial output of TVEs (RMB billion)	Growth rate of gross industrial output value of TVEs (%)	Growth rate of gross industrial output value of SOEs (%)	Share of TVEs in gross industrial output (%)
1978	49.31	-	14.4	11.6
1979	54.84	11.2	8.88	11.7
1980	65.69	19.8	5.6	12.7
1981	74.53	13.5	2.53	13.8
1982	85.31	14.5	7.05	14.7
1983	101.68	19.2	9.39	15.7
1984	170.99	68.2	8.92	22.4
1985	272.84	59.6	12.9	28.1
1986	354.09	29.8	6.2	31.6
1987	474.31	34.0	11.3	34.3
1988	649.57	36.9	12.6	35.6
1989	742.84	14.4	3.9	33.7
1990	846.16	13.9	3	35.4
1991	1162.17	37.3	8.6	43.6
1992	1797.54	54.7	12.4	52.0
1993	3154.07	75.5	5.7	65.2
1994	4258.85	35.0	6.5	60.7
1995	5125.92	20.4	8.2	55.8
1996	5553.74	8.3	5.1	55.8

Sources: *China Statistical Yearbook*, 1997 and previous years.

zhen, Zhuhai, Shantou, and Xiamen) reached RMB 215.5 billion and accounted for 3.8% of the total GDP in 1996. Total export-import volume accounted for 20% of the whole economy in 1996 and grew by 36.8% per year in the 1990s.

Use of Foreign Capital

China has had great success in absorbing and utilizing foreign capital. By the end of 1997, the volume of foreign capital flowing into China was growing at 30.5% annually. Accumulated foreign capital, including foreign direct investment (FDI), foreign loans, foreign securities, and so on, exceeded U.S.$360 billion; FDI was U.S.$220 billion. At present, about 240,000 foreign funded enterprises (FFEs) are operating in China. China has been first among the developing countries in absorbing FDI for four years from 1993 and in the world, second to the United States. In 1997, foreign capital inflow reached U.S.$64.4 billion, increasing 13% over the previous year (Table 15.3).

In order to attract foreign investors, the central and local governments implemented many preferential policies, of which taxation concessions and exemptions were dominant. For example, in the SEZs and EEAs, the income tax rate for FFEs is 15%, and the tax rate on profit remittances is 10%. For high-tech and export enterprises, the income tax rate is only 10%, and profit remittances, capital goods imports, and product exports are all tax-free. New enterprises are granted a tax holiday for two years, and the income tax is levied at half the normal rate in the following three years. These policies are more favorable than those of Hong Kong (now a part of China), Macao, Taiwan and other Southeast Asian countries.

With the increase in the use of foreign capital, some contradictions and problems arose in connection with the operations of FFEs. In order to attract foreign capital, a favorable environment and preferential policies were not enough. Laws that protected the benefits of foreign investors and standardized the treatment of foreign enterprises needed to be enacted. Beginning in 1989, China published a series of laws: the taxation law, the labor law, the law of exchange management, the law of enterprise registration, the law of foreign economic contracts, and so on. At the same time, the Chinese government signed agreements with many countries concerning protection of investment and avoidance of dual taxation. With the implementation of some local laws and regulations, an environment suitable for international investment was established.

Some problems of using foreign capital were connected with two issues. One was related to unequal industrial distribution. Most foreign capital was concentrated in labor-intensive processing industries, while foreign capital inputs into technology-intensive and basic industry were comparatively small. The other issue was the unequal regional distribution. The FDI flows were mainly focused on the eastern coastal regions. According to industrial surveys, the accumulated contract volumes of FDI in the eastern regions accounted for 90.4% of total FDI at the end of 1995. To stimulate development of the middle and western regions, the central government put most foreign government loans into infrastructure and basic industrial

Table 15.3
Use of Foreign Capital

Year	Foreign capital inflow ($ billion)	Growth rate (%)	Foreign loans ($ billion)	Direct foreign investment ($ billion)	Share of foreign capital in fixed investment (%)
1979-1983	14.4	19.8	11.8	1.8	2.6
1984	2.7	36.5	1.3	1.3	3.9
1985	4.6	71.8	2.7	1.7	3.6
1986	7.3	56.2	5.0	1.9	4.4
1987	8.5	16.5	5.8	2.3	4.8
1988	10.2	21.0	6.5	3.2	5.9
1989	10.1	-1.6	6.3	3.4	6.6
1990	10.3	2.3	6.5	3.5	6.3
1991	11.6	12.3	6.9	4.4	5.7
1992	19.2	66.2	7.9	11.0	5.8
1993	39.0	102.9	11.2	27.5	7.3
1994	43.2	10.9	9.3	33.8	9.9
1995	48.1	11.4	10.3	37.5	11.2
1996	54.8	13.9	12.7	41.7	11.7
1997	64.4	17.5	12.0	45.3	na

Sources: China Statistical Yearbook, 1997; A Statistical Survey of China, 1998.

projects in those regions and provided incentives to encourage foreign capital to flow there. According to statistical sources, 47% of the loans of foreign governments and 40% of the loans of international financial organizations were put into the middle and western regions in 1996.

The use of foreign capital makes up for shortages of construction funds, promotes the level of industrial technology and management, and advances economic growth. It also makes use of, and improves, available human talent, increases employment, raises tax collection, stimulates imports and exports, and adds to foreign exchange reserves.

With the increase of the numbers of FFEs and the fields they entered, the problem of competition between the FFEs and domestic enterprises became troublesome. As mentioned before, the central and local governments formulated many preferential policies, especially taxation reductions and exemptions, to attract foreign capital. These concessionary policies were not available to domestic enterprises. Already at a disadvantage because of the heavy burdens of the old economic system, state-owned enterprises and collective enterprises were unable to compete with foreign enterprises. Some township and village enterprises (TVEs) and individually owned enterprises that experienced rapid growth in the initial stage of the reform were also hurt by competition because of their unequal treatment. The Chinese government realized the seriousness of the problem and adopted some appropriate measures. China adopted a policy to give FFEs "national treatment," hoping it would help its effort to join WTO. In addition, new measures are being implemented to improve the investment environment and to attract foreign capital.

Foreign Trade

China's foreign trade developed rapidly since reform and the opening-up policy. From 1978 to 1997, the total value of imports and exports increased by 14.5 times from U.S.$20.6 billion to U.S.$325.1 billion, and the average annual growth rate was 15.5%, 5.7% above the GDP growth rate (Table 15.4). China ranked 10th in the world in international trade in 1997, up from 32nd in 1978. The expansion of foreign trade served to stimulate economic growth. It is estimated that in the period 1991–1995, a 1% increase in exports could make the economy grow 0.2%. The share of exports in GDP reached more than 20%, up from 5% in 1979. The foreign trade structure has also changed greatly from agricultural and mineral primary products to industrial manufactured products. The ratio of primary products exports to industrial manufactured products exports has changed from 1:1 in 1980 to 1:6 in 1996. From 1990, service trade increased as rapidly as goods trade. Although there are still many restrictions on FFEs seeking to enter Chinese services markets, in 1995 import of insurance and other services doubled over the previous year.

Table 15.4
Imports and Exports

Year	total value of imports & exports ($ billion)	Growth rate (%)	Imports ($ billion)	growth rate (%)	Exports ($ billion)	growth rate (%)
1978	20.64		10.89		9.75	
1979	29.33	42.1	15.67	43.9	13.66	40.1
1980	38.14	30.0	20.02	27.8	18.12	32.7
1981	44.02	15.4	22.01	9.9	22.01	21.5
1982	41.61	-5.5	19.29	-12.4	22.32	1.4
1983	43.62	4.8	21.39	10.9	22.23	-0.4
1984	53.55	22.8	27.41	28.1	26.14	17.6
1985	69.6	30.0	42.25	54.1	27.35	4.6
1986	73.85	6.1	42.91	1.6	30.94	13.1
1987	82.65	11.9	43.21	0.7	39.44	27.5
1988	102.78	24.4	55.27	27.9	47.51	20.5
1989	111.68	8.7	59.14	7.0	52.54	10.6
1990	115.44	3.4	53.35	-9.8	62.09	18.2
1991	135.63	17.5	63.79	19.6	71.84	15.7
1992	165.53	22.0	80.59	26.3	84.94	18.2
1993	195.7	18.2	103.96	29.0	91.74	8.0
1994	236.62	20.9	115.61	11.2	121.01	31.9
1995	280.86	18.7	132.08	14.2	148.78	22.9
1996	289.88	3.2	138.83	5.1	151.05	1.5
1997	325.06	12.1	142.36	2.5	182.7	21.0

Sources: *China Statistical Yearbook*, 1997; *A Statistical Survey of China*, 1998.

Reform of the Foreign Trade System

Decentralizing export management was the most important aspect of the reform of the foreign trade system. During the experimental stage from 1979 to 1986, controls on imports and exports of commodities were gradually eliminated. Reform of the foreign trade system started in 1987 by implementing a contract responsibility system on foreign trade offices. In order to encourage exports, the government implemented an export subsidy policy in addition to operating a duty drawback scheme. Controls on the use of foreign exchange were modified so that the exporting enterprises unilaterally used the "retained" portion of the foreign exchange earnings. Based on the success of experiments giving firms responsibility for their own profits and losses in light industries, crafts, and clothing exports, the old foreign trade system was abolished. Instead of turning their foreign exchange over to government agencies and using trade quotas, exporting enterprises could use a large part of their foreign exchange earnings. A foreign exchange revenue settlement system was also started. This basically completed the reform of the foreign trade system.

Reform of the Foreign Exchange System

The reform of the foreign exchange system and the reform of the foreign trade system are connected. The exchange rate is an important tool to manage and control foreign trade. Before the reform, the main problem of China's pegged exchange rate system was the overvaluation of the renminbi (RMB), also known as the yuan. In 1978, U.S.\$1=RMB1.5. This noncompetitive exchange rate system had unfavorable effects on import and export trade. China adopted a dual foreign exchange rate system in 1981, with different exchange rates for trade and nontrade items. Under the dual exchange rate system, China adjusted the exchange rate again and again in 1985, 1986, 1989, and 1990. In effect, the RMB was gradually devalued.

However, the system of foreign exchange management changed very little. The means of managing and adjusting the exchange rate were mainly administrative, and there was no market-adjustment mechanism. As a consequence, the exchange rate for the RMB did not fluctuate in accord with changes in the value of foreign currencies, nor did it adjust in response to the demand and supply of foreign exchange. The persistent overvaluation of the RMB seriously affected the development of foreign trade. Moreover, the black market and other rent-seeking actions caused by overvaluation and the dual-track system did great harm to the Chinese economic environment. After the violent fluctuation of the foreign exchange market in 1993, the Chinese government decided to reform the foreign exchange system thoroughly.

Four major reforms of the foreign exchange system established a new foreign exchange mechanism for China in 1994:

—Unifying the official and swap market exchange rate at the swap market rate, U.S.$1=8.7RMB;

—Permitting the RMB to be converted freely for current account items;

—Setting up a foreign exchange market among the banks in place of the swap market;

—Adopting a managed floating exchange rate system that permits those banks operating foreign exchange businesses to float the bulletin exchange rate above or below the standard rate of the Central Bank within a limited range.

In 1996, the Chinese foreign exchange authority abolished many remaining restrictions on exchange to make the RMB completely convertible with respect to current account transactions. The Chinese government also declared that the next target of foreign exchange reform was to make the RMB freely convertible on capital items as well so that the RMB will ultimately become a completely convertible currency.

Import and Export Policy

The rapid growth of foreign trade should mainly be attributed to the non-state-owned economy, especially the FFEs and TVEs (Table 15.5). With regard to exports, the FFEs accounted for over 40% of the total exports in 1996, up from 1.1% in 1985, and contributed more than 60% to the growth of exports in 1996, up from 18% in 1988. First, the FFEs knew the demands of the international market better and had more experience with international competition than domestic enterprises. Second, most products of the FFEs and TVEs were labor-intensive and, thus, embodied the comparative advantages of China in the international market. Processing trade played an important role in China's export trade; it accounted for 50% of the total exports in 1995. By choosing appropriate directions for development and suitable products. the FFEs and TVEs advanced China's comparative advantages in international trade and fostered the transformation of trade policies from import-substitution to export orientation.

To stimulate exports, China implemented flexible tariff policies. Although China's published tariffs were high for some time after reform and opening up had begun, 33% in the early 1990s, the real tariff level was very low owing to policies such as duty drawbacks for exports, duty reductions and exemptions for FFEs, and so on. This phenomenon is reflected in the low share of tariff receipts in total fiscal revenue. For example, the share was only 5% in 1993.

The development of import trade also benefited from the policy of foreign capital use and the flexible policy on real tariffs. Most FDIs and foreign loans entered China as goods imports. According to research (Niu Nanjie, 1998), about U.S.$85 billion of foreign capital flowed into China as goods imports during the 14 years from 1983 to 1997. For FFEs, imports were higher than exports all along, and their share in total imports was rising year after year, from 40% in 1993 to 54% in the first half

Table 15.5
Imports and Exports of Foreign-Funded Enterprises (FFEs)

Year	Exports ($ million)	Share of FFEs in total exports (%)	Imports ($ million)	Share of FFEs in total imports (%)
1980	8.24	0.05	34.41	0.17
1981	32.35	0.15	110.87	0.50
1982	52.87	0.24	276.42	1.43
1983	330.36	1.49	288.01	1.35
1984	68.94	0.26	399.21	1.46
1985	296.70	1.08	2064.10	4.89
1986	582.03	1.88	2430.31	5.67
1987	1208.09	3.06	3122.18	7.23
1988	2456.42	5.17	5746.71	10.40
1989	4913.20	9.35	8796.17	14.87
1990	7813.79	12.58	12306.33	23.07
1991	12047.25	16.77	16907	26.50
1992	17356.19	20.43	26370	32.72
1993	25237.17	27.50	41833.20	40.24
1994	34712.97	28.68	52934.17	45.76
1995	46876.00	31.51	62942	47.66
1996	58531.00	40.91	67442	52.42

Source: *China Yearbook of Foreign Economic Statistics.*

of 1997. Most of these imports, 44% in 1995, for example, were imported as processing trade that was duty-exempt in China.

In recent years, as China has campaigned to enter the WTO, it has decreased the level of import tariffs significantly and removed most nontariff barriers. The average import tariff rate decreased from 32% in 1992 to 19.4% in 1996. The proportion of import and export goods controlled by licenses fell from 43.5% in 1992 to 25.3% in 1995. At present, import tariffs on agricultural products, gauze, sugar, iron and steel, and automobiles still remain high in order to reduce competitive pressures on national priority industries and immature industries.

With the deepening of reform, the opening of the economy, and the strengthening of China's economic power, the Chinese government has started to encourage domestic enterprises to invest abroad directly. Investment abroad can make up for domestic resource shortages. Although China has developed some products with international competitiveness, the share of Chinese products in the international market is very small, and export trade has been restricted by many tariffs and nontariff barriers. Investing and establishing factories abroad allow Chinese firms to exploit foreign markets directly.

MACROECONOMIC DEVELOPMENT STRATEGY AND POLICIES

Economic Development Strategy

The relationship between growth and efficiency was an important aspect of China's new development strategy. Before 1978 China made the speeding up and promoting of extensive development its first priority. Beginning in 1979, the government put forward measures to reform enterprises seeking to improve technology and to deepen their productive capability. When the target of doubling GDP was put forward in 1983, the emphasis was on "constant improvement of economic efficiency." The 13th Communist Party of China (CPC) proposed that the development of science and technology and education should get top priority and that economic development should focus on technical progress and the improvement of labor quality. In 1995, the Central Committee of the CPC advanced the strategy to "promote the nation by science and education" and stressed that the growth mode should be transformed from an extensive to an intensive one.

In terms of the speed of development, Chinese authorities have changed course several times. The Chinese economy has experienced several "stop-go" cycles. The extremely high growth rates of 1983–1984, 1986–1987, and so on caused severe economic overheating and inflation. In order to solve these problems, the Chinese government had to slow growth. What constituted an optimal growth rate was hotly debated among economists in late 1980s. Most economists suggested that an excessively high growth rate was harmful to the Chinese economy. However, Deng Xiaoping pointed out during his inspection trips to southern China in 1992 that it was not appropriate for backward countries like China to develop slowly; China must seize any opportunity to achieve high-speed growth. His opinion won broad support, and the Chinese economy soon heated up again and experienced another high-growth period from 1992 to 1995. Fortunately, the Chinese economy realized a "soft landing" after three years' effort. Nevertheless, to achieve several high-speed growth periods is still the basic objective of the Chinese government.

Although the old egalitarian income distribution policy played a great role in wiping out large-scale poverty in the early period after the founding of the PRC, it did not offer necessary incentives to labor and was inefficient in improving productivity. In 1978, the Chinese government advanced the idea that it was all right for some people to become wealthy by honest, hard work. This represented a great change in ideology and in the distribution policy, which was to be "efficiency first and fair considered also." This policy inspired people to be active and creative in developing the economy.

However, the income gap was growing with the rapid economic growth, and the problem of unfair distribution is now serious. According to recent research (Zhao and Li, 1997; Li et al., 1998), the Gini coefficient of the nation as a whole is 0.445, while that of rural people increased from 0.21 in 1978 to 0.34 in 1995 and that of urban people increased from 0.16 in 1978 to 0.28 in 1995 (it was 0.30 in 1994). The per capita income of urban people was 2.5 times of that of rural people. From the perspective of the common Chinese people, the most unfair aspect of the income distribution is that most of the richest people are those who earn big money illegally or by special privilege. The enlarged income gap discourages most Chinese much more than it creates incentives. Thus, new policy measures for solving the unfair distribution should be enacted to maintain the healthy, sustainable development of the Chinese economy. This is one of the hard tasks faced by the Chinese government.

Macroeconomic Stability Policy

The growth pattern of the Chinese economy in the 1978–1997 period shows four growth cycles: 1978–1983, 1984–1986, 1987–1991, and 1992–1997 (Figure 15.2). The GDP and inflation movements correspond to the fluctuations of investment.

The instability in the process of Chinese economic development was mainly caused by inconsistencies between the macroenvironment and micromechanisms during reform. As China's reform measures were introduced, they were often in contradiction with the macroenvironment (Figure 15.3). On one hand, the contradictions pushed the reforms ahead. On the other hand, it was just such contradictions that occasionally caused either overheating and inflation or, alternatively, increased unemployment. On a number of occasions, the central government had to try to stabilize the economy or even to "brake suddenly," which was often followed by a slowdown.

Figure 15.2
GDP Growth, Investment Growth, and Inflation

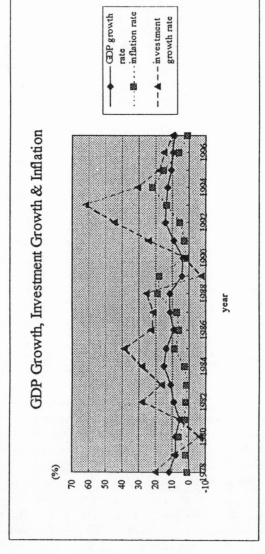

Source: China Statistical Yearbook, various years.

Figure 15.3
Fiscal Expenditure, Money Supply, and GDP Growth

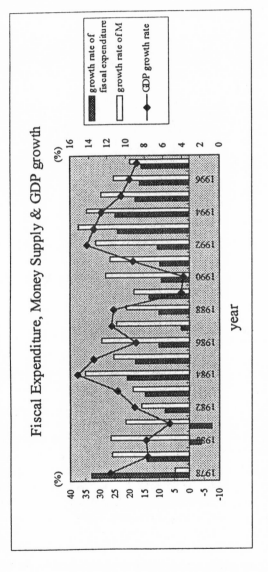

Fiscal Expenditure, Money Supply & GDP growth

Source: China Statistical Yearbook, various years.

221

Table 15.6
Fiscal Revenue of the Central Government before and after Taxation Reform

	1993	1994	1995	1996	1997
Fiscal Revenue of Central Government (RMB billion)	95.75	290.65	325.65	366.11	421.65
Growth Rate of Fiscal Revenue of Central Government (%)	-2.2	203.6	12.0	12.4	15.2
Share of Central Government in Total Fiscal Revenue (%)	22.0	55.7	52.2	49.4	48.8

Fiscal System Reform and Fiscal Policies

Under the planned system, the finances of the central government played a key role in national economic development. All of the profits of enterprises were turned over to the national finance department, and the budget of the central government was the main channel of fund allocation.

The main focus of fiscal reform during the 1980s was decentralization, that is, giving part of the government's fiscal authority to local government bodies. This focus encouraged local governments to expand this revenue base and to develop the local economy. Reforms strengthened local finances; local revenue accounted for half of total fiscal revenue in the late 1980s. At the same time, the revenue stream of the central government fell sharply, and the budget deficit grew. This fiscal problem weakened the ability of the central government to control and manage the national economy.

In order to stop this trend and establish an efficient system of macroeconomic management and control, a dramatic step of setting up a "tax-sharing system" was taken at the beginning of 1994. The reform of the "tax-sharing system" divided the authority and responsibility between the local and the central governments and regulated the taxation drawback and transfer payment system. This reform strengthened the finances of the central government greatly (Table 15.6).

As a result of these fiscal system reforms, the role of public finance in economic development was reduced. Fiscal policy has been tightened several times since 1979. For example, in order to control overheating of the economy and inflation, tighter fiscal policies were adopted in 1980–1981, 1985, 1987, 1989–1991, and 1995–1997 to control investment and to reduce consumption. In spite of that, fiscal policy remained expansive in general. In another words, the central government budget was more slack than tight. The slack fiscal policy was mainly reflected on three aspects:

—The proportion of fiscal revenue in the national income kept decreasing, and the growth rate of fiscal revenue was much lower than that of national income, even negative in certain years.
—The fiscal deficit remained high. There was a budget deficit not only in years of rapid economic growth but also in years of tightening.
—Investment and the individual income have increased rapidly. The average annual growth rate of the investment was 23% from 1981 to 1997 and that of the total wages was 16% from 1978 to 1997.

Financial System Reform and Financial Policy

Until the early 1980s, financial policy had very limited impact on economic development, and the financing function of banks with respect to resource allocation was negligible. In the old financial system, the People's Bank of China (PBOC) served both as a central bank and a commercial bank. The financial market was undeveloped, and there was little direct financing. The interest rate was fairly low with few financial options. This was the source of what could be called "financial depression."

Financial system reform started by adding new financial organizations such as the Agricultural Bank of China, the Bank of China, the Industrial and Commercial Bank of China, the People's Construction Bank of China, and so on. With the establishment of these specialist banks, the PBOC began to act solely as a Central Bank. At the same time, nonbank financial institutions, including insurance companies, trust and investment corporations, finance companies, and security corporations, were established one after another. They now play an increasingly important role in the financial market.

Financial reform was greatly deepened in 1994. Three policy banks were established: the State Development Bank (lending for major infrastructure projects); the China Import and Export Bank (providing finance for foreign traders); and the China Agriculture Development Bank (providing funds for agricultural crop purchasing). These policy banks took over the function of policy-oriented loans from the four state-owned specialist banks, which were allowed to develop into commercial entities. Finally, the Central Bank functions of the PBOC were strengthened. The new PBOC Law promulgated in 1995 was an important landmark in financial reform, giving the PBOC the power to perform the Central Bank functions of stabilizing currency and supervising financial institutions. In 1997–1998, several foreign banks in Shanghai and Shenzhen were granted the right to undertake limited RMB business.

Financial markets grew rapidly. In 1985, several interbank markets and acceptance markets were established. In 1986, the PBOC carried out rediscount business for the specialist banks. In 1996, a nationwide interbank relending market was established. At the same time, direct financing developed gradually. In 1984, the first joint-stock company was established, which marked the beginning of stock issues. Then, stock exchanges in Shanghai and Shenzhen were set up, respectively, in 1990 and in 1991, which marked the formation of the stock market. By the end of 1997, there were more than 800 quoted companies, and the total market value of stock had reached about RMB2,000 billion.

Interest rate policy occupies an important position in macroeconomic management. However, while China maintained a low interest rate policy, the instrument of interest rates was not used effectively. Since the beginning of the 1980s, the PBOC raised the nominal interest rate several times. But, until 1996, the central government strictly regulated the interest rate, and the state commercial banks could adjust their lending rates only within a specified band around the officially determined rate. Interest rates were not determined by the Central Bank through open market operations, or by the commercial banks on the basis of market supply and demand. Regulated interest rates were well below potential market interest rates, even negative, as in 1994–1995. The low interest rate policy limited the full use and the efficiency of monetary policy instruments.

Dramatic changes occurred in 1996. In January, the nationwide, unified, interbank market opened. In June, interest rates in the short-term interbank market were fully liberalized. In the same year, China started to issue national bonds through a bid market that determined the interest rate of national bonds. Since then, interest rate policy has played a real role in Chinese macroeconomic management.

Macroeconomic Policies from 1995

With the reforms of the fiscal, monetary, and financial systems, the Chinese government started to use fiscal and monetary instruments to regulate the economy. The soft landing of the Chinese economy from 1995 to 1996 was the result of successful utilization of those instruments. To deal with the overheated economy and severe inflation of 1993–1994, the Chinese government adopted both a tight monetary policy and a tight fiscal policy. But unlike earlier periods, the central government used the indirect monetary policy instruments effectively, along with quite cautious direct credit controls. In early and mid-1995, the interest rate for refinancing and the rates on debts of financial institutions were raised twice. It was the first time that money supply was controlled by open market operations. The success of these monetary polices can be seen in the statistics of Table 15.7.

After the successful "soft landing," facing the impact of the recent Asian financial turmoil, the Chinese government is again seeking economic growth as its most important accomplishment. A GDP growth goal of 8% was set for 1998 and was almost attained. A series of fiscal and monetary policies was implemented to create incentives for the economy to reach this goal.

In early 1998, the government made infrastructure construction and residential construction the focal points of economic growth and increased funding twice. In August, the central government adjusted the budget program to expand the budget

Table 15.7
Soft Landing and Monetary Policy

Year	Growth Rate of M0 (%)	Growth rate of M1 (%)	Growth rate of M2 (%)	Growth Rate of Retail Price Indices(%)	GDP Growth Rate (%)
1994	24.2	26.8	34.4	21.7	12.6
1995	8.2	16.8	29.5	14.8	10.5
1996	11.6	22.1	25.3	6.1	9.7
1997	15.6	18.9	19.3	0.8	8.8

Sources: China Statistical Yearbook, 1995–1997; A Statistical Survey of China, 1998.

deficit to RMB90 billion from the initially planned budget deficit of RMB40 billion. At the same time, the government issued additional national debt of RMB100 billion to financial institutions to invest in infrastructure and stimulate domestic demand.

With regard to monetary policy, the central government issued special national bonds to replenish the capital of commercial banks so that the ratio of capital of the commercial banks reached the legal level of 8%. On the other hand, the interest rate was lowered twice in early and mid-1998 to 4.77%. It was lowered five times after May 1996, when the interest rate on one-year deposits was 9.18 %. The rates of bank reserves and the rediscount rate were lowered correspondingly.

In addition, the central government increased the rate of duty drawbacks to encourage exports. All of these actions indicate that comprehensive and effective utilization of macroeconomic policies plays an important and increasing role in economic developments in China. They also indicate that the Chinese government is becoming more and more mature in using policy instruments to manage the national economy.

INDUSTRIAL POLICY

Before reform, the development of Chinese industries was out of equilibrium. Tertiary industry developed slowly and accounted for only 23.7% of GDP. The ratio of heavy and chemical industries in secondary industry was too high, while the light industrial products that closely related to consumer living standards were insufficient. That was an important reason that the Chinese economy appeared to be a "shortage economy."

After 20 years' efforts, the industrial structure was rationalized, and the ratio of the three sectors, primary, secondary, and tertiary, was 18.7: 49.2: 32.1 in 1997. That can be attributed to four adjustments in China's industrial policy.

The first adjustment started from 1979. The objective was to switch from the priority on heavy industry to light industry and agriculture in order to solve the problem of an inadequate supply of consumer goods. The rapid development of light industry was realized by changing the direction of investment and the growth of TVEs, while agricultural development depended on the new household responsibility system that linked remuneration with household output.

The second adjustment started in 1983. With the rapid economic growth, the investment scale in light manufacturing industries increased dramatically, and there were increasing demands for energy, raw materials, and transportation. The central government formulated industrial policies to quicken the development of infrastructure and basic industries such as agriculture, energy, raw materials, and transportation. Developing basic industries required large-scale investment over a very long period of time. Moreover, prices were controlled by the central government. As a result, local governments and non-state-owned investors were reluctant to invest in these industries and continued instead to invest in light industries and processing industries. The task of developing basic industries became one of the major responsibilities of the central government. However, with fiscal decentralization, the proportion of fiscal revenue to GDP decreased, and the investment capability of central government was weakened. The low rates of development of basic industries caused by inadequate investment led to disequilibrium in the industrial structure. There was heavy pressure on railway transportation and the supply of electricity, and there were shortages of all kinds of raw materials. This situation generated a high rate of inflation in 1988. Thus, the industrial policies of 1983–1988, although thought to be correct, were unsuccessful.

The third stage of adjustment was from 1989 to 1993. The central government promulgated the first real industrial policy in 1989. It proposed to "reduce and control the production and construction of the long-term oversupplied goods, improve and enlarge the production and construction of the goods in short supply, especially concentrating on the production and construction of food, cotton, coal, electricity, traffic especially railway transportation, and textile and other light products with great demand but short supply." By 1993, the industrial structure had been improved greatly from the perspective of matching demand and supply.

The fourth stage started in 1993. At this point, the important tasks became raising the efficiency of allocating and utilizing resources and improving quality and competitiveness. In 1993, the State Council promulgated "The Outline of National Industrial Policy in 1990's" and further emphasized the importance of the development of agriculture, basic industries, and "pillar" industries. In February 1994, the State Council approved an "Industrial Policy for the Automobile Industry." For the first time Chinese authorities promulgated an industrial policy for a specific industry. This marked a new stage of China's industrial policy.

In 1995, as we have noted, the authorities proposed to switch growth policy from an extensive approach to an intensive, efficient model. In their view, the way to realize this transformation was to formulate effective industrial policies to quicken the speed of technical progress and to improve the returns of scale. In 1998, the new State Council established the Bureau of Industrial Policy of the Committee of Economy and Trade to take charge of the research, formulation, and coordination of national industrial policy.

Regional Development Policies

With the reform of the economic system and political system, the central government transferred many economic management powers to local governments. At the same time, the incentives of local governments to develop the regional economies were strengthened. Local governments played more and more important roles in the development of regional economies.

Meanwhile, the breakthroughs in the systems of economic management, ownership, and distribution created a loose policy environment for local governments in which they could experiment and gain new experience. In some regions, the nonpublic sector, sometimes privately owned but more often collective, grew rapidly and became the driving force in local economic development.

With the development of regional economies, new problems emerged. First, pursuing their own economic interest, some local governments abused their authority of economic management and invested in short-term projects. As a result, processing industries expanded rapidly, while the construction of infrastructure such as energy and transportation lagged, and the raw material industries developed inadequately. The myopia of local investment resulted in excessive competition among the domestic enterprises. In the violent competition, many inexperienced enterprises incurred losses or were even closed down. Thousands of workers were laid off, and employment was under heavy pressure.

Second, local protectionism arose. Regional trade barriers obstructed the formation and development of a nationwide unified market. Local protectionism took the form of prohibiting exports of cheap local raw materials and prohibiting the imports of products from other regions. This protectionism distorted local enterprises' behavior and industrial structures and was harmful to long-term upgrading of industries.

Perhaps the most serious problem, also most difficult to solve, was the increase in regional disparities emerging from regional economic development. In 20 years of high economic growth in China, the different regions, mainly the coastal, central, and western regions, developed unevenly. From 1980 to 1994, the ratio of the average annual growth rate of the three regions was 10.69:8.72: 8.68. The gaps between them in per capita GDP were even larger; for example, the ratio is 2.31:1.24: 1. The coastal region produced 60% of national total GDP using 20% of the land and 40% of the population.

The inequality of policy treatment, especially the opening-up policy, is commonly regarded as the main reason for the regional disparities in economic development and income. As mentioned before, China opened to outside gradually, and the coastal regions benefited first from the policy because of their favorable natural endowments. In order to attract foreign capital, the central government formulated a series of preferential policies for opening regions and gave the governments of these regions more decision-making power than those of other regions.

Resource allocation was another reason for regional disparities. The regional distribution of China's industries depended on attributes of the regions. The advantage of coastal regions mainly lies in process industry, the center regions are fit for agriculture, and the western regions are rich in natural resources, especially minerals. In the process of reforms, the prices of industrial products were liberalized, while the prices of major agriculture products and minerals were artificially held at low levels, which meant that coastal regional development came at the cost of center and western regional growth.

The unbalanced development of the regions' economies continues to threaten the long-term stable development of the Chinese economy. The center and western areas are the home of minorities and the large gaps of incomes and living standards tend to make the society unstable. Differences in the direction of reform and in the objectives of different regions make the reform more difficult. For example, the coastal regions are the birthplace and driving power of market-oriented reforms. The regions seek a maximum of economic authority and independence. In contrast, the western regions want the central government to be more powerful so that they will get more fiscal support through redistribution.

The fact is that promoting the economic development of the center and western regions is necessary for maintaining the high rate of growth of the Chinese economy. The growth of the coastal regions is slowing down because processing industries are reaching saturation. The center and western economies will be the new driving force of Chinese economic development if their potential of rich resources and lands with little population can be exploited.

The central government has formulated some policies to reduce regional disparities:

—Developing resource industries and infrastructure in the center and western regions;

—Encouraging foreign capital to flow to center and western regions;

—Strengthening cooperation between the coastal regions and center and western regions.

Regional cooperation is developing rapidly. However, there is, as yet, no indication that foreign capital is going to the center and western regions. The siting of foreign investments is determined by market forces, and most of these investments still flow into the coastal regions. There is a long way to go to resolve the problem of regional disparities.

SUMMARY: OUTLOOK FOR CHINESE ECONOMIC DEVELOPMENT

Since 1990, Chinese economic development has shown three interrelated, long-term tendencies. The first is the tendency of continued rapid growth. The average annual GDP growth rate from 1978 to 1997 is 9.8%. It is expected that growth will be 8% annually in the years before the end of this century and that the growth rate will stay at about 7% during the first 10 years in the next century. The second is the tendency for changes in demand and industrial structure to accelerate. The third tendency is the deepening of the market-oriented economic system and its internationalization.

However, some serious problems remain to be solved:

—The weak agriculture base cannot satisfy the increasing demands for agricultural products as the population grows, and living standards improve.

—The centralized management and operations of the state-owned enterprises do not fit with the market economy.

—Strong inflationary pressures, the deficient fiscal system, and the lack of a powerful macroeconomic control system pose obstacles to rapid economic growth and transformation.

—The low quality of the national economy and the irrational industrial structure cannot generate sufficiently high incomes.

—The large population and the growing surpluses of workers create large needs for employment.

—The deficiency of resources per capita makes ecological problems more serious.

Now, facing severe domestic and international dislocations after the Asian financial turmoil, China is making great efforts to ensure attainment of the target growth rate of 8% in 1998. We believe that, as long as the Chinese government sticks to its basic national policy of reform and opening up and adjusts the policy measures according to the world economic situation, the Chinese economy will make great progress in the twenty-first century.

REFERENCES

Development Research Center of the State Council. (1995). *Economic Reform and Policy*. Beijing: Press of Social Science Documents.

EAAU (East Asian Analytical Unit) Report. (1997). *China Embraces the Market*. Barton: Commonwealth of Australia.

Fan Gang. (1998). "Growing into the Market: Economic Transition in China." Working paper.

Institute of Industrial Economy. (1997). *China's Industrial Development Report, 1996–1997*. Beijing: Economic Management Press.

Li Shi, Zhao Renwei, and Zhang Ping. (1998). "China's Economic Transition and the Change in Income Distribution." *Economic Research Journal* 4.

Li Wuwei. (1998). "Policy Analysis of Chinese Regional Economic Development." *Social Sciences* 3.

Lin Justin Yifu. (1995). "Chinese economic reform and the development of economics." In *Economics and Chinese Economic Reform*. Shanghai: Shanghai People Press.

Niu Nanjie. (1998). "An Analysis of Economic Effect by the Use of Foreign Investment in China." *Economic Research Journal* 5.

Wang Tongsan and Qi Jianguo. (1996). *Industrial Policy and Economic Growth*. Beijing: Press of Social Science Documents.

Yi Gang (1996). "Analysis and Its Policy Implication on the Financial Capital Structure Construction." *Economic Research Journal* 126.

Zhang Shuguang. (1996). "On the Economic Reform and Macroeconomic Situation of China in the 90's." *Economic Research Journal* 6.

Zhao Renwei and Li Shi. (1997). "Increasing Income Inequality and Its Causes in China." *Economic Research Journal* 9.

16

An Analysis of China's Regional Economic Development Policy

Li Wuwei

China is a developing country with vast area and large population, but it is not so rich in natural resources. Due to the large differences of China's various regions in natural environment, resource conditions, and economic infrastructure, the economic development of various regions is uneven.

BALANCED DEVELOPMENT POLICY IN THE PERIOD OF TRADITIONAL PLANNED ECONOMY

Before the policy of economic system reform was adopted, the target of the central government's regional development policy was to realize balanced regional development. Under the traditional, planned economic system, it was possible for the central government to carry out balanced development among regions through planning directives. The main method was forcing the coastal developed region to hand over a large proportion of its financial revenue to the central government and giving subsidies to the underdeveloped regions in the middle and western part of China. For example, 85% to 87% of the financial revenue of Shanghai and Jiangsu Provinces had to be given to the central government each year. Second, the state's capital construction investment leaned toward the middle and western regions. This policy restricted the economic development of the coastal region, making the growth rate in the middle and western regions a little higher than that of the eastern region. From 1953 to 1978 the ratio of average GDP growth rates of the east, middle, and west was 5.75:5.73:6.8, respectively, which enabled the economic development gap between the eastern and the middle and western regions to be narrowed gradually. However, because of the poor natural environment and economic base in the middle and western regions, the economic rate of return in these two regions is obviously much lower than that in the eastern region. Such balanced development as was emphasized before inevitably could be realized only at the expense of efficiency.

FROM 1980 TO 1994: REGIONAL DEVELOPMENT POLICY SEEKING EFFICIENCY

Since 1980, China's regional development policy changed to a policy centering around efficiency with the fairness taken into consideration. From a long-term point of view, China's target is still to narrow the gap in regional economic development in "becoming rich together." However, requiring a synchronized, egalitarian development policy at the expense of efficiency would postpone China's development, as a whole, and result in poverty. Therefore, policies must be adjusted around efficiency, that is, allowing some areas to become rich first, so as to rapidly raise national economic strength, and then to support the underdeveloped regions' development, gradually realizing the target of equalization through financial transfers and technological cooperation.

The main policies adopted to quicken economic development in the coastal region were:

1. Capital construction leaned toward the coastal region. From 1980 onward, the percentage of investment in the coastal region was gradually increased. This trend lasted till 1994.

2. The coastal region took the lead in adopting a policy of opening toward the outside world. China's opening toward the outside world pushed forward gradually from the south to the north and from the east to the west. The so-called opening policy mainly refers to access to foreign capital and to preferential policies in taxation and finance to attract foreign investment and to increase development. Table 16.1 lists the timetable of opening toward the outside world or various locations. Inland and border cities, provincial capitals, and cities along rivers did not open to the outside world until 1991. As a direct impact of this policy, the technological level of the coastal region was raised quickly, as a result of foreign investment. From 1980 to 1994, 88% of China's foreign investment receipts went to the eastern coastal region.

The regional development policy centering around efficiency speeded up the economic development in the coastal region and thus rapidly raised national economic strength as well.

Although the economic growth rate of the middle and western regions during this period was also much faster than before, due to even faster development in the eastern region, the gap between China's eastern and western regions was widening rapidly. From 1980 to 1994, the average annual GDP growth rate among China's three regions—the eastern, middle, and western regions—was 10.69%, 8.72%, and 8.68%, respectively, and the ratio of GDP per capita of the three regions changed from 1.81:1.21:1 in 1980 to 2.31:1.24:1 in 1994. The rapid widening of the economic gap between the east and the west caused serious economic, political,

Table 16.1
The Timetable of the Places Opening to the Outside World in China

1979	Special policies were adopted for Guangdong and Fujian Provinces, and these two provinces took the lead in carrying out local economic management reform and the local government were allowed to keep more financial revenue.
1980	The four special economic zones—Shenzhen, Zhuhai, Shantou, and Xiamen (Amoy)—were established.
1984	Fourteen cities along the coast were opened to the outside world.
1985	The economic open area along the coast was enlarged to 253 counties and towns.
1988	Hainan Special Economic Zone was established.
1990	Shanghai Pudong New District was established (with the policies of the special economic zones applied in the district).
1991	Thirteen cities in the interior and along the border, 5 cities along the rivers and all the capitals of each province were opened to the outside world.

and psychological disequilibrium, resulting in the emergence of some social instability. With macroeconomic regulation and control starting in the second half of 1993, an adjustment of regional development policy was also put on the agenda.

COORDINATED REGIONAL DEVELOPMENT POLICY: CHANGING TOWARD A MARKET-ORIENTED ECONOMIC SYSTEM

The development of the market economy will promote the flow of resources toward areas with better economic results, which will be advantageous to the development of regions with better natural conditions and economic base, widening the economic gap between different regions. It is unnecessary for the state's regional development policy to lean toward the coastal region. Policy must focus on the promotion of coordinated development of different regions and the gradual narrowing of the development gap between the regions. Since the second half of 1993, when macroregulation and -control started, and when the state's ninth five-year plan and the outlines of long-range targets for the year of 2010 were made, the central government adjusted regional development policies. The main ones are as follows:

1. State investment gives priority to resource development and infrastructure construction, piloting resource processing and labor-intensive industry into the middle and western regions. As of 1995, the share of investment in the inland region increased to 48.84%, 7.3 percentage points more than that in 1993. Among the 151 key projects started in 1994, 91 were in the middle and western regions. However, because of the reform of the investment system and the declining share of state investment in total investment, the percentage of state investment in total investment is falling year by year. In 1994, it was only 3.3% of total investment of the country, so such a shift has little direct impact upon the total volume of investment in the eastern coastal region.

   Because of the large scale of investment in the coastal region in the 1980s, the marginal return of industrial investment has been falling. By 1994, the rate of capital tax and profits of the three regions of the eastern, middle, and western parts of China had approached one another. Under the pressure of the large increase in land and labor cost, labor-intensive industry and resource-processing industry in the coastal region began to move toward the middle and western regions.

2. Financial policy: adopting a standardized central financial payment transfer system, gradually increasing financial support for the middle and western regions. In 1994, a tax reform was carried out nationwide. The new tax system changed the distribution pattern between the local governments and the central government and greatly increased the central government's regulation and control ability. This change makes the local governments' expenditure dependent upon the central government's tax receipts in different degrees. So far as the middle and western regions are concerned, the new tax system is beneficial to their development. On one hand, the central government allows all the natural resource taxes to be kept by local governments (except the sea-oil resource tax). On the other hand, while defining the increase of the VAT and consumption tax of the various regions, it was decided that the increase of the rate of tax payments to local governments should be linked to national average growth of revenue collected from VAT and the consumption tax.

3. Opening policy: quickening reform and steps for opening in the middle and western regions, guiding more foreign capital to the middle and western regions. At present, most of the cities in the middle and western regions have also been opened to the outside world. In the meantime, the policy of attracting foreign investment was adjusted. The zone-oriented opening policy adopted in various places in China to attract foreign investment changed to an industry-oriented policy. If the foreign investors invest in export-oriented or import-substitution projects or invest in agriculture, raw materials industry, infrastructure, and high-tech projects, preferential treatment will be provided, including appropriate tax reductions and market access. This will be good for the middle and western regions, to bring their advantage in natural resources and lower land and labor cost into full play as well as to promote their market development. In addition, the central government decided that over 60% of the loans provided by international financial organizations and foreign governments will be used in the middle and western regions.

4. Regional cooperation policy: encouraging and strengthening economic and technological cooperation between the eastern coastal regions and the middle and western regions.

The aim of "The Law on Demonstrating Co-operative Projects of Enterprises Run by Townships and Villages between the East and the West," approved by the State Council, is to promote the combination of the more advanced technology and management and stronger capital strength in the eastern region with the rich raw materials, energy, and labor force resources in the middle and western regions, speeding up rural industrial development in the middle and western regions. In more than two years, over 30,000 cooperation projects have been signed between the eastern and the western regions.

Another approach is to encourage the eastern developed provinces and cities to support and cooperate with inland underdeveloped provinces and regions. For example, Shanghai provided support geared to the needs of Yunnan Province and the Three Gorges Reservoir region; Jiangsu Province helped Guizhou Province, Zhejiang Province assisted Sichuan Province, and so forth. Such support included cooperative investment projects and technological services, qualified personnel training, and so on. For instance, Shanghai has signed 81 cooperative project agreements with a total investment of RMB2.5 billion with Yunnan Province. Such cooperation is beneficial to the coastal region as well. As the cost of land and labor force has risen, the coastal region is faced with the problem of industrial upgrading and structural transformation and needs to transfer part of its industries into the middle and western regions.

5. The policy supporting the poor: strengthening the support for the poor regions. The way to support the poor regions has changed from relief to development. In 1994, the state laid down the "eight-seven" plan of supporting the poor, striving to get rid of poverty from the middle and western regions within this century. The state added RMB1 billion appropriations and RMB1 billion loans with discounted interest rates to the original base supporting the poor regions.

Although regional coordinated development policies are recent, they have achieved preliminary results and quickened economic development in the middle and western regions. In 1996, the rate of increase of investment in the middle and western regions outstripped that of the eastern region, and the economic growth rate also approached that of the eastern region. The three provinces with the fastest industrial growth rate in 1996 in the whole nation—Anhui, Hubei, and Jiangxi—were all in the middle region. Their industrial growth rates were 20.9%, 20.4%, and 19.7%, respectively, which enabled the GDP of the middle region to reach 0.9 percentage points higher than that of the eastern region. It is expected that these policies will gradually narrow the economic development gap between the east and the west in China. Moreover, such development is not achieved at the expense of efficiency in the eastern region of China.

17

Public Policies in the Vietnam Economy

Vu Tuan Anh

For years, Vietnam followed a Soviet-inspired, centrally planned economic model in the north that clashed with a quasi-colonial economy highly dependent on U.S. assistance in the south. Since the unification of Vietnam in 1975, the country began a trial-and-error process to find a suitable path of development. Despite the enormous constraints placed on Vietnam's economy by its state of underdevelopment and by war damage, a long-term process of economic reform has been conducted. Public economic policy changes led to comprehensive reform in many fields.

Three main lines of reform are being put into practice:

—First, in the economic field, a shift from a centrally planned economy to a market economy;

—Second, in social life, intensified democratization and building a legally authoritative state.

—Third, in international relations, an open-door policy to step up communication and cooperative relations with the outside world.

Among these three economic reform orientations, economic policy reform is the most advanced. Under the influence of economic restructuring and globalization, the socioeconomic situation in Vietnam has undergone fundamental change.

This chapter examines the contents of economic policy reform in Vietnam, its impacts on economic growth, and perspectives of future socioeconomic development.

THE PROCESS OF ECONOMIC POLICY REFORMS

After unification of Vietnam in 1975, the majority of Vietnamese were optimistic about what the cessation of the war would bring. They expected that quick success in the economic field could be obtained by means of a centralized mobilization and distribution mechanism. This mechanism had proved to be most effective and successful in wartime. The model of centralized economic planning was first applied in North Vietnam, where it took shape and underwent an experimental stage of over 20 years, and then it was expanded to the whole country. But the expected result did not come about. During the years 1979–1980, the economy encountered a serious crisis whose direct causes were repeated crop failures to say nothing of considerable cutbacks in foreign assistance. The country was once again involved in political and military conflicts with China and Cambodia. The U.S. embargo isolated Vietnam's economy from international trade and investment flows. Vietnam's economic policies proved utterly incapable of resolving the requirements of development.

Since the 1980s, many new business forms and activities were devised by grassroots economic establishments in defiance of the restraints and arbitrary interdictions imposed on them by governing institutions. These spontaneous "reform experiments" in industry, agriculture, and trade helped to prepare conditions for the next step of reform. Government leaders were highly sensitive to these new changes and showed a readiness to institutionalize them. Economic restructuring has taken place, step by step, to readjust policies in order to make them more adaptable to economic development. Since 1986, particularly since 1989, the Vietnamese governments have undertaken the most important and comprehensive reform, called Renovation Policy or Doi Moi. Unlike reforms in the past, this reform program is marked by a new quality and totally different direction as well as by paramount dimensions and depth. The reforms have taken place at the same time in the following ways:

—turning a centrally planned economy into a market economy with guidance from the state,

—developing and diversifying international economic relations, and

—reforming state administration.

In agriculture: at the beginning of the 1980s, a product-based contractual quota system assigned to every household replaced the direct and centralized management of all rural economic activity by cooperatives. The purchase and sale of farm products and production materials were allowed freely on the market. This policy stimulated peasant households to invest their labor and funds so as to exceed the quotas they were obliged to deliver to the cooperatives. In the contractual quota system, the cooperative still played an important role in production and distribution because it decided on the business orientation and on farm product distribution. The renewal of a system of agricultural management in which the peasant household is considered to be a self-governing economic unit, to which a plot of land is entrusted for long-term use, and which has the right to make business decisions is a step forward in the move toward privatization of agriculture. It brought about a series of great socioeconomic changes in rural area, namely, in land use, social division of labor, production organization, and so on. In turn, these changes would create many new requirements in terms of policies such as land policy, rural credit loan regulations, and social policies.

In industry: in the centrally planned economy, enterprises had very limited rights to do business independently. They were forced to follow the state plan in material supply, production, and distribution of their products. From the early 1980s, state-owned enterprises began to be authorized to conduct business without being bound by the plan. The free market for materials and consumer goods prevails and operates actively. The state has minimized its intervention by reducing legally binding quotas for items under the state's pricing system and by extending the rights of enterprises to make business decisions. Then came the separation of the financial system of state-owned enterprises from the national budget, entrusting decisions in matters of finance to enterprises and eliminating state subsidies to wages and materials as well as low depreciation rates and low interest rates.

The transfer of the operational mechanism of the national economy from concentrated management by the state to cost accounting and market competition has compelled enterprises to restructure their production and business procedures, change the variety of goods produced and technologies used, and improve their management knowhow. A few enterprises did not meet the requirements of that transfer. They are being transferred to ownership by collectives and private individuals, or they will have to close down.

Policies aimed at encouraging the private sector to engage in business undertakings have also been promulgated. In 1988, the development of the private sector started with small household business: the introduction of freedom to carry on business and lifting the restrictions on the amount of privately invested capital and on the number of employees. Laws on companies and on private business were passed in December 1990, providing a legal framework for the establishment of large private companies in different forms. A series of private establishments began operating, especially in urban areas. Commerce and services constitute the domains most attractive for private business. By early 1995, 20,000 private enterprises had been registered. Of these, 72.4% were one-owner businesses, 26.9% were limited liability companies, and only 1.8% were shareholding companies. The overwhelming majority of the private sector in Vietnam is still operating at the household business level.

The process of shifting from centralized planning to the market economy in Vietnam unfolded gradually. The state gave up its unlimited and direct intervention in business activity and is keeping only the role of regulation, largely through macroeconomic instruments.

In 1989, the Vietnamese government introduced a packet of concerted reform measures that are similar to a limited shock therapy. These included:

—Canceling all direct subsidies

—Introducing a market price system

—Depreciating the Vietnamese currency and unifying different exchange rates by introducing an officially managed floating exchange rate

—Establishing a two-tier banking system and introducing positive real interest rates

—Liberalizing domestic trade, allowing leasing of land for construction and trading of gold and jewelry

—Reducing tariffs for commercial and noncommercial imports

These measures and the deregulation of foreign trade, moving from the state monopoly of foreign trade to more open and diversified participation of the private sector in exports and imports, helped to increase domestic market supply as well as exports. Inflation has dropped very quickly.

National financial policy was reformed in an effort to advance toward a balanced budget. The centralized direction of taxation has increased tax revenue. Current expenditures and investment were separated. The creation of the State Treasury in the Ministry of Finance improved budget operations. Since 1992, the government has ended the use of credit from the Central Bank to cover budget deficits. State Treasury bonds have been sold domestically and, beginning in 1995, in international markets.

The banking system was transformed into two systems: the Central Bank and commercial banks. The latter have developed rapidly. In addition to four state-run commercial banks, there are also joint-stock banks, collective credit organizations, and joint venture banks with foreign partners and branches of several foreign banks.

Strict financial and monetary control policies have curbed inflation.

Another part of economic policy reform is the change of industrial policy toward consumption goods and, at the same time, providing supplies to international commerce. Structural policy has shifted from giving priority to the development of heavy industry to pushing ahead with agricultural development and promotion of production of consumer goods and commodities for export.

In external economic relations, the changes in the former Soviet Union's and East European countries' political institutions and the disintegration of the Council of Mutual Economic Assistance (CMEA) constituted a shock. Vietnam lost important markets for exports and suffered economic decline in a number of activities. Exports were reduced to a minimum. Vietnam needed rapidly to change its import and export structure.

A policy of integration into the world market has been implemented through liberalization of foreign trade, promotion of exports by exemption or reduction of taxes, and encouragement of import of materials. Attraction of foreign investment is regarded as an important policy aim.

Tremendous efforts have been made for the creation of a legal framework in accordance with a market economy. The 1992 constitution legalized the economic reforms, including private ownership and the market mechanism. Many laws have been passed dealing with private and state-owned companies and bankruptcy. Vietnam has signed many international conventions, and bilateral agreements and has accepted international arbitrage for settlement of business disputes. Licenses have been provided for foreign international law firms to operate in Vietnam.

Public administration has been streamlined. From the beginning of 1995, a major program of public administration reform started, including the establishment of administrative courts and general deregulation of procedures and formalities. State agencies are more interested in feedback from business circles and search for a dialogue with people. More economic information has been made available.

In conclusion, economic policy reform in Vietnam has the following specific features:

—It was a combination between grassroots initiatives and the readjustment of economic policies by the policymakers at the central level. This two-way relationship between the grass roots and the center has contributed to understanding, perception, and response to the needs of readjusting economy policy. A relatively harmonious combination of spontaneous reforms at the microlevel and decisive action of the highest political leadership area are major reasons that the Vietnam's economic reforms have not produced a deep recession as took place in some other formerly centrally planned economies.

—The Vietnamese economy reform does not mean a change from an old economic model to another one taken from another country. It was a process of "learning by trial and error." It seems that the economic reforms in Vietnam have developed without a general road map. Sometimes they did not bring about the results that were hoped for. But, on the whole, the outcome has proved to be manageable.

—The reform was a combination of a gradualist approach and limited shock therapy in 1989. According to Vietnam's experience, in reform some measures need to be implemented promptly and resolutely. These are price, exchange rate, and interest rate policy. Other measures must be introduced gradually according to financial possibilities. These are policies with respect to salaries, societal protection, and reforming of state-owned enterprises.

—The reform was successful without foreign financial aid. Only very recently has Vietnam received credits for the construction of physical and social infrastructure. On the contrary, the economic blockade and embargo against Vietnam and the involvement of the country in various political and military conflicts have compelled Vietnam to consume resources that should have been used for its socioeconomic development.

—The economic reform has a high social component and humanistic approach. The government has paid much attention to reduce the burden of reform on vulnerable groups of the population. The program "to eliminate hunger and reduce poverty" has had strong support from the population and could improve the situation of rural regions.

IMPACTS OF ECONOMIC POLICY CHANGES ON SOCIOECONOMIC DEVELOPMENT

Under the influence of economic policy reforms, the socioeconomic situation in Vietnam has undergone fundamental change. On one hand, Vietnam has made impressive achievements in economic growth and institutional transformation. On the other hand, it faces a lot of problems in both economic and social transitions.

Economic Growth

The economic policy reforms have had significant positive impacts on economic growth. Economic stagnation and recession have been overcome: a fairly high, continued, and relatively comprehensive growth rate has been achieved in the 1990s.

GDP achieved an average increase of 8.2% per annum in the period 1991–1995 compared to 5.2% and 5.9% in the periods 1981–1985 and 1986–1990, respectively. Average annual industrial growth is 13.3%, much higher than in the previous period. Agricultural production achieved an average annual increase of 4.5%. Service industries increased at an average annual growth rate of 12% in 1991–1995.

Agricultural production still constitutes a branch of primary importance in Vietnam's economy, attracting 70% of the work force and producing nearly 40% of GDP. Due to improvement of irrigation systems, the supply of new varieties of seeds, and reform policies, since 1989 Vietnam has ensured self-sufficiency in food supply and could export rice. Total food output was 21.4 million tons in 1990 and reached approximately 29.1 million tons in 1996. Food production per capita increased significantly: 304 kg. in 1985, 324.4 kg. in 1990, and 372.5 kg. in 1995. Rice exports are 1 to 2 million tons per year, one of the most important export items of the country.

Diversification in the structure of agricultural production away from rice has also occurred. The production of nonfood crops increased substantially in the last decade. Average annual growth rates for these crops were significantly higher than for food crops. Vietnam became a considerable exporter of such products as coffee, rubber, cashew nuts, and tea.

The difficulty now in agriculture is the lack of additional processing. Products destined for export are mainly in crude form.

After a period of recession in 1989–1990, industrial production has recovered and started to record high rates of growth. A number of important products like electric power, crude oil, cement, steel, and paper have gained a high and steady growth rate due to significant capital investment. However, industry is now facing great trials no matter how high the growth index. Machinery and equipment are not adequate, not to mention the low technical skill and poor technology of indigenous industrial establishments. These cannot compete with imported goods. A number of foodstuff-processing industries and industrial branches such as textiles and mechanical engineering are in a state of stagnation and decline in the face of harsh competition from imported goods. This problem will be more serious in the future when Vietnam begins to implement agreements on AFTA, including reduction of tariffs to 0–5% and abrogation of nontariff barriers.

Although it would be possible to maintain the GDP growth rate for a number of years with increased investments from home and abroad, structural change will be necessary to avoid a declining growth rate by the end of the decade.

Structural Change

In the past few years, the sectoral structure of the Vietnamese economy has been changing. The proportion of sector I (agriculture, forestry, and fisheries) was reduced from 42.9% in 1985 to 28.4% in 1995. After a period of recession and decrease of its proportion in GDP, sector II (industry and construction) began to regain its share in GDP, declining from 29.4% in 1985 to 22.7% in 1990 and increasing again to 29.9% in 1995. Sector III (services) has increased considerably from 27.7% in 1985 to 38.6% in 1990 and to 41.7% in 1995.

Macroeconomic Environment

Vietnam's recent success consists mainly in improvements of the macroeconomic environment. The 1997–1998 crisis in East Asia will pose new challenges.

The most striking feature was the curbing of galloping inflation. The rate of price increase in three digits in 1988 was gradually reduced and stood at only 4.5% in 1996. Prices have been set according to supply and demand on the market since 1989. The official exchange rate and the market exchange rate drew closer to each other, and, since mid-1991, a single exchange rate has prevailed. The government has been intervening in adjustment and regulation to secure relative stability for Vietnam's currency. Though this policy is still being hotly discussed, particularly with regard to its effect on competitiveness of exports, it has a positive impact on the mentality of domestic investors and consumers. Of course, the 1997 crisis and depreciation of currencies in East Asia have affected the competitiveness of Vietnamese products and are likely to impact on the exchange rate.

Vietnam has been successful in cutting public expenditures and in controlling inflation, thereby building an effective public finance policy. The budget deficit is still large, though it went from 8% of GDP in 1990 to 1.5% in 1995.

The taxation system is being reformed to suit the new circumstances. The present Vietnamese tax system comprises 10 taxes, with some special stipulations applied for foreign investors. Tax reform has brought about fundamental changes for revenue raising in Vietnam. In 1986, taxes accounted for only 20% of the total annual budget, while 70% of budget revenue came from state-run enterprises. In 1995, taxes and other fees made up 85% of total revenue and became the main source of revenue for the state.

In 1995, the government started an extensive reform of the tax system, referred to as the second stage of tax reform. One of the important reform measures was to do away with the overlap of the turnover tax by implementing a value-added tax (VAT). Besides VAT, a corporate income tax and an individual income tax are being implemented.

External Economic Relations

An important event is the admission of Vietnam as the seventh member of ASEAN. Together with the normalization of relations with the United States and the signing of an agreement on cooperation with the European Union, Vietnam's admission to ASEAN creates opportunities to broaden economic relations with other countries in the Southeast Asian region and in the world in general.

Vietnam's export growth has been fastest in food products and light manufacturing. The share of two main products, crude oil and rice, decreased from nearly half of exports in the early 1990s to less than a third by 1995. Concurrently, exports of textiles, clothing, and footwear have grown rapidly and are approaching the value of oil exports. The appearance of crude oil and rice on the export commodity list in the last 10 years has improved Vietnamese export turnover considerably. Both items, together with marine products and some other agricultural export products, remain products of "industries exploiting crude materials," with low value-added content, though their quality has recently been enhanced.

Most imports are made up of capital goods and raw materials used for investment and production. The most important individual import items are fuel, steel, and fertilizers, but imports of semifinished products, such as electronic components and textiles, have also grown rapidly in recent years. Consumer goods imports have been remarkably small. This import structure is determined by trade policy rather than by pure market forces. Import tariffs are higher and license requirements more stringent for consumer goods than for machinery, equipment, and intermediates. In fact, trade policy has been explicitly aimed to restrict consumer goods in order to provide a captive market for domestic producers.

Neighboring Asian countries are major markets for Vietnamese foreign trade (covering 75% of exports and almost as much of imports). Japan has become the biggest purchaser of Vietnam's export commodities. Singapore is the second biggest market for Vietnam's exports. Clearly, this trade orientation is the source of serious problems during the current crisis in Southeast Asia.

Vietnam seeks to attract foreign direct investment. Compared to corresponding laws prevailing in other countries in the Asian region, Vietnam's foreign investment law, promulgated in 1987, is quite open and more suited to the investors' requirements.

PERSPECTIVES ON DEVELOPMENT

Vietnam's economy has passed through the critical period and commences toward a takeoff. The good results obtained from rice production, oil extraction, and manufacture of important items such as electricity and cement, to say nothing of an explosion of commerce and services, have contributed to maintain GDP growth at a good level. The centralized planning mechanism in the economy was dissolved and replaced by the market mechanism. Both state and private economic sectors have been stimulated to further development. The macroeconomic environment has been relatively stable with an acceptable rate of inflation and, until recently, a steady currency exchange rate.

Despite tremendous progress in economic growth in the last few years and important achievements in economic reform, the Vietnamese economy faces great challenges and needs to continue economic and public administration reform. Vietnam is still a very poor country and a developing economy. Its per capita GDP, calculated in U.S. dollars using the official exchange, was $274 in 1995. Per capita GDP calculated on a purchasing power parity (PPP) basis was $1,010 compared to Indonesia's and China's $1,950.

The huge gap in development between Vietnam and regional countries can be reduced only by higher, but sustainable, growth rates over several decades. However, the challenge is that Vietnam's economy is still based mainly on natural resource exploitation. Agriculture, forestry and fisheries still account for 27% of GDP, and over 70% of the population are still living in rural regions. The competitiveness of Vietnamese products is low, even in domestic markets. Vietnam's exports include mainly crude oil and unprocessed agricultural and seafood products. The share of processed and manufactured goods is increasing but remains very modest.

The population growth rate of 2.1% per year is still too high in the context of a poor country. It offsets a great part of the GDP growth. Unemployment and underemployment are common everywhere, especially among working-age youth. The long-term development of human resources requires much more investment in education and health care systems.

In the future, Vietnam has to continue economic reforms on a consistent basis:

—The first priority is reforming and strengthening the financial sector, including public finance. A system of commercial banks, insurance and securities companies, and a stock exchange needs to be established and linked with international financial markets to attract foreign and domestic capital. The performance of banks needs to be enhanced, and all relevant financial transactions in the economy have to be conducted through banks.

—Controlling dollarization of the economy, step by step, creating convertibility for the Vietnamese currency, and managing the exchange rate of the Vietnamese dong in the interests of an export-oriented economy also have high priorities on the reform agenda.

—Further reforms of the taxation system and public finance must be implemented in order to reduce the overly big budget deficit and to keep inflation under control.

—State-owned enterprises (SOEs) must be reformed according to a well-prepared program. On one hand, the SOEs must be reorganized and upgraded in order to be competitive. On the other hand, small and medium-size SOEs, which are no longer relevant in the market economy, have to be reformed within programs of privatization.

—The private sector needs more assistance and promotion from the state in order to make a bigger contribution to development of the national economy.

In the Vietnamese economy, social considerations have a high value. Income needs to be redistributed to keep income inequality at an acceptable level and to assist the poorest people. The government needs to provide all groups of the population equal access to education, employment, and health care and to sustain a steadily improving welfare system. The main idea is to combine economic progress with social progress, to have all people, regardless of their ethnicity or religion, participating in economic progress.

REFERENCES

Le Dang Doanh. (1997). "Vietnam's Economy after 10 Years of Economic Reform." *Vietnam's Socio-Economic Development Review* 11.

Nguyen Quang Thai. (1997). "Industrialization and Modernization Policy." *Vietnam's Socio-Economic Development Review* 11.

Vu Tuan Ahn, ed. (1995). *Economic Reform and Development in Vietnam*. Hanoi: Social Science Publishing House.

————. (1993). *Economic Reform in Vietnam: Results and Problems*. Hanoi: Social Science Publishing House.

World Bank. (1993). *Vietnam: Transition to Market*. Washington, DC: World Bank.

III

Perspectives on East Asian Development

18

The Lessons and the Outstanding Questions

F. Gerard Adams

What are the principal conclusions that can be reached about policy with respect to East Asian development and the crisis?

Despite the fact that economic views tend to range widely, there has been wide consensus about the forces behind the East Asian "miracle." Though policy concerns and implementation differ considerably among the East Asian countries, there has been only a little less agreement about the appropriate policies. With the collapse of the East Asian development boom, however, new isues have arisen, and some views about policy that were once widely accepted have been called into question. This summary chapter outlines the principal conclusions and considers the points of disagreement.[1] We deal first with the growth period and then turn to the period of crisis.

EAST ASIAN GROWTH

There has been substantial agreement about the growth process in East Asia and the policies that were behind it. Some of the principal conclusions can be summarized as follows:

—East Asian development is a linked process, sometimes called the "flying geese" pattern or the "development ladder." Its essential characteristic is the change of industrial structure as countries develop from primary production, to labor-intensive manufacturing, to more advanced manufacturing, to services. In the process, sectoral activities are shifted from the more advanced countries to those following in development behind them.

—Reliance on private entrepreneurship in the market economy, albeit frequently with close cooperation between government and private enterprise, has allowed the East Asian countries to adapt to changing competitive conditions.

—Outward orientation to supply products competitive in the world market has turned out to be more fruitful for economic development than import-substitution and protectionism.

—Appropriate policies have contributed to the growth process. There is surely agreement that these must include macropolicies like fiscal and monetary policies for macroeconomic and balance of payments stabilization and broad, "activity-specific" approaches like a favorable exchange rate and export promotion, attraction of foreign investment, public investment in infrastructure and education, and encouragement of saving and private investment.

In certain respects, however, the story of East Asian development remained subject to controversy even before the onset of the crisis in 1997. Some of the important controversies can be summarized as follows:

—The role of technical change. East Asian development has, of course, been greatly aided by high levels of saving and investment. The debate has been about whether technical change has played an important role (Lau, 1998; Saito, 1998). This represents largely a methodological issue, whether technical change is accounted for separately or whether it is embodied in capital, as is likely. The issue does not materially affect one's conclusions about policy.

—The role of government. The principal controversy has been with respect to what Wade (1990) and others have called the "developmental state." How big and how interventionist should the state be in the development process? Should state intervention guide sectoral priorities? Should public sector directives support efforts to build technical advantage in promising new industries? Should there be state-owned enterprises, or should business be privately owned and controlled? Even in countries like Korea and Taiwan, where state guidance initially played an important role (Wade, 1990), the trend has been in the direction of liberalization and privatization, at least until the 1997 crisis. But there remains controversy on the need to apply political tools, particularly sector-specific measures, to advance growth and technical change. In other words, does strategic development policy like industrial policy or introduction of high-tech industries accelerate growth?

—The opening of East Asian markets to foreign competition. Progress toward import liberalization has been considerably slower than export promotion in most countries. But there has been significant progress, and market opening is seen widely as one of the steps leading to greater product availability and competition. Further steps in that direction through the mechanisms of AFTA and APEC can be expected to promote integration and economic growth and technical change. On the other hand, there is still much protectionism. Do trade barriers to protect infant industries help development, or do they lead to inefficiency and technological backwardness?

—Capital flows and foreign investment. What should be the role of policy with respect to capital flows, foreign direct investment, and foreign ownership in the domestic economy? In many countries, growth has been facilitated by capital inflows, and, by direct foreign investment. But in many of the East Asian countries there is great reluctance to rely on foreign capital or to face competition from foreign-owned firms. Should a country rely heavily on inflows of foreign capital? Should a country allow widespread foreign ownership in its manufacturing, finance, or service sectors?

Resolution of these questions is very important as a guide to long-term policy in East Asia.

THE CRISIS AND ITS POLICY IMPLICATIONS

The 1997 crisis represents an unanticipated interruption in the growth process. We have discussed the cyclical, policy-related, and institutional background behind the meltdown in Chapter 2 and in the individual country chapters. We will summarize policy thinking in terms of consensus and in terms of disagreement. As the crisis has evolved, dissatisfaction with the policies of the IMF has increased, so that the initial consensus has broken down. Nevertheless, there are still important points of agreement.

There is no question about the need to restore confidence. This may, after all, call for many of the conservative policies proposed by the IMF—higher interest rates, restructuring of the banking system, fiscal balance, increased competition, and accounting transparency, and so on—regardless of whether the country is working with the IMF, like Thailand, or is struggling independently, like Malaysia. A critical component is the need to restructure and recapitalize the financial system and to provide adequate prudential supervision. That represents a significant challenge. Finally, there is the need to deal with foreign obligations and to reestablish foreign exchange equilibrium and inflows of capital. Political stability is a *sine qua non* of reestablishing confidence.

Disagreements are motivated, in large part, by the social consequences of the restructuring programs. Radelet and Sachs (1998) question the implications on political and economic stability of raising interest rates—that might damage solvent businesses—and of cutting public expenditures at times when social considerations like unemployment are increasingly serious. Others have questioned the rescue of developing country institutions from a moral hazard perspective, arguing that reckless financial behavior is being encouraged. Still others are concerned about the role of foreign speculators as a cause of the crisis, particularly in Malaysia. Throughout East Asia, the need for foreign financial assistance is in tension with fear that assets are being sold at "fire sale" prices and/or that foreign companies will greatly enlarge their role in the national economy.

The East Asian crisis has called into question the movement toward liberalization of trade and financial movements. Some have argued that financial flow liberalization, particularly flow of foreign capital, is destabilizing (Soros, 1998). It is tempting for public authorities to intervene in response to the difficulties presented by crisis conditions. As we have noted, Krugman (1998) has argued in favor of exchange controls, taking the position that international capital flows have been speculative and destabilizing. It is probable that many countries, in addition to Malaysia, will go back to regulating capital flows and may impose trade barriers. Public sector interventions may also proliferate in the domestic economies of the East Asian countries if traditional free market methods do not produce a turnaround.

At this time, it is difficult to estimate when a turnaround might come. That depends greatly on conditions in the country itself. Some like Thailand are beginning to show some evidence of stability, while others are still seeing increasing problems. Much depends on whether policies can restore confidence. Finally, much depends also on the state of the world economy. Continued world wide efforts will have to be made to help the East Asian countries escape from the crisis. It is too early to tell how far the crisis will spread and what the nature of the international efforts to deal with it will be.

THE FUTURE OF EAST ASIAN DEVELOPMENT

What are the implications of the preceding discussion for the future of East Asian development? A sustained development process was under way during the past three decades. Despite current difficulties, there is reason to be optimistic that it is likely to resume and spread to the lower-income East Asian countries as the more advanced ones move their industries into high-tech manufacturing and services.

Increasing integration between the economies of the East Asian countries, themselves in the framework of AFTA, and between them and the other countries of the industrial world is likely to continue. The APEC initiatives are likely to expand this interaction, as the high level of foreign direct investment originating in the West and in Japan resumes.. Thus, in spite of the crisis interruption and policy failures, we believe a sanguine perspective about East Asian growth is appropriate in the long run. Much depends on the policy posture of developing and industrial countries alike.

NOTE

1. For a comparable discussion, see Hughes (1995).

REFERENCES

Adams, F. Gerard, and I.-M. Davis. (1994). "The Role of Policy in Economic Development: Comparisons of the East and Southeast Asian and Latin American Experience." *Asian Pacific Economic Literature* 8(1) (May), pp. 9–26.

Adams, F. Gerard, and Shinichi Ichimura, eds. (1998). *East Asian Development: Will the East Asian Growth Miracle Survive?* Westport, CT: Praeger.

Hughes, H. (1995). "Why Have the East Asian Countries Led Economic Development?" *Economic Record* (May), pp. 88–105.

Krugman, Paul. (1998). "Saving Asia: It's Time to Get Radical." *Fortune* (September).

Lau, Lawrence J. (1998). "The Sources of East Asian Economic Growth." In F. Gerard Adams and Shinichi Ichimura, eds., *East Asian Development: Will the East Asian Growth Miracle Survive?* Westport, CT: Praeger, pp. 41–68.

Radelet, S., and J. Sachs. (1998). "The East Asian Financial Crisis: Diagnosis, Remedies, Prospects." *Brookings Papers on Economic Activity* 1, pp. 1–90.

Saito, Mitsuo. (1998). "The Stages of Technical Progress: An International Comparison." In F. Gerard Adams and Shinichi Ichimura, eds., *East Asian Development: Will the East Asian Growth Miracle Survive?* Westport, CT: Praeger, pp. 69–88.

Soros, George. (1998). *The Crisis of Global Capitalism.* New York: Public Affairs.

Wade, R. (1990). *Governing the Market: Economic Theory and the Role of the Government in East Asian Industrialization.* Princeton, NJ: Princeton University Press.

Index

About the Contributors

SHIGEYUKI ABE is professor of Economics at the Center for Southeast Asian Studies at Kyoto University. He has published extensively on trade and investment, modeling, and exchange rates.

F. GERARD ADAMS recently moved from the University of Pennsylvania to the McDonald Professorship at Northeastern University in Boston. He had many years of association with the Asian Graduate School of Business Administration in Bangkok. His recent work has focused on East Asian development.

FLORIAN A. ALBURO is professor at the School of Economics at the University of the Philippines in Manila.

BOEDIONO was a director of the Bank Indonesia. He is in charge of the Indonesian Ministry for Development Planning. He has been a professor at the University in Jakarta, Indonesia.

HIDEFUMI IMURA is a professor at the Institute of Environmental Studies at Kyushu University in Fukuoka, Japan.

WILLIAM E. JAMES is director of research at the International Centre for the Study of East Asian Development (ICSEAD) in Kitakyushu, Japan. He has published extensively on issues of trade regulation.

TAKESHI KATSUHARA, formerly director of research at the International Centre for the Study of East Asian Development (ICSEAD) in Kitakyushu, Japan, teaches environmental economies at Toa University.

MINGSARN KAOSA-ARD teaches at Chiang Mai University and has been associated for many years with the Thailand Development Research Institute.

KYU UCK LEE, a member of the Competition Policy Advisory Committee, Fair Trade Commission of Korea, is professor of economics at Ajou University in Seoul.

HSIEN-FENG LEE works with the Council for Economic Planning and Development in Taiwan.

LI WUWEI is research professor at the Shanghai Academy of Social Sciences.

HARTADI A. SARWONO is deputy director at Bank Indonesia.

AZMI SETAPA is senior research fellow and head of the policy studies division of the Malaysian Institute of Economic Research (MIER).

CHI SHIVE is vice chairman of the Council for Economic Planning and Development and professor of economics at National Taiwan University in Taipei.

KONG YAM TAN is head of the Department of Business Policy, Faculty of Business Administration at the National University of Singapore.

HEIDI VERNON is professor of international business at the College of Business Administration, Northeastern University, in Boston. She has taught and traveled widely in Asia, particularly in Indonesia.

VU TUAN ANH is a researcher at the Institute of Economics, Hanoi, Vietnam and is associated with Vietnam's *Socioeconomic Development Review*.

TONGSAN WANG is a senior researcher at the Institute of Quantitative and Technical Economics, Chinese Academy of Social Sciences, Beijing.

Y. C. RICHARD WONG is director of the School of Business at the University of Hong Kong.

TORU YANAGIHARA is a professor at Hosei University and does research at the United Nations University in Tokyo.

ISBN 0-275-96444-2

HARDCOVER BAR CODE